The Year's Best
Sports Writing
2021

The Year's Best Sports Writing 2021

Edited and with an introduction by Glenn Stout

TRIUMPH
BOOKS

Library of Congress Cataloging-in-Publication Data available upon request

This book is available in quantity at special discounts for your group or organization. For further information, contact:

Triumph Books LLC
814 North Franklin Street
Chicago, Illinois 60610
(312) 337-0747
www.triumphbooks.com

Printed in U.S.A.

ISBN: 978-1-62937-887-9

Design by Sue Knopf

"Walk, Run or Wheelbarrow" by Allison Glock. First published in espnW, December 31, 2020. Copyright © 2020 by ESPN Enterprises, Inc. Reprinted by permission of ESPN.

"What Happens When Two Strangers Trust the Rides of Their Lives to the Magic of the Universe" by Kim Cross. First published in *Bicycling*, March 26, 2020. Copyright © 2020 by Hearst Magazine Media, Inc. Reprinted by permission of Hearst Magazine Media, Inc.

"Pre-Game Interview" by Jay Martel. First published in *The New Yorker*, January 13, 2020, and on newyorker.com January 6, 2020: https://www .newyorker.com/magazine/2020/01/13/pre-game-interview. Copyright © 2020 by Jay Martel. Reprinted by permission of Jay Martel.

"The Ramshackle Garden of Affection" by Ross Gay and Noah Davis. First published in *The Sun*, June 2020. Copyright © 2020 by Ross Gay and Noah Davis. Reprinted by permission of Ross Gay and Noah Davis.

"The Inheritance of Archie Manning" by Wright Thompson. First published in ESPN+, December 11, 2020. Copyright © 2020 by ESPN Enterprises, Inc. Reprinted by permission of ESPN.

"'There Might Be a Family Secret'" by Jayson Stark. First published in The Athletic, September 11, 2020. Copyright © 2020 by The Athletic. Reprinted by permission of The Athletic Media Company.

"This Woman Surfed the Biggest Wave of the Year" by Maggie Mertens. First published in *The Atlantic*, September 12, 2020. Copyright © 2020, Maggie Mertens, as first published by *The Atlantic*. Reprinted by permission of Maggie Mertens.

"Hook Shot Charlie Is Spreading Hope Throughout Charlotte. If You Want Some of It, Just Try The Hook" by Michael Graff. First published in Axios

Contents

Introduction   xi

Walk, Run or Wheelbarrow   1
ALLISON GLOCK   FROM espnW

What Happens When Two Strangers Trust the Rides   5
of Their Lives to the Magic of the Universe
KIM CROSS   FROM *Bicycling*

Pre-Game Interview   25
JAY MARTEL   FROM *The New Yorker*

The Ramshackle Garden of Affection   29
ROSS GAY AND NOAH DAVIS   FROM *The Sun*

The Inheritance of Archie Manning   49
WRIGHT THOMPSON   FROM ESPN

"There Might Be a Family Secret"   71
JAYSON STARK   FROM The Athletic

This Woman Surfed the Biggest Wave of the Year   81
MAGGIE MERTENS   FROM *The Atlantic*

Hook Shot Charlie Is Spreading Hope Throughout   89
Charlotte. If You Want Some of It, Just Try The Hook
MICHAEL GRAFF   FROM Axios Charlotte

The Most Magical Place on Earth   95
TAYLOR ROOKS   FROM *GQ*

Is College Football Making the Pandemic Worse?   111
   LOUISA THOMAS   FROM *The New Yorker*

The Confederate Flag Is Finally Gone at NASCAR   127
Races, and I Won't Miss It for a Second
   RYAN McGEE   FROM ESPN

Twelve Minutes and a Life   131
   MITCHELL S. JACKSON   FROM *Runner's World*

Kobe Always Showed His Work. So We Have to   149
in Remembering Him, Too
   BRIAN PHILLIPS   FROM The Ringer

How Kobe Bryant's Death Brought Bobby McIlvaine—   159
an Athlete, a Scholar, the Friend I Should've Known
Better—Back to Life
   MIKE SIELSKI   FROM *The Philadelphia Inquirer*

Andrew Giuliani, Official Sports Guy of the White   171
House, Sees a Score in Big Ten's Return
   KENT BABB   FROM *The Washington Post*

Baseball's Fight to Reclaim Its Soul   181
   TOM VERDUCCI   FROM *Sports Illustrated*

Inside the Rise of MLB's Ivy League Culture: Stunning   193
Numbers and a Question of What's Next
   JOON LEE   FROM ESPN

Shades of Grey   207
   ASHLEY STIMPSON   FROM Longreads

A Nameless Hiker and the Case the Internet Can't Crack   229
   NICHOLAS THOMPSON   FROM *WIRED*

The Master Thief   239
   ZEKE FAUX   FROM *Bloomberg Businessweek*

The Bout   255
  CARY CLACK   FROM Truly*Adventurous

The Bubble of a Dream   281
  PETER BROMKA   FROM Medium

Out There: On Not Finishing   311
  DEVIN KELLY   FROM Longreads

Fifty Years After Its Unfathomable Loss, Marshall   323
Spends Another Nov. 14 with Pain and Memories
  CHUCK CULPEPPER   FROM The Washington Post

Their Son's Heart Saved His Life. So He Rode   329
1,426 Miles to Meet Them
  A.C. SHILTON   FROM Bicycling

Advisory Board   343

Notable Sports Writing of 2020   347

Introduction

No one saw *this* coming.

It seems as if every time we think we've seen it all in the arena of sports there is always a surprise, but I don't think anything quite prepared us for the events of 2020.

As I write this we are barely a year removed since the word COVID entered our common lexicon. I remember thinking, upon first hearing of the emerging pandemic, that "this could be bad." How bad? I recall telling someone "it will be June or July till things get back to normal."

I was only off by about a year, more or less.

It was no accident that sports played a role in first underscoring the scope of the pandemic, first represented by the NBA's Rudy Gobert's unfortunate mocking of the severity of the virus on March 9 when he famously made sure to touch all the microphones at a press conference only to come down with the virus himself a few days later. Soon, the NBA and nearly every other sports league suspended operations.

Entirely by accident, it was because sports are so ubiquitous in our society that it was through sports that most Americans and Canadians became aware of the severity and potential danger that COVID posed. The result, as we now recognize, was that virtually all sports activities of any kind took place for the remainder of the calendar year and beyond—when they took place at all—under the specter of the virus.

But that's not all that happened.

In what, by any measure, is certainly the most unique year in the history of sports this century, if not the last one as well, COVID disrupted almost everything. We also had to confront a long overdue racial reckoning, a recession, and civil unrest in a toxic political climate. Tragedies like the death of Kobe Bryant were swept away and recent championship celebrations almost forgotten. At a time when some expected sports, as it continued, albeit haltingly, to provide a kind of escape from grimmer realities, that really didn't happen. In a sense, perhaps never before has sports—at least the commercialized, institutionalized, athlete-as-commodity kind of sports—seemed to matter so little. Compared to the time before COVID, fans and athletes alike were forced to reconsider their relationship to the games.

It just didn't feel or look the same without fans in the stands, with seasons cancelled, suspended and then resumed, NFL games played mid-week, and a host of other disruptions. Far from being an escape or respite from reality, in many ways sports made reality more present. For every fan that turned to the games for solace, others turned away, finding the intrusion of reality too uncomfortable to bear. Super Bowl ratings were the lowest since 1969. Ratings for the 2020 NBA playoffs were down 37% compared to 2019; the NHL (38%), MLB (40%), and college football (30%) suffered similar drops. ESPN even began airing *cornhole* competitions, *cherry-pit spitting*, and *lawn mower racing*, the kind of "sports" the network would have never considered even in its nascent days.

Professional and most other institutionalized sports, in just about every way possible, played truncated schedules and operated in ways that, in the future, will result in very large asterisks placed next to every champion. Who, really, was the best at anything in 2020? We'll never really know.

Writers, or course, were no less affected. Those who covered sports for a living found themselves watching video feeds or sequestered in the nether regions of arenas and ballparks, with access to the athletes themselves, with few exceptions, nearly non-existent. Print publications and digital outlets pared back considerably if they managed to stay in business at all. The freelance market dried up almost entirely (even, if we're playing the ratings game, as book buying increased by 8%). Those of us who imagined that their careers had reached a place of stability were reminded, yet again, that the only constant is change. All of us, in ways large and small, were forced to adapt.

Fortunately, however, sports have never been the sole province of the leagues, associations, and their related acronyms. Those have never been more than the bottom of a very big funnel that shuffles and sorts and spits out athletes and sports for our mass consumption. Yet sports itself, the actual games and competition that pit one human being tested against another, or even against themselves, still took place. The venues may have been less visible, even so personal as to be solitary, but it is there that the value of sports during such a time was revealed. Maybe the myopic focus only on wins and losses, on *beating the other guy*, finally began to run its course, and some of the older, more essential but recently considered less valuable traits of sports began to re-emerge. The mere act of survival, of perseverance, or somehow still managing to join with others in any kind of shared activity suddenly seemed important again. I didn't miss playing baseball or watching it nearly as much as I did not being able to play catch. And if basketball didn't take place in an arena before thousands of fans, there remained, somewhere and someplace, a ball being dribbled and bounced off a backboard and games of "HORSE" played on opposite ends of the court, even if no one was watching. And to those who indulged in lone pursuits, finding competition only with the imagination, sports continued to play an essential role and helped us go on.

I think in this, the strangest of seasons, we can give some credit to the writers for showing how sports continued, and what roles it survived to play. While some writers struggled to provide content, throw-away filler as fungible as the age, the situation pushed others to reach elsewhere, into the more hidden places of our hearts where we find value in what we do. I've long argued that despite the various strains and struggle writers may face in a business that, in many ways, makes no sense, that despite all the obstacles placed in their way, they nonetheless continue to produce work that is vital, proving their value again and again.

This book is evidence of that, and 2020 was no exception. As the prospects for this volume began to take shape, others may have wondered what would become of sports writing during this time and whether it would even be worthwhile to put together such a collection—I never did. I knew that despite everything—in fact, *because of everything*, that the writers that aspire to write about sports and perhaps appear in a book such as this would meet the challenge. They would penetrate our uncertainty and ambiguity and somehow translate our collective anxieties and fears to locate that solid center that still remained, the core that makes us all still care.

Perhaps that's what this past season revealed. As I read through the thousands of stories that were considered for this volume, those I found myself and those that were recommended to me, something true and lasting seemed to surface. Whether a given story was overtly COVID-centric or not, it became clear to me that although we might not always give a damn about the games—and in the long run that may not even matter—we sure as hell do care about each other. That's what the best writing can do, by words alone uncover what no other medium can do in quite the same way, and reveal what really matters. That's also something readers cherish and desire. That they still looked forward to a book such as this provides some proof that this is so.

I'm a firm believer that the value of writing comes from the degree it enables us to know each other, and if there is a thread that unites most of the stories in this collection, it is precisely that. Writing about sports occupies a special place in our culture, because sports are one of those few subjects we share an interest in with almost everyone, a topic that can inspire communication between strangers. Standing in line somewhere or sitting in a bar—even socially distanced—you can turn to a stranger and make a comment about a game or a player and usually get a reaction. You start to speak to one another and before long find yourself sharing memories and opinions and observations, the *stories* that make up our lives. The instant that happens the gap between us begins to narrow. The stranger is not so strange, even if we might disagree, and even if he or she might be wearing a hat or a T-shirt that might cause us to blanch. The sharing of words and stories brings us closer to each other and makes the world a less lonely and less frightening place, even if you love the Red Sox and I cheer myself hoarse for the Yankees, I bleed Maize and Blue and you go gaga over Scarlet and Gray, I say Kobe and you say LeBron, and then the next person weighs in and mentions Dr. J and MJ. The moment we tell and share stories, we begin to know each other and begin to understand, however narrowly, there may be a place where we overlap and stand on the same side.

None of this is to say this collection is entirely pandemic-centric. It's not. Sports took place before we knew Brooklyn's Dr. Fauci ever played point guard for Regis High School, and even after we all joined team COVID. This book continues a long tradition that began when the *Best Sports Stories* series was first published in 1945, and continued (with one exception due to the illness of its editor) until 1990. Then, in a fortunate coincidence, the venerable *Best American Sports Writing* series began its 30-year run, taking its place on the shelf each year for a longer period of time than Nolan Ryan took the mound, but not quite as long as Gordie Howe laced on the skates.

Year after year the dedicated readers of each volume of those two collections made the case for the necessity of their existence. Neither book ever "stuck to sports," for the moment we give more than the final score, we're not sticking with sports but placing sports in the context of our larger world, a world not defined by statistics but by people who live and breathe and love and die. Sports are just another place where humanity, at its best, its worst, and all places in between, is on display. In that confined space it is perhaps a little easier to see each other a bit more clearly than to try to comprehend the world in its entirety.

So we begin again, and go on from here.

THIS BOOK REPRESENTS both the old tradition of those previous two series, but also a fresh start. While this series may resemble those that came before, it is not quite the same. I was honored, after the demise of *The Best American Sports Writing*, when hundreds of readers lamented its passing, and grateful when Triumph Books approached me and asked if I had any thoughts as to how another collection might take root. I did, and over the course of a number of months shared my ideas as to how that might look.

Over the final years of *The Best American Sports Writing*, as my name became familiar as the only constant over its 30-year lifespan, many made the understandable assumption that it was in some way "my" book. I never did and it never was. In my role as series editor I never selected a single story for inclusion, yet the perception gained traction. That is why the first recommendation I made in regard to *The Year's Best Sports Writing* was that there would be no "Glenn Stout" at the helm feeding stories to a guest editor. While he or she was always free to select any story they wish, admittedly some took that responsibility more seriously than others.

In this new collection, the annual editor, which the publisher will select, will change each year. He or she will again have the responsibility of making the final selections, but our expectation is that the annual editor will take a much more active role in making the annual selections. Instead of a "series editor" to provide assistance with that daunting task and ensure that the editor sees as wide a range of material as possible, an eight-member advisory board will be on the lookout for stories over the course of the year, just as we expect the annual editor to do. The makeup of the board, as the reader can see from those in this inaugural edition, is designed to represent the full scope of this industry:

freelancers and staffers of every age and background, male and female, people with experience in newspapers and magazines and digital publications, both those who cover sports exclusively and those who do so only occasionally. This year I made the selection of the advisory board, choosing writers I trusted and respected, some that I knew quite well and some I knew hardly at all. Collectively, the board will help ensure the annual editor sees stories of all kinds, from as many places and perspectives as possible, because the "best" can come from anywhere. They did a terrific job of not only alerting me to stories I had missed, but it was also illuminating to see those stories that multiple members of the board put forward. This was particularly helpful in the selection of the story by Kim Cross that appears in this collection. Although works by board members are eligible to appear in the book, none of us wanted any such selection to appear to be the product of any favoritism. Suffice to say that Kim's story was not only cited by a number of aggregators as one of the best stories of the year but was also independently submitted by a majority of the board members.

This year's book was a bit of a challenge for all of us, for until publication was certain we could not recruit members to the board. Nevertheless they took their task seriously and mined their memory banks—and those of their colleagues—for work that appeared over the entire course of the year. Knowing that this book might happen since last spring, although I was unable to solicit submissions I took a flyer and nevertheless paid close attention, setting stories aside in the event this book was published according to the same criteria I always have: searching for stories that reading once, I wanted to read again and share with friends. Although it was impossible this year, in the future we may well have a mechanism by which writers and outlets can again nominate their own work.

In many ways serving as the first annual editor of *The Year's Best Sports Writing* also marks the end of my role in this series. Over the next few years my role will diminish and become primarily custodial, then dwindle to nothing. That's my choice, for as I said, just as *The Best American Sports Writing* was not "my" book, neither is this, and I've occupied this space long enough. It's time for others to take over. Each year another writer will serve as annual editor and write the introduction. My major role is only to plant a new seed in the ground and work the soil for a couple of years to give it a chance to grow on its own. As ever, the book really belongs to the writers that aspire to appear in its pages and the readers who look forward to such a collection each year, and my thanks first goes out to each and every one of them. I'd also like to thank everyone at Triumph Books who believed in this project, colleague Bill Ruthi, the members of the advisory board—Ben Baby, Alex Belth, Howard Bryant, Kim Cross, Roberto José Andrade Franco, Latria Graham, Michael Mooney, and Linda Robertson—and Siobhan and Saorla for putting up with the work of a book such as this for one more year.

Serving as the first annual editor does satisfy a long desire, one that I now must admit was much more difficult than I believed it would be. Making the final selections is much tougher than simply making suggestions, and the circumstances of this year made that much tougher still. I wish all those who follow the very best.

By then, I'll be settling into the same role that set me on this unlikely path more than 50 years ago, when the full shelf of *Best Sports Stories* in my small town library helped sparked a lifelong interest in writing. I'll just be turning the pages as a reader again, settling in each year to read a volume that we hope proves to be as entertaining, inspirational, and essential as those of the past.

—Glenn Stout
Alburgh, Vermont
Summer 2021

The Year's Best
Sports Writing
2021

Walk, Run or Wheelbarrow

ALLISON GLOCK

FROM espnW • DECEMBER 31, 2020

It's 5 o'clock and the sun is beginning to dip as my daughter pulls on her coat and heads out for her daily walk. She is 20 and has been living at home since the onset of the pandemic, a stark shift from her former independent life in New York City, and a tight arrangement that chafes us both.

Her 19-year-old sister is also home, remote learning away from her college campus, and while we are grateful beyond imagination to thus far be healthy and to have a house in which to quarantine, bumping up against each other every day for nearly a year while we pretend the world isn't melting has made cornered ferrets of us all.

At our worst, we snarl and hiss, longing fervently for THE MOMENT when we can rejoin society and, with it, a version of ourselves we recognize. The outside version. The active, animated, alive person we once saw reflected in the eyes of others, one beyond the (not so) funhouse hall of mirrors we currently stare into.

Until then, my eldest walks. She carries a backpack loaded with her journal, a beanie, whatever book she's reading. She dons her mask and canvasses our Atlanta neighborhood at New York speed, striding purposefully as if she has somewhere to be. When the sun starts to set, she sits on a patch of grass or a park bench to catch her breath and stares into the sky, tracking the light until it bleeds into darkness.

She does this every evening because, as she explains, it gives her "something to look forward to."

When she comes home, cheeks flush, hair windswept, my daughter does seem happier, lifted. The simple act of walking underscoring her autonomy, reminding her that she is still a human capable of breathing fresh air, of shuttling from point A to B, that she is still a human at all.

For her part, my younger child runs. I hear her in the early morning, tiptoeing past the sleeping dogs, her lanyard key jangling around her neck. She hates running.

What she really wants is to be back on her university campus with friends. To be engaged and challenged and eating crappy cafeteria food and working on the local farm and stressing about grades and wondering what color she should dye her hair next. Instead, she is in her childhood bedroom Zooming in front of a screen stacked with largely silent black squares, doing her best to act as if this is still worthwhile, her sorrow an anvil on her chest. So she runs. She runs as fast as she can.

At night, we talk a lot about "The COVID Lessons." The education of the past 10 months. The Marie Kondo-fication of our souls. We pretend we are learning what actually matters.

I tell my children to trust in facts, which still exist and carry the weight of centuries. I tell my children I want them to recognize who benefits if we are confused, if we are unclear, if we are off-balance, if we are afraid, if we are split from the herd by our otherness. Hint: not us. (Not anyone, really.) Mostly, I tell my children that I love them and they matter. My children who don't want to have children anymore.

Maybe they hear me. But I doubt any of it registers as appreciably as the immediacy of their feet hitting the earth during their walks and runs. The rib-deep assurance they feel when they pound and stomp and the ground does not give way.

I recently took a long hike of my own through a historic cemetery in my neighborhood. My dog bounded ahead, racing across the expansive potter's field, a resting place for the forgotten and overlooked, now blanketed with Bermuda grass and magnolias. I jogged to keep pace, the tread of my sneakers sticking slightly in spots of damp mud. We both came to rest, panting under the shadow of a century-old oak, branches nearly bare, the few remaining leaves cupping the light like jewels. My dog snorted, rolled, peed—shamelessly lived his id-rich life. In the distance, another visitor waved our way, then shrugged and moved on.

As I stood there, I thought about an Olympic hopeful I'd interviewed years ago. I met him at a high school athletic field, where he was running drills after his shift at his day job. Weeds clogged the edges of the neglected track. Empty beer bottles and greasy burger wrappers had blown into the lanes, and the surface itself was cracked and buckled in spots. But the track was close to his house, so that's where he trained, unsung and alone, for an event that is years into an uncertain future, for a team he might not even make.

I remember watching him round the curve back then, cheeks puffed, eyes glazed with pain, and wondering what kept him running. I remember thinking how difficult it must be to sacrifice that much. To believe so blindly in a story as yet unwritten.

Over the past year, almost all of us have become prisoners in our own M.C. Escher print made real, bit players in an unfolding Samuel Beckett novel. You must go on. I can't go on. I'll go on. Every day we are neck-deep in cruel absurdity, in absurd cruelty, grasping for meaning in a vacuum. Left with nowhere else, we return to the body because, among other gifts, the body does not lie.

A girlfriend told me she's been laboring to keep her sanity during quarantine by hauling a wheelbarrow loaded with mulch up and down her driveway, shoulders burning, the Sisyphus of the suburbs. Another 40-something colleague is teaching herself to ride a skateboard because, why not? There is so much death.

Choking levels of despair. Countless dreams deferred. The numbers—the stats—simultaneously unbearable and impossible to fathom.

You must go on. I can't go on. I'll go on.

There is, mercifully, a vaccine, offering a promise to reenter the world beyond ourselves. This is good news. This year and its season of grief are almost over. But that release remains many months away. Leaving us to linger betwixt and between, on the threshold of a hope we dare not imagine, believing blindly in a story as yet unwritten.

Until then, we walk.

Until then, we skate. We hike. We wheelbarrow. We run. We chase our dogs. We meander in cemeteries, searching for signs of life. We propel our bodies forward. We tread the ground. And we do not fall through.

A journalist for 20-plus years, ESPN senior writer and producer **Allison Glock**'s work has appeared in *The New York Times, The New York Times Magazine, The New Yorker, Esquire, Rolling Stone, Men's Journal, Marie Claire, GQ,* and many other publications. She is the author of seven books, including Whiting Award winner *Beauty Before Comfort.* In 2018, Glock co-wrote and produced the groundbreaking sports documentary *Man Made.*

What Happens When Two Strangers Trust the Rides of Their Lives to the Magic of the Universe

KIM CROSS

FROM *Bicycling* • MARCH 26, 2020

> *Sometimes, their caravan met with another.*
> *One always had something that the other needed—*
> *as if everything were indeed written by one hand.*
> *As they sat around the fire, the camel drivers*
> *exchanged information about windstorms,*
> *and told stories about the desert.*
> —PAULO COELHO, *THE ALCHEMIST*

Once upon a road in Kazakhstan, two men converge in the desert. Strangers born an ocean apart, riding bicycles burdened like camels, they emerge from either horizon, slowly approaching a common point. Day by day, hour after hour, they make their way through a land as flat and featureless as a page without words. Thousands of miles spool out behind them. Thousands more lie ahead.

One rides east. The other, west.

For months now, each has been pedaling, alone, through sun, wind, rain, and snow, climbing mountains, crossing plains, and loading his bike onto boats to float across minor seas. Now, on a Sunday morning in August, they soldier down an unpaved Soviet road that never seems to bend. The only sound is tires crunching on gravel and, now and then, the lonely roar of a truck hurrying between two somewheres.

The earth spins. The sun rises. Long shadows shrink into puddles of shade beneath their spinning wheels. From dawn to dusk, in every direction, the landscape looks the same.

The only thing that changes is the angle of the sun.

Then, through the shimmering heat, a blur appears on their common horizon and gradually comes into focus: a simple white box of a building on the edge of the dusty road. Next to it, a metal shipping container marked by a hand-painted word, ШАЙХАНА. Translation: *chaikhana*, a teahouse, where travelers can find water, food, and shade. The nearest city, on the Caspian Sea, is 235 miles away.

Here, under a noon Kazak sun, two sagas, by chance, eclipse.

The American is six feet tall, 200 pounds, smiling through the scraggly beard of a traveler who hasn't seen a shower in days. He is 27 years old.

The Brit is five-foot-seven, 143 pounds, smiling through a blue bandana and a slightly darker beard. He is 26 years old.

"What the hell are *you* doing here?" says the American.

"What the hell are *you* doing here?" says the Brit.

It's the first time in days they have opened their mouths to speak their native tongue. When had they last encountered a fellow traveler on two wheels? Each ogles the other's bicycle—two wildly different animals beneath the same desert dust. The strangers introduce themselves.

"I'm Noel," says the American, who is riding east.

"I'm Leon," says the Brit, riding west.

LEON
Leon Whiteley had been meandering west for 309 days and 11,337 miles. His journey began in Gumi, a South Korean city

where he'd spent the year teaching English. When his tenure ran out, he came up with the boldest, daringest overland voyage he could fathom: riding to England by bike—solo. So far, the trip had not gone as planned. But Leon thrived on misadventure.

Leon did not fancy himself a "cyclist," at least not of the Lycra-clad, leg-shaving sort. When he was a boy growing up in Yateley, a town in South East England, a bicycle was his primary means of getting from here to there. He had never had a driver's license.

When he was older, the bicycle became a vehicle for exploration. He once pedaled 874 miles from the northern edge of the British Isles to Land's End, the southernmost tip. Riding with a friend for those 11 days, he tasted a glorious freedom. No trains to catch, no rooms to book. As Leon wrote on his 323-page blog, "We fell into our own rhythm, generally dictated by how much pedaling our legs could take between sunrise and sunset."

Now, after years of traveling the world with a backpack and a hunger to stray as far as possible from the ever-beaten path, he cycled "to avoid the herd." He craved an epic adventure, a trip that was "more akin to a quest." His dream: "to ride from one edge of the map to the other."

A proper touring bike was well beyond Leon's budget. So he settled on an aluminum Gary Fisher hard-tail mountain bike with V-brakes, a triple chain ring, and a heavy fork. It cost around $400. It was better suited for a spin around the block than a hemispheric odyssey, but it would do. He added bar ends, four water bottle cages, rear saddlebags, and a handlebar bag. The nicest thing about the bike was the Schwalbe Marathon tires.

Leon took pride in this make-do bike, in the $18 Gore-Tex jacket he found on sale, and the discounted two-man tent that looked a little less like a "vulnerable caterpillar" than a lightweight one-man bivy that would "leave no illusion that I was a singleton if happened upon by forces of ill intent." He whittled his belongings to the barest necessities and mailed everything else home to England.

One Saturday in October, Leon embarked a day past sched-
ule, wheels rolling at 10 a.m. The first few miles out of the city
squandered 50 miles worth of patience, but soon he was passing
red peppers drying on the side of the road, a man threshing grain
with his feet, and an official highway sign pointing the way to the
"Grave of a Loyal Dog." (He paid respects.)

Leon loved the motto of the British Special Air Service: *Who
Dares Wins.* He lived by this tenet, embracing the price of authen-
ticity: the risks, the fear, the unknown dangers of sketchy places
and dodgy strangers. He believed in the "Tao of travel, where
things just flow and you're carried by a randomness through a
string of highly fortunate and unlikely experiences."

NOEL

One hundred seventy-six days and 5,388 miles before meeting
Leon in the desert, Noel Kegel pulled bike parts out of a cardboard box and reassembled them on the floor of the airport in
Lisbon, Portugal. He imagined the endless road across Eurasia,
the world's largest landmass.

Noel had dreamed up this bike, part by part, before knowing where it would take him. Its soul was a Rohloff Speedhub,
a weatherproof constellation of planetary gears as precise as a
luxury timepiece. It drove a lugged steel Waterford frame cus-
tom-made near his home in Viroqua, Wisconsin. Each wheel he
had lovingly built by hand, adjusting the tension of 32 spokes so
the circle was perfectly true.

Raised in his family's bike shop, Noel could repair a flat
tire by age ten. During high school summers he earned money
by wrenching, and he rode his bicycle 900 miles to college in
Montreal—three times. As a young man, he felt a wanderlust.
His dream: "to ride ocean to ocean."

His own continent seemed too easy, too tame. So he ran his
fingers over a globe, searching for the longest ride. The one he
found spanned 19 countries and 130 degrees of longitude. One
side of the globe to the other.

He wasn't driven by any of the reasons that inspired other long-haul travelers. He wasn't doing this to escape a dud job, to heal from a breakup, or to mourn a loss. He didn't need to find himself. This wasn't about raising money for a cause. He didn't want sponsors, or even attention.

"I just wanted to see a few more corners of the Earth at 10 miles per hour," he said.

People told him he was crazy. The world, they warned, is a dangerous place. Noel believed otherwise. "If you listen to people, you'll never go anywhere," he said. "It's best to go out and explore and realize the world is a good place."

In Lisbon, Noel rattled over cobblestones, rolled by a 145-year-old arch, and climbed a hill to a 15th century castle. Before heading east, he rode west to the coast, where he stood on the edge of Europe, watching the sun melt into the Atlantic. Before falling asleep, he thought of the woman waiting for him on the other side of the water. Then he rose with the sun, turned his back to the sea, and pedaled toward the Pacific.

LEON
From Korea, Leon planned to cross the Yellow Sea by ferry, then ride due west through China. His plans were immediately thwarted: the Beijing Olympics complicated the visa process. He would have to ride *around* China, a circuitous detour of island-hopping through the Philippines and Indonesia, stuttering up through Malaysia, Thailand, and Cambodia, entering China from the south.

This detour would take 99 days.

Leon pedaled north to Seoul, where airport officials treated his bike as if it were made of uranium. In Manila, he reassembled it before a captivated audience of janitors, who passed him tools like surgical nurses and asked, "Don't you have any friends?"

He wove through Manila with one loose pedal, dodging mopeds, rickshaws, and Jeepneys as gaudy as carnival floats. "I felt just like another clown in the circus," he wrote, "and even started to enjoy it." On a glorious descent along the coast, distracted by the view, he missed a turn and wound up three bays and 37 miles from where he needed to be. He had no GPS—only a compass, a map, and his gut. (They were right more often than locals.)

Leon loved the idea of setting off every morning not knowing where he'd sleep that night. This dream became a recurring nightmare. Many towns had no hostels, just hourly rooms. Wild camping had its charms and jinxes. As he set up camp in the woods by the side of a road, a murmuration of starlings "danced in great swirling flocks" above his tent, "then proceeded to poo all over it."

One very long night in Borneo, he lay wide-eyed in his tent as a gathering drumbeat filled the jungle. It was joined by moaning and human screams, then howling dogs and a woman shouting words in some exotic tongue. Afraid to draw attention to himself by turning on his lamp, he crawled out of his tent in the dark and stood, half-dressed, in the full-moon light, armed with a ballpoint pen ("the most dangerous weapon I could find in the dark"). The devil's symphony crescendoed with a blood-curdling scream, and then—silence. Only the sound of a coconut crashing to the ground.

He often awoke, dog-tired, to endless climbs that disappeared into the mountain mist. He was honked at by lorries, mocked by locals, stoned and cursed by children, and stymied by bad directions. Some days the road only seemed to go up, and no matter which way he turned, it was always into the wind. Caught in a monsoon, he struggled through water that lapped at his pedals. But when strangers offered a ride through a sandstorm, he resisted.

"Wouldn't have been able to hail a lift if I was fighting at Stalingrad, or halfway up Everest. But no, I had to be born at the first point in human history when adventure must be sought out and contrived, and isn't just thrust upon you."

Dogs terrorized him at every turn, snarling and snapping at his ankles. Leon filled his pockets with stones to hurl at these "wretched beasts of Beelzebub." At a bookstore, a big white dog lumbered over to greet him. When he patted its head, the dog snapped at him. Leon imagined festering rabies and fantasized about turning the miserable beast into a fur coat. Better yet, "a pencil case, and one of those fluffy toilet-lid covers that were fashionable back in the eighties." At the border, a customs dog peed on his bike.

Riding into a blistering headwind after fixing his third flat tire in three days, he was ambushed by two dogs. Startled, he sped up, swerved, and crashed, hitting his head and scattering water bottles in the road. He leapt to his feet and kicked a fence post to dislodge it for use as a club. Instead, he dislodged his big toe. Limping back to his bike, hurling stones at the hellhounds, he didn't notice his front tire going flat.

One day Leon heard pitiful whelps coming from the roadside. It was a bedraggled puppy pawing desperately at the sides of a scum-filled drainage ditch. He reached into the filthy water, rescued the pup, and set him free. Riding away, he secretly hoped the God of Dogs was watching.

NOEL

Noel did not believe in a God, but he believed in a world where he could wander alone into a vast unknown and find his way safely home.

"When you're on a bike you are vulnerable," Noel said. "People sense that. And they want to help you."

In Turkey, old men playing backgammon at small cafes hollered "*Oy! Çay!*"—inviting him to tea. In villages, people waved him out of the rain and into their threadbare huts, where he sat on dirt floors, telling stories with his hands and breaking stale bread with strangers. In one town, a middle-aged mother wanted to buy him a bus ticket so he wouldn't have to ride his bike.

In Croatia, he took a detour from the Adriatic coast to visit the ruins of his grandfather's village. He stood inside a roofless church, saw abandoned houses crumbling back into earth, and searched weed-choked cemeteries for leaning stones engraved with his family name. He pressed wildflowers into his journal and wondered how, in a parallel world unravaged by war, his life might look here.

He crossed the Caspian Sea on a freighter, a 24-hour trip approaching the very mid-point of his journey. On the ship, afloat between Europe and Asia, he met a fellow passenger who owned a car wash in Uzbekistan. The man did not speak much English, but he invited Noel to his home.

Five weeks later, after meeting Leon, Noel would roll up to the only car wash in Chust and speak the man's name. The man, so moved by Noel's visit, would welcome him like a king. The next 36 hours would be a whirlwind of feasting, touring the town, and gathering with curious, smiling Uzbeks. Noel "almost had to escape this typically Central Asian uber-hospitality for fear of becoming too indebted to his kindness."

Noel would pedal away with a full belly, a free haircut, and a treasured gift: a knife engraved with the names of new friends.

LEON

Pedaling in his granny-gear up the steepest roads in Malaysia, Leon discovered that pushing his bike was equally expedient and a welcome reprieve from the saddle. (He had no bike shorts.) As he trudged up a soul-crushing hill, a man ran at him, shouting.

"My friend, you look like you could need one of these?"

The man held out a can of Carlsberg, a Danish pilsner. Leon smiled and cracked it open. The next thing he knew, he was drinking too much rice wine at a traditional Malaysian fête. He pitched his tent in the family's garden and fell into a deep slumber.

At 4 a.m., Leon awoke with a start, smothered by ripstop fabric. A tent pole had snapped, collapsing his shelter. Just his luck. He left at first light, thanking his hungover hosts and grimly facing the soul-crushing hill.

Another day, a van slowed down to offer a lift to town. Leon said thank you, but no, he had to make it on his own. The man said there was a big rain coming—really, it was no trouble. Again, Leon politely declined. A few miles later, the monsoon arrived. Drenched, with night swiftly closing in, Leon saw he had a flat.

In Kuching, he noticed a broken spoke. He carried the answer—a shiny chrome spoke key—but had no idea how it worked. "I've been carrying it more as a magical amulet," he mused, "rather than an actual tool I might have to use."

Another spoke broke on the way to the bike shop in Kuala Lumpur, where he discovered all bike shops were closed on Sunday, and Monday was a national holiday. Back at the hostel, he griped about his two-day delay. A Swede reading Paulo Coelho looked up from his book and declared, "The universe is not working in your favor."

NOEL

The universe had a peculiar way of working in Noel's favor. Things often went wrong in all the right ways.

In the Balkans, Noel joined a fellow rider named Fabien for three days of riding with company. That first morning, Fabien's rack broke. Noel was already pedaling 100 pounds of gear and bike, but he cheerfully strapped Fabien's bags to his rig. That afternoon, Noel heard a nauseating noise—the crack of a brazed joint on his custom steel frame. They transferred both loads to Fabien's bike and made haste to the nearest town, where Noel found a welder and felt lucky.

"Without each other we would have had a different experience," Noel said, "and might have had to hitchhike."

Thousands of miles later, Noel would have a fortuitous flat while descending a steep mountain pass. Fixing it drew his attention to a more serious problem. His brakes, slowing 300 pounds of man and bike, had worn his rear wheel paper-thin. The aluminum rim showed a hairline crack—an omen of imminent and catastrophic failure. Noel disengaged his rear brake and crept down the mountain accompanied by the scent of burning rubber, stopping every so often to let his front rim cool down.

In the next big town, Noel tried to buy a new wheel. No luck. He called home to Wisconsin and had his family shop, Wheel & Sprocket, place an order. Four days later, a Soviet-era Lada with DHL spray-painted on the door pulled up and handed him a package with a new wheel.

While waiting for this delivery, Noel befriended another solo bike tourer, a German named Christian. He was headed east. They rode together for a few hundred miles, then picked up a third rider, a Dutchman named Ron. The trio rode together like migrating birds, each laboring in the front for a spell, then resting in the flock's wind-shadow. They traced the edge of the Taklamakan Desert, climbing out of the endless sand to 11,726 feet, celebrating the high points and sharing the lows.

It was nice to ride with company. But off-bike, each moved at a different pace. Erecting Christian's German tent required half an hour and an engineering degree. In the morning, Noel was ready to roll in 10 minutes, while Christian took a couple of hours to dry and meticulously pack his gear. When his friends decided to hitchhike a tedious stretch of road, Noel was grateful to continue his unbroken line alone.

LEON

Leon rode alone until mile 2,787, when he finally encountered a fellow bike tourer. At last—a kindred spirit! Alas, the man ignored him.

Then, in China, Leon befriended Carsten, a German with waterproof maps, WD-40, a little book with pictures of things you might need to request in a language you do not speak, and "a divine messenger of what lay ahead"—a GPS. Carsten was headed west.

Leon discovered the wonder of drafting, even if it meant staring at another bloke's arse. Freed from the constant stress of figuring out where on earth he was, Leon found himself laughing at things he once cursed, like the "bugling freight lorries handled with mystifying inconsideration." Such things irritated Carsten even more. "Why are zey doing dis?" Carsten fumed. "What is the mentality of deez people?"

But the GPS was a fickle oracle. It gave inaccurate distances, led them miles in the wrong direction, and constantly changed its mind. It gave its holder "the illusion of control," which Leon came to resent. "You'd be much better off carrying a crucifix, clasping a rabbit's paw to your breast, and chanting Hail Marys every thirteen paces."

In China, less than 200 miles from the Eurasian Pole of Inaccessibility, the furthest point in the world from any ocean, Leon's rim came apart at the seam. He lucked upon a bike shop 12 miles down the road, but instead of fixing the rim, the mechanics broke something else.

"It really couldn't have happened at a worse place," he noted. "Directly halfway between Lanzhou and Ürümqi, the only two places in a thousand miles where one is guaranteed to get the required parts."

The nearest town where he *might* find help was 250 miles ahead. The bus stop was miles behind. Leon hitched a ride back, only to find the bus didn't take bikes. (The police convinced the bus driver to reconsider this policy.) In the next town, the bike shop removed the wheel, put it back on, and then it would not turn. Defeated, Leon found a hotel, where he walked into a door and split open his forehead. Then he spotted a familiar bike. Carsten heard a *tattarrattat* upon his door. He opened it to find Leon—bloody and bloody exhausted.

After a few hundred miles, Leon and Carsten decided to part. It was for the best. "With Carsten following his GPS and me following Carsten, I've effectively stopped thinking," Leon said. "Whilst progress has been quicker and more efficient, it has effectively ceased to be my adventure."

A day or two from the Chinese border, Leon's rear hub began to squeal. Getting to a bike shop 500 miles away took 10 hours on an overcrowded sleeper bus whose driver screamed "Fack you Inglishi!" In the city, the mechanic fixed the problem—no charge. On the bus ride back, he met a young man leaving the university "because I'm always anxious and afraid and my head is sick." Leon replied, "I know how you feel, mate."

But the Tao of travel ensured that for every yin moment, there was a yang. No shadow can exist without light.

In Kyrgyzstan, Leon met a mother who was raising four children on a roofless platform that served as living room, dining room table, and family bed. Leon joined them on the bed-thing for a simple meal of melon, bread, and tea. They asked for no payment, but Leon gave them cash, a flashlight, and a few family portraits he had printed in town.

While napping by a tranquil lake, Leon was awakened by a drunk man waving a serpent in a bottle. Miming across the language gap, the man conveyed his desire to cook the snake, which he believed to have medicinal qualities that would heal his bad knee. He reconsidered this plan when a waitress, seeing the serpent, screamed and ran away.

In Uzbekistan, a woman with gold teeth gave Leon brand-new socks and lollipops. That same day, after showering in a leaky irrigation channel, he was invited to tea at a local's house. Four generations welcomed him into a lush courtyard, passed him babies, and fed him grapes growing on the arbor above. Days later, another meal left his body "alternately evacuating itself from both ends."

Leaving China, Leon traced the border of Uzbekistan and Turkmenistan, where the Kyzylkum and Karakum deserts meet. One morning he woke up to two flat tires and ended the day with a broken tent zipper, through which he fed the mosquitoes. The next day, British chaps in a battered Mongol Rally racecar gave him one of their tents.

On a Sunday morning in August, Leon awoke at dawn in the last oasis of civilization before the longest stretch of emptiness. He loaded up on water and entered the desert, pedaling toward the Caspian.

NOEL

After crossing the Caspian Sea, Noel would not see another major body of water for 5,000 miles. He would stay on the same road through western China for half as long. As the days grew shorter, the nights would grow colder. He would boil bottles of water to put in his sleeping bag. He would wake under veils of ice formed by his frozen exhalations.

He would face his hardest day and his darkest night alone in the Chinese desert. After seeing a rare intersection on his map, he would ride furiously toward the crossroads, which gave him hope for a meal, a warm bed, or at least a peasant selling drinks. His body would be a machine, fueled by a handful of nuts, able to go 80 miles without stopping.

Racing the setting sun, he would stop only to pee or flag down a truck when he ran out of water. As dusk fell like a curtain on an empty theater, he would crest the final hill before the crossroads, only to arrive at...*nothing.*

"Just two roads meeting in the desert."

At the end of this longest day—113 miles over ten and a half hours—he would pitch his tent in the dark and fall asleep without eating. But he would not break. Or even come close. Not here, not once in months of pushing farther and harder than he knew he could, would he ever glimpse his limit.

LEON

Somewhere around mile 11,000, Leon approached his limit. It wasn't his body. It was his bike.

He was two days into a 10-day stretch of desert in the middle of Central Asia. To make room for 30 pounds of water—enough for two or three days—he had ditched his warm coat and other belongings. Ahead lay six hundred miles of desert and steppe, a treeless desolate grassland. Most bicycle tourers took buses and planes to bypass this hopeless void.

That would have been "the sensible option," Leon mused, "considering the heat, hundreds of kilometers without towns or water stops, Soviet uranium dumps, and occasional outbreaks of bubonic plague along the way."

As he entered this vast stretch of emptiness, Leon heard a foreboding sound: PING!

It was the sound of a breaking spoke. "This was my worst nightmare," Leon said. "Overloaded with water and on the bad roads ahead, breaking spokes was my greatest fear." There would be no bike shops in the desert. No buses to catch to nonexistent towns.

"But what could I do?" Leon lamented. It was his own fault, he knew, for embarking without the tools or knowledge. "But sod it, I was going to throw caution to the wind and keep going till I couldn't go on any further, and then, who knows? After all, it was only 1,000 kilometers of inhospitable terrain in furnace-like heat, with just a few possible water stops. Shouldn't be too bad."

A few miles later, another *PING!*

Then another.

And another.

Under the weight of his panniers, his rear wheel sagged badly out of true. The circle no longer a circle, his bicycle was limping. Pedaling against a rubbing brake and the added insult of a cross-wind, Leon could hardly move faster than walking. He passed a turtle trying to hide in the shade of a blown-out tire.

The next real city, on the Caspian Sea, was 800 unpaved miles ahead. Would his bike rattle to pieces before he could reach it? At this pace, would 10 days of desert stretch into 20? Did he have enough food? Would he run out of water?

In the inane vacuity of this desperate place, existence became existential. He was fiercely present, running on instinct, living "moment by moment at a higher pitch." His fate lay in his hands alone, his future hinging on every decision, and "the sheer lack of options was itself the liberating factor."

By and by, a building appeared on the horizon, a concrete island in a sea of dust. *Water!* After four hours of labor, he reached a decaying structure with a few petrol pumps overseen by a boy. He asked the boy for water and was shown to a pipe coming out of the ground. *Uranium contamination*, he thought, and rode on.

Three days from now, Leon will meet another cyclist in this sea of dust, and the alchemy of that meeting will remind him that "there is an almost magical aspect to life, but to find it one has to go to the edge and expose oneself to the possibility."

Unable to see this glimmer of hope on the endless path ahead, he begins to think the unthinkable:

"I'm never going to make it."

NOEL

Not once would it occur to Noel there was a chance he might not make it.

The question was, would he make it in time? He had a self-imposed deadline, a promise to keep. There was a woman waiting on the other side of the world, and he said he'd be home for Christmas.

After meeting Leon, Noel would race against time, crunching his stats at the end of the day, counting down sunsets, ticking off miles. He had planned to finish in Singapore, the farthest point he could find from where he started in Portugal. But as the deadline neared, he would revise his target, first to Vietnam, then to Hong Kong, and finally to Shanghai. What mattered most was riding ocean to ocean.

One wind-whipped day in November, on the eve of his 28th birthday, Noel would stand alone on the edge of China, gazing over the pewter sea. With his bike and his camera as his only companions, he would film a little victory speech.

"Well, after crossing deserts, climbing over mountains, riding through valleys, and across plains, here I am—at the Pacific Ocean." Fifty pounds leaner, cleanly shaven, he would look like a younger version of himself, as if he had ridden time into reverse. He would look to the horizon and say, "There's nowhere else to go."

With gray waves pounding the riprap, he would level his camera, stand by his bike, and shake a cheap bottle of Chinese champagne. He would twist the cork and the cork would break, and he would shrug and laugh. "Well," he would say, to no one in particular, "that was anticlimactic."

This is how Noel's ride—287 days from coast to coast, 175 days in the saddle—would finally come to an end. Total mileage: 10,610. Almost a palindrome.

Along the way, his future had come into focus: go home, get married, and take over his father's bike shop. After 10 months of riding and dreaming, he would return to the woman who waited. But he would find that in his year away, the world at home had changed. Their relationship would slowly unravel. For Noel, the struggle lay not in the journey but the price he would pay in the aftermath.

"Had I been too selfish, too focused on my own needs on the far side of the world?" This question would remain "the painful scar on an achievement that was otherwise wholly fulfilling."

He would ride through Canada, Iceland, Patagonia, and Alaska. He would meet another woman and marry her. Ten years after the meeting, he would be looking ahead to the 50th anniversary of his late father's business, which would grow into nine bike shops. Only close friends and family would know about his odyssey, because he almost never spoke of it.

"You do something like this and you're supposed to have an epiphany," he would say. He would not have an epiphany. He would wonder: "Did I fail?" No, he would decide.

"I went on a bike ride, and that's enough."

LEON

In the Czech Republic, Leon would pore over a map, an act that had become a near-religious ritual. He loved tracing his path behind him and deciding the route ahead. There was a part of him that was ready to finish, but also a part that yearned to keep going. "Could I get to the Arctic Circle?" he mused. On his map he saw new lines to be drawn, new mountains to be conquered. "My map was a two-dimensional representation of possibility, and the longer I looked at it, the more the possibilities multiplied."

The next day, riding toward Prague in the pouring rain would dampen this enthusiasm. His deified notions about the "Grail-like romanticism of the eternal ride" would give way to the desire to be warm, dry, and still.

One soggy night in November, with rain and darkness as his only companions, Leon would pedal into Berlin. Lost on mysteriously empty roads, soaked to the bone, he would find his way to the city center, where a crowd would be celebrating the 20th anniversary of the fall of the Berlin Wall.

He would wake up and decide, for the first time in 15,376 miles and 402 days, he could not bear to get on his bike. Back in Europe, the adventure would fizzle. The ride would feel like a chore. He would realize: *The quest is over.*

Hoping to resolve this strange malaise, he would take a train to Hamburg to visit Carsten, the German he'd met in China. But the spell would be broken. He would fly home to England, leaving his bike in Carsten's tiny apartment. With Leon's permission, his friend would throw the bike away.

Leon would spend a year in England doing odd jobs, fighting ennui, and feeling homesick for the endless road. He would even miss the parade of horribles that made for the rough days and epic tales.

He would visit Afghanistan and North Korea, walk across the U.K., and move to Manchuria in search of "the thing that had made me feel so alive." Ten years after the meeting, he would be finishing his eighth year teaching at a Chinese university.

Would he ever find it again, the thing he had chased across a continent?

"Sometimes, if I keep moving."

LEON + NOEL

This future hangs in the balance, beyond the horizon, as Leon meets Noel.

On this August day, under the noon Kazak sun, Leon rides up to the *chaikana* and sees Noel walking out. The two men stop and stare at each other. *Could this be a mirage?*

"What the hell are *you* doing here?" Noel says to Leon.

"What the hell are *you* doing here?" Leon says to Noel.

Here is Noel, a Sagittarius, born on a Monday in the Chinese year of the Rooster. Here is Leon, a Virgo, born on a Tuesday in the Chinese year of the Dog. Incompatible under both zodiacs, antithetical in many ways. But here they are, colliding in a moment of perfect synchronicity. As if their stories were, indeed, written by one hand.

"My bike is falling apart," Leon says.

"I would love to help you," Noel says, "but I don't have the right tools."

Leon shows him the spoke key. "I have the spokes, too."

"Why didn't you just fix it?"

"I don't know how."

Noel runs his hands around Leon's wheel, feeling for spots where the balance is off. With each twist of the key, he restores the pivotal harmony of diametric forces, adjusting the tension of 32 spokes so the circle is perfectly true.

They go into the *chaikana* and share a meal. Sitting on a carpet, like camel drivers, they swap information about water and share stories about the desert.

They laugh about their inverse names and parallel sagas, but they don't make too much of it. The "cosmic improbability," as Noel describes it, will not occur until later. It soon comes time to go their separate ways, drawn onward by the call of the road. They say goodbye, never to meet again.

On a lonesome road in Kazakhstan, two men diverge in the desert. One is riding into the sun. The other is chasing his shadow. Each finding his own true way through the world, they move toward opposing horizons, lone travelers crossing the hemisphere on circles turning circles.

Kim Cross is the *New York Times* bestselling author of *What Stands in a Storm*, a narrative account of the biggest tornado outbreak on record. A national champion water skier, she has competed in more than 10 sports, some of them laughably obscure. She loves wheelies, dirt jumps, and fly fishing in Idaho, where she coaches her son's school mountain-bike team. Find her at kimcross.com.

Pre-Game Interview

JAY MARTEL

FROM *The New Yorker* • JANUARY 6, 2020

(On the sidelines.)

REPORTER: So this is it, the big event, something you've worked toward, well, not just for your entire career but for eternity. How do you feel?

SISYPHUS: Really good, Bob.

REPORTER: Now, you're the underdog in this matchup. How are you planning on turning things around?

SISYPHUS: Well, I need to go out there and give a hundred and ten per cent. If I stay within myself, I'll take it to the next level.

REPORTER: Any thoughts on the conditions? It's pretty hot out there.

SISYPHUS: Well, it is the underworld.

REPORTER: Right.

SISYPHUS: I like to think that the heat gives me an advantage: firmer footing.

REPORTER: Well, best of luck.

SISYPHUS: Thanks, Bob! I'm not gonna stop till I reach the top! Yeah!

REPORTER: Now let's go to the booth for our live coverage of this exciting matchup. Ted and Pythagoras?

(Minutes later.)

REPORTER: So that was clearly not the result you were hoping for today.

SISYPHUS: No, Bob, it was not. But you try not to get too low from the losses or too high from the wins.

REPORTER: You have no wins.

SISYPHUS: Exactly, but I'm still feeling good about where I'm at. I feel like if just a couple of things had gone differently I could've come out on top.

REPORTER: What things?

SISYPHUS: Well, like if I had been able to keep that rock on top of the hill.

REPORTER: Right. Any thoughts on your opponent's performance?

SISYPHUS: I just have to give the rock credit for what it did out there. In all of our matchups, it's used a similar strategy, and, I have to admit, it's working.

REPORTER: Gravity?

SISYPHUS: Exactly, Bob. And I feel like maybe the rock just wanted it more? A rock that big, you really have to bring your A game to roll it up the hill and get it to stay there.

REPORTER: Which you haven't been able to do yet. Ever.

SISYPHUS: That's right. But I'm not gonna stop till I reach the top! Yeah!

REPORTER: Let's go back up to the booth. Ted and Pythagoras?

(Minutes later.)

REPORTER: So that was…rough. A crushing defeat. Literally.

SISYPHUS: Yes, Bob, it was.

REPORTER: Has it rolled over you like that on the way down before?

SISYPHUS: No, and there's a part of me that's disappointed. But the rest of me is saying, "Go out there and do it!"

REPORTER: Seriously?

SISYPHUS: Yes. If I keep playing my game, that rock doesn't stand a chance! It might as well be getting its mail forwarded to the top of that hill, because that's where it's going to stay!

REPORTER: I admire your fighting spirit—as well as the anachronistic analogy—but aren't you even a little bit discouraged?

SISYPHUS: I am not, because there's no "I" in "fail," Bob.

REPORTER: Actually, there is.

SISYPHUS: There's no "sissy" in "Sisyphus."

REPORTER: So you don't do anagrams.

SISYPHUS: There's nothing I can't do!

REPORTER: Back to the booth.

(Minutes later.)

REPORTER: So, from the replay, it looks like the rock rolled over you, then was delayed by some brush while you slid down the hill, and then it crushed you again. And again and again. Is that right?

SISYPHUS: Yes, Bob. And I won't lie—this one hurts. But it's all mental, and if…

REPORTER: Hold on. We just watched your body being repeatedly pulverized by a huge boulder.

SISYPHUS: You gotta give credit to my opponent. It had a solid game plan today and executed it well.

REPORTER: Rolling over you repeatedly?

SISYPHUS: Exactly, Bob. I just need to get back to my basics, and, boom—I'll be taking it to the next level.

REPORTER: Do you ever wonder what you did to be stuck at this level? Because I do.

SISYPHUS: It's just character-building adversity that, in the end, is gonna make me stronger.

REPORTER: I keep thinking over my life, wondering what I did to anger the gods.

SISYPHUS: The gods are on my side, and I'd like to take this opportunity to thank them for my success, because I'm just one man out here.

REPORTER: You have had absolutely no success. All right, it's time for you to get crushed by the big rock again.

SISYPHUS: Not this time! I'm gonna make you a believer, Bob!

REPORTER: Please, someone make this stop.

(Minutes later.)

REPORTER 2: How do you feel?

SISYPHUS: Really good, Bob.

REPORTER 2: Uh, it's Bill. Bob ran onto the course during that last round and into the oncoming rock.

SISYPHUS: Geez, that's rough. It's a tough game, but you hate to see that happen to anyone. Bob, we're rooting for a speedy recovery, buddy!

REPORTER 2: Bob's dead.

SISYPHUS: Well, my sympathies. I'm not gonna stop till I reach the top!

(They watch the grounds crew working at the bottom of the hill.)

SISYPHUS: As soon as they clean up that mess.

Jay Martel is a novelist, essayist, screenwriter, director, actor, and TV producer. His first novel, the science-fiction comedy *Channel Blue*, was published by Head of Zeus in 2013; his latest novel, *The Present*, is currently available as an Audible Original. He's a contributor to *The New Yorker*, where his humor appears regularly.

The Ramshackle Garden of Affection

ROSS GAY AND NOAH DAVIS

FROM *The Sun* • JUNE 2020

Shortly after Noah Davis enrolled in Indiana University's MFA program, where I teach poetry, we discovered that we're both pretty serious ballplayers. Noah had just finished his basketball career at Seton Hill University, and I had kept up a decent (if intermittent) basketball regimen. We began playing one-on-one together, and while warming up or shooting foul shots in between games, we would talk—about teaching, poetry, family, college sports, gardening. After a couple of months we thought it might be interesting to write letters back and forth. We could make an independent study of it, an exercise in epistolary essay writing. After the semester ended, we kept going, until now we have almost a book's worth of these little missives. They are about basketball, and, as such, they are about gender and masculinity and race and capitalism and touch and care. And, as we're both poets, they're very much about language and the imagination. And, as we're friends, they're also about friendship.

—Ross Gay

Dear Ross,

We play full-court, one-on-one basketball. Every basket is worth one point, every airball is minus one, and every offensive rebound plus one. First to five wins.

You might have your own philosophy on this, Ross, but how are you able to sleep at night? How are you able to sit comfortably by the fire? How are you able to eat barbecue lentils with avocado in a tortilla and talk with Stephanie? How can you live in the warmth of all that when you win by intentionally missing a shot so you can grab an offensive board?

Winning on a *missed shot.*

It's fundamentally wrong, like what I learned in church to call a "sin." It rips and tears at me. It takes away the beauty of scoring.

You can say that jazz and blues have beautiful rips and tears, and they do. That similes and metaphors and line breaks and cadences and titles often have beautiful rips and tears, and they do. And I guess it's gorgeous when you move me—twenty-years-younger-than-you me—out of the way and grab the rebound.

There's also beauty in your caring enough about me and my game to make me suffer, endure, agonize, ache, hurt, and writhe under the fact that I have lost games in which you have scored only one bucket.

And there's a beautiful struggle in putting the ball in the basket. It's hard to put the ball in the basket. It's infinitely easier not to put the ball in the basket. That's why even pros usually miss more shots than they make.

I see a miss as a failure.

Maybe you're better at failure than I am. But how can you miss on purpose? If I'm late getting back on defense, you'll bounce the ball off the bottom of the rim and catch the "rebound" for a point. Alone under the basket. Missing.

When I was in a shooting slump in college, I'd visualize the ball going in, and you're out here missing on purpose. What the hell, Ross!

Why do you mock the skill of making the shot?

What is lost when you miss on purpose?
What is it, Dr. Gay? Professor Gay? Mr. Gay? Ross?
    Love,
    Noah

Dear Noah,

My mother says I was like a little old man when I was a kid. She doesn't mean it the way parents do when they talk about their kids being "old souls," some way of bragging about the wisdom those kids were born with, which never seems to be quite accurate. My mother is not complimentary in that way. She is from the Lutheran-inflected, Calvinist-inspired regions where, when you leave the country for two years, your parents might not hug you and weep and beg you to stay; they might simply shake your hand goodbye. Regions where compliments are bestowed sparingly, where the word *love* is bequeathed rarely. Which is to say, I think she is being more descriptive than complimentary. She is saying that when I looked at a caterpillar crawling on my finger (there is a photograph of this, from the days before the perpetual photographing of everything, though now I can't recall if the photograph is of my brother or me), I looked at it like an old man would. I believe my mother on this—and I do not always believe my mother—in part because her observation has been verified elsewhere, including, alas, on the basketball court.

It seems that from a fairly young age—probably middle school, though maybe toward the end of elementary—I have had what is called an "old man's game." I don't have to tell you, the phrase "old man's game" implies playing as though you are a step slower, with less bounce than the fleet kangaroos who have so graciously permitted you to join them on the court.

Let me make a point here that should be glaringly evident to all who have played the beautiful game of basketball, which is that it is a young person's game. A game that affords no particular benefit to youths would not produce the phrase "old man's game," and with it the anxiety, the looming sense of mortality, that basketball so plainly does. But let me also make a point here that when I visited my pal Jay in Menlo Park, California, a couple of years back, I saw a half-court game consisting of women who all looked to be in their seventies.

The quality of the old *person's* game, then, includes what some might call "cheating." By "cheating" I mean techniques like tugging on an opponent's shorts or jersey to negate the lost step. (Where did the step go, you ask? That's a good question!) Or, my favorite, a simple spin move in close quarters with a touch—more like a thud—of elbow to your man's chest, so he can't sky and block your shot. Or, of course, all the things you can do to get a rebound: hold someone's wrist; pin someone's arm beneath yours; and, beloved standby, grab someone's shorts. In a pickup game the consequences of cheating are, at worst, someone threatening blows. It seems mean to threaten an old man, though, even if the old man in question is only forty-four and four months (and three days).

Now, I'm not saying that I'm smarter than you, Noah, Baby Noah, Big Baby Noah, Sweet Noey. (I have so many names for you that you've not heard me use, which is among the many indications of my love for you, along with the elbows.) But I am kind of saying that. Bouncing the ball off the bottom of the rim is, as you say, a poorly missed shot, but also a perfectly missed one, because it results in a point in our game, which means it's a way for me to stay on the court. If there were a way I could stay on the court without cheating—without those perfectly, beautifully missed shots—believe me, I would do it.

I've been ruminating on today's intramural game, particularly on the discussion I had with the other team's big kid on the line after he was sort of draping himself on me, and I swung the ball quickly by his face, without the least intention of hitting him (which, naturally, I have done to others by accident, and have had done to me; I have several mostly invisible scars through my eyebrows as evidence). I was trying just to get a little space and to stop his hanging on me, which was not, in this game, a foul. When there was a stoppage in play shortly after, I tugged his jersey and said, quietly, soothingly, amicably, in the spirit of reconciliation, "I wasn't trying to hurt you. I want you to know." First he told me to let go of his jersey. He then told me that I'd had bad intentions, a pouty argument that I debated to little effect. Finally he told me not to smack his ass. I think that was the order. And then, in conflict with what I was actually feeling, which was something along the lines of *Oh, shut the fuck up*, I said, "Sorry." And then, stumblingly, "I thought this was an adult game."

I felt myself withdraw somewhat from the game after that, in part because I didn't want this kid to feel attacked, which, evidently, he had. I could not quite tell if he was angry at me for my, shall we say, contact-y play or because, after we would tussle on the court, I would say something to the effect of *Good fight,* or *Good work*, and, shamefully, I would smack him on the ass. When he did not smile at me once, I wondered, flickeringly, *Is he displeased?* Which didn't make sense to me, because we were having fun. Weren't we?

When I feebly suggested, more to myself than to him, that this was an adult game, I was in some way talking about the way basketball (especially the best games, which include, for me, our one-on-ones) elicits or even *requires* a kind of consent. The consent is to many things, and many of those things might fall under a larger umbrella of touch. When you walk onto the court, you are consenting to touch, to being touched. That's basketball. None of which suggests that the nature of the touching is not to be negotiated, as evidenced by the occasional long, high-volume debates that ensue at all the best courts I've ever played on, which sometimes woefully devolve into courtrooms. But usually it's just players working out how to touch one another so that beauty might flourish.

As you mentioned after the game, it's tricky, when we play with other people, figuring out how to dial it back from our game, which includes lots of touching, pushing, scratching, hugging, diving, screaming, sprinting, laughing, ass-smacking, shoving, hurting, cheering, and sometimes bleeding. All of which falls under the umbrella, to be more precise, of affection.

When you dunked on me the other day, it was affection. When I drop my shoulder into your sternum to make a little room for myself, it's affection. When it heats up and we're not laughing and an orbital bone might bust or a tooth loosen, it is, and always will be, affection. When you recover the loose ball I poked from your dribble and drop that thing through the rim and smack me in the ass running back; and when I hit a runner in the game after missing them all during warm-up and I smack my forearm into your back and holler, Gamer! Affection. Which, I'm discovering as I write this, is why I even play basketball: to consent to this ramshackle garden of affection.

     Love,
     Ross

Dear Ross,

I saw you withdraw during today's game.

I feel like some of the problem was me. I let my man score twice early on, their team went up 8 to 4, and they thought they could hang with us, which they couldn't. This early success might have caused an inflated self-image in the big man, who was then deflated by one of your affectionate but, I'll admit, sharp elbows, which I have consented to taking.

I was hurt that you withdrew. You left some boards for others to chase, there wasn't as much talking on defense, and your arms didn't flail with the measured recklessness I've come to expect. This hurt the team, but, as your friend, I was angry that their big man couldn't see what a seven o'clock game on a Monday night meant for his growth as an individual. He couldn't see the sweetness in the competition. He was used to a game centered on violence and domination, and the dissonance of *Good work* and *Good fight* after the bumping and shoving on the court knocked him so off-kilter that he slapped your arm away and ordered you to curb your body movement.

I, too, didn't take this seven o'clock Monday-night game as an opportunity to mature. I had some young-male issue with the fact that you weren't receiving the respect you deserved. I knew that you, a professor, couldn't give this player a less-affectionate touch—not that you should have, because we're trying to spread intense, competitive sweetness and affection. So I trotted to the opposite side of the court and put my shoulder into the big man's chest as he ran back on offense. I wanted him to feel me. I asked him with my eyes, as I backpedaled, if he felt me, if he knew there was another big body he had to recognize.

Big man, if you're reading this, I hope you and I have grown since Monday night. I hope you've found affection in many different places. I hope I can learn to give affection to those who actively reject sweetness. I hope I don't search out other people who offend me and make them recognize my body. I hope you've forgiven my bump.

Ross, the next day a young man playing with us slammed his elbow into your eyebrow while going for a rebound, splitting it open, and I affectionately asked you to go bleed off the court, so we wouldn't have to stop the game. You tried to stop the flow with a band-aid, but blood ran down your nose and into your mouth. Damn, damn, damn. I should've brought you more paper towels.

But you didn't ask for that.

You asked me to keep playing. Not to shy away from this kind of affection.

Love,
Noah

Dear Noah,

The other day I was heading to Cincinnati to hole up and knock out this poem about Dr. J I've been working on since April 4, 2015. Actually I've been working on it since December 3, 2013. More accurately I have been working on it since the 1980 NBA Finals, when the shot I want to meditate on—the best layup in the history of the NBA—actually transpired. Though when does anything actually transpire? Maybe I've been working on it my whole life.

I pulled up near a coffee shop that I'd visited once before, and a block or so away was a nice city ball court, well maintained, right next to a busy playground. There might have been a sprinkler for the kids to enjoy. It was hot. I think the date was May 25. The mulberries in Cincinnati were coming on, the smells of spring hustling toward summer, people out and about in the sun. And on the court I could see that a game was petering out. When a guy walked off dribbling his ball, I asked if this was a regular game on weekend mornings, and he said it was, but there was also one about to start up on 8th Street, or maybe 6th; I can't remember. I made my way toward the street he'd mentioned, which was five blocks away. When I got there, people were laughing, getting loud, shooting around, finding their touch—the good milling about that happens before the work. Another young guy walking down the street asked me, "Are they starting?" I said I thought so, and he took off running—I'm sure to get his gear so he could join. The sun was every bit of out. I looked from across the street beneath a bar's awning because I was shy about standing on the sideline and being asked to play, which I so badly wanted to do. I knew I wouldn't be able to say no, though I needed to say no, because my wrist still hurt from when you'd landed on it. (Don't worry; you're forgiven.) Just picking up my backpack that morning had been a wincing ordeal. I watched for a while as people gathered like they were going to water, which, of course, they were. God, I was thirsty.

One of the benefits of aging is having the wherewithal to hold off from playing when you're hurt—to hang on in the parch when you know that the fun you have today might result in another month or two or more of thirst. Knowing how to sit on your ass and watch the game instead of jumping in. I did such damage to my left big toe when I was twenty-six: I sprained it and wouldn't stop playing, because I was at the height of my flying, and giving up basketball for a few months was unfathomable. And so, for twelve or thirteen years after that, until I finally got it fixed, I had a toe that hurt to touch, was constantly inflamed, and needled me with shards and flecks of bone. I like to have no regrets, everything's a learning experience, etc. But even though I learned something (slow your roll and recover), I kind of regret that.

All the same, it reminds me how much this game makes me think about dying. It makes me think about our precious, brief visit on earth, and how the visit to the court is even more brief, and just as precious. That's what I was feeling, watching people tie their shoes and trot over to get their warm-up shots in and squeezing the ball in their hands. Picking teams and starting to play. God, how soon we die. How beautiful this game.

Love,
Ross

Dear Ross,

I've been up in northern New Hampshire catching brook trout on small mountain streams. The fish are beautiful—some of the most aesthetically beautiful life I've had the joy of encountering. And that list of beautiful life I've encountered is very long.

Like most wild things—like most *living* things—these trout are always on the verge of dying. Floods, drought, ice, eagles, ospreys, mink, pike, bass, other trout, and me. Even though I wish only to hold them for a moment, to meet with this other life quickly before returning it to the stream, they know my shape as one that can bring death.

Because I'm young and confident in my legs, I step quickly over slick rocks in currents strong enough to move even my big frame. My dad walks behind me, and, because he loves me, he's told me five times this year that I'm not invincible and must be careful with my step. I've fallen and slammed my knee, my elbow, and my shin this spring, but there's only been blood and bruises, no sprains or breaks.

He's likely closer to death than me, and is preparing for his own mother's death. I found his mother, my grandmother, on her floor in February. Her face smashed on a chair. She's now in a memory-care unit in Wisconsin, close to my aunt. My father is making sure I don't rush the death that will find me, and I thank him for this. I try to listen. I truly do.

I'm a better listener now than I was in high school when he told me not to force my dunks and I did force one, in the fifteenth game of my senior year, against a team we were beating by thirty. When my fingers didn't wrap around the rim, I swung up under the basket like a bag of groceries in the hand of a child. My wrist and right ankle were beneath me when I landed. While I was on the floor, the gym was silent, and I called, "Dad! Dad!" and he came down out of the stands, and I said sorry over and over, and he said it was fine and he wasn't angry. He and Mom took me to the hospital, where the doctor told me my left wrist was cracked and my right ankle sprained.

On the drive back from the hospital, the moon was as large as a pregnant mother's belly, and, being young and thinking everything revolved around my basketball season, I was amazed that it was still shining when I was so sad. I told my parents this, and Dad said, "Yes, isn't it nice that the moon will be there long after we're all dead?" And, before I could answer, Mom said, "Yes, it is."

The doctor at the hospital said I wouldn't play another game that year, but my mother, who knew I was far from death and who I pray is still far from hers, got me an appointment with the orthopedist at Penn State with the help of a friend, the women's basketball coach. That doctor sawed my cast off, and I played a few more games before we lost far earlier in the tournament than we'd ever thought we would at the beginning of the season.

Even with all the falls I've taken from ledges and into deep water, the closest I've ever felt to death was when I swung off that rim. Mom and Dad were there to see me fall from so high. I was so high, Ross.

Love,
Noah

Dear Noah,

Today I saw the year's first crocuses—purple and gold—tipping their chins to the early-morning light. And the light, too, has a slightly different drape this morning, something beckoning. The daffodils are about to come out, and don't you know they look about to burst, not unlike a baby bird just tapped out of its fragile cell, not quite knowing how to open its eyes.

When I was about your age, my buddy's father collapsed on the court, all six feet nine inches of him. My friend sprinted over to his dad and put his hand immediately to his father's neck and, listening to his breathing, knew he had to start chest compressions, and he did, alternating with the breaths, while his father stared into the lights above, his body rocking with his son's love. The father's body a boat his son was trying to steer. His son was steering. We all were standing there watching this son take his father home.

All the while I was watching this dying, this loving and dying and living, I heard basketballs bouncing, an almost rain-patter of them, though they do not make the sound of rain, unless it is rain on the biggest corrugated-steel roof you've ever seen, and, Lord, I want to play on the court that protects. I want to dance around those puddles.

One day soon the trees I planted with my own father's ashes will have to come down. In the past few years they've been taken over with black rot, a quick-moving disease that will eventually girdle the branches and cut off nutrients to the leaves. It looks like tumors, little knotty growths crawling all over the bark. My father died of a large, knotty growth in his liver, but I don't, I won't, connect my father's death to the death of the trees. It's just the humidity and the spores of fungus riding the winds. It's just that life sometimes requires a little death.

Love,
Ross

Dear Ross,

During a summer-league game, a boy on the sideline slipped away from his mother and stuck his toy into an electrical socket. Sparks the color and shape of the tiger lilies on the east side of my family's house bloomed around his arm.

I was guarding a man who hadn't hit a shot all night, and the boy and the socket were behind him. I saw the blossoming.

The other team's point guard, the boy's father, ran to his son, who wasn't crying, and told him there was nothing to worry about. The man I was guarding said, "It's not OK, though." The father said, "I know, but, God damn, shut the hell up." The burns on the boy's skin followed his muscles like roots.

In spring, before the leaves are out, birds would careen into the glass backboard of our driveway basketball hoop, and my brother, Nathan, and I would pick them up and lay them between the exposed roots of the tulip poplar behind the basket.

I would hear them thump against the glass.

Sometimes they would still be warm. They filled my palm like a dinner roll.

Give us this day our daily bread.

Dear Lord, songbirds died so I could learn to shoot a bank shot.

I've never pictured Nathan and me doing that before, but now that's all I can see: both of us bending down to the driveway's black surface, brown ball beneath an arm, to pick up a yellow goldfinch, neither of us afraid of this death on the court where we hoped to map our future lives with jump shots and rebounds.

Boys gathering dead birds before they play basketball.

After we played, we would take the birds to the woods, where a skunk or fox might find them and live another day.

Did anyone keep shooting after your friend's father died on the court?

We finished the game while the point guard took his son to the hospital.

Nathan and I believed we had to keep shooting.

> *Love,*
> *Noah*

Dear Noah,

There's still laughter, though. When you and I worked out on Thursday, there was some explicit, and explicitly fun, holding or grabbing or tackling. I think you were keeping me from scoring, or from one of my (many) offensive rebounds, and you were like *That's enough of that!* (Since we have stopped counting offensive rebounds as points, I have gleefully been forced to become a better ball-in-basket scorer—a good thing to learn at forty-five!) Anyway, you wrapped me up or near tackled me or shoved me, which made me laugh hard. Other times you got a long rebound and were off to the races, and I hacked you like eight times between the three-point line and the rim (and sometimes you still scored, despite those hacks; ah, youth), and we laughed. Last time it happened, I laughed so hard I had to take a breather, hands on my shorts, the whole deal—not from the three quick full-court points, nor from the sweet fighting we were doing, but from the goofy hold or hapless hack, and the laughter that followed. (An aside: try to write about laughter—not cruel or vicious laughter but joyful, reaching-toward laughter—and see if you don't smile; see if the pelicans don't start lifting off inside your chest.) It occurred to me, and I think I said so, that cracking up is like doing five wind sprints or, better yet, ten burpees in the middle of a point, and that is hard!

I do not know exactly how to articulate this, but I think that these moments of silliness that interrupt the game are the point of the game: when the artifice of the ball and hoop—the machinery of the play—becomes irrelevant to our bodies breathing irregularly, convulsively, our teeth glaring in peace, both of us stumbling toward some mutuality, our laughter saying, *You are safe here. As am I.*

Just across the street, on a grassy hill next to the post office parking lot, I can see two kids—maybe brothers, one big and one little—play-wrestling. The big one tosses the little one around but is careful. It is among the most beautiful sights, bigger children knowing how to play with smaller ones. It is a mutuality, an understanding, or an attempt to understand someone else's body and how to care for it. They are both laughing hard, almost hugging each other to stay upright. Do you know what I'm talking about? They seem to be the point of the game. They are the point of the game.

> *Love,*
> *Ross*

Dear Ross,

I was a big brother who didn't toss his little brother carefully. In high school, every time I raised my hand around Nathan, he would flinch. Even if I was only scratching my head. Even if I was reaching to hug him, which we did more than other brothers we knew. I could even kiss him on the back of his head, and all through middle school he'd ask to sleep with me in my twin bed, and I'd let him. But there were enough times in our playing when I used my hands to strike him that, once he grew big enough to strike back, he did, and I flinched, too. Both of us over six foot three and strong, we flinched from each other.

Each time the other flinched from a movement not soaked in malice, the one who'd raised a hand would bend close, cradle the head of the other, and say, "I'm sorry you're scared." We always meant it. Oh, Mom and Dad, we really meant it.

But, to this day, at twenty-five and twenty-two, we still sometimes strike in malice, then quickly apologize. After years of this we should know better.

Even in our worst times as brothers, we built rafts of laughter to float on together. (Nathan laid most of those planks.) And, just

like you said about how the laughter in our games at the ridicu-
lous shoving is the same as wind sprints and burpees, Nathan's
and my laughter makes us weary enough that the tension coiled
in our muscles, left there by years of flinching from each other,
slackens and lifts like tundra swans flying from cut cornfields.
We're so exhausted from our laughing that we cannot, will not,
move quickly in malice, only slowly in tenderness.

Once, Nathan and I had been playing in the backyard for so
long that our feet were green with grass stains and the fireflies
had come out. We'd played until our veins had risen to our skin's
surface, and we were tired. On our way into the house, we started
to grab and push, the last motions our bodies could muster, and
we moved closer, torso to torso, and then Nathan said something
that he knew would make me laugh, because it had made me
laugh a thousand times before, and we drifted on the wave of
our hooting and hollering around the side yard and the rest of
the way to the garage. Laughed so loud the tundra swans high
above us could hear.

> Love,
> Noah

Dear Noah,

That's exactly it, isn't it? The tenderness is so beautiful, so
precious, because we know life is so often otherwise. Because we
know tenderness is something we need to be shown, and shown
is good. I remember a fight with my own brother. One time, after
we'd done our paper routes (I usually finished before him), I got
home and straightened up the house: folded the throws, put the
newspapers in their place, whatever else a nine-year-old thinks
straightening up entails. My brother came home and promptly
unfolded one of those blankets to snuggle into the couch as the
New Zoo Revue was wrapping up and *Fat Albert* was about to
come on. I had it in my head that he couldn't use the blanket
I'd just folded, so we fought. After I got the better of him, he
retreated to our bedroom.

But I wasn't done. I followed him upstairs to find him under the blankets, and I sat next to him on the bed and started slapping him, methodically, in the mouth, where he had just gotten braces on his teeth. I slapped him again and again until he asked, in a way that still kind of pierces me, "What are you doing?" And I left. My father must've heard him sniffling, because a few minutes later Dad came down in his robe to where I was lying on the couch, enjoying my cartoons, and he commenced to rebalance the scales—which is to say, he made my mouth feel like my brother's must have felt.

You have to be taught tenderness. You have to be shown tenderness. You have to notice tenderness. You have to revere and exalt tenderness. You have to play at tenderness. You have to practice tenderness.

I feel like part of becoming a grown-up person is no longer being shocked by many of the awful things we do to one another—is seeing in every awful thing something very close to something I've done or thought or said. Is knowing that all that is awful outside of me is also present inside of me, in some form or other. And I also know that all that is sweet and beautiful outside of me is also present inside of me, in some form or other. I see my nine-year-old self beating on my brother. I see my brother trying to turn away. I see my father trying to make it better by smacking me in the face. Poor things, every one of them. All of them hurting. All of them wanting to make the hurt stop. All of them tender. All of them needing tenderness.

All of us needing tenderness.

I think it is tenderness you and I are practicing, Noey. I'm sore and bruised and bloody sometimes, my knee sounds like a pepper grinder, and my toenail's about to fall off again, but I think it's tenderness we're practicing: Some balm to the boy who would break his brother's smile. Some balm to the dad who would do the same to his son. Some sweetness to make the malice go soft. The hands for holding. The hands for tending. Some tenderness by

which we kiss the broken thing in us. Kiss and kiss the breaking
thing in us that it might fly away.

> *Love,*
> *Ross*

Dear Ross,

When you contested my shot, putting your long arm as close
to my body as you could without fouling me, so close your sweat
flew into my face, and I made the shot anyway—that's when my
shot became beautiful.

People can make beautiful things alone, but that is not the
effort you and I are invested in. We're invested in the study of
beautiful collaboration that needs others. The kids on the other
court were there to recognize and witness the beauty of that
moment. I think they even huddled together, bumping each other
in excitement at the made shot, chirping like starlings, which
made the shot even more beautiful. We needed their witness,
just as I needed you there to create the shot. We needed them to
carry the embrace and the hollering and the kiss I laid on your
cheek beyond the lines of the court, beyond our joined lives.

Everyone I've ever stepped onto a court with has become a
part of my life. I see it clearly when I recognize a familiar face
on the bus and remember his behind-the-back move into a jump
shot, or when I walk in the arboretum and smell the sweat that
I smelled last semester when another player and I were fighting
for position beneath the hoop. At home in Pennsylvania, players
I haven't seen in years will pass me at Sheetz, and I'll remember
their running form or how they called out to their teammates.
This lingering is a kind of muscle memory, to know someone so
physically, so intimately that their motion on the court is the first
image to cross your mind's eye. I remember their moves before
I remember their names.

Yesterday morning, while I was riding my bike to go talk
poetry with Adrian, I passed a group of men who were hauling
ladders to the side of a rental home to work on the roof. My red

basketball shoes hung off my backpack strap like a pair of giant cherries, and one of the men did a double take.

As I braked at the stop sign, he yelled to me, "Go play some ball, young man!" There was a yearning beneath his exclamation. He had a day ahead of him of nailing shingles in the hot sun. I had basketball in front of me. I couldn't tell if my shoes had reminded him of the beauty of his former basketball life, or if he was lamenting the fact that he was missing some beauty in a gym not a mile away. But I also think he was happy that I'd taken the time to tie my basketball shoes together and would play that day.

His call was a command in the most wonderful sense.

And because of the work you and I are doing, Ross, I could hear a choir of voices harmonizing with his shout:

Go make some beauty, young man!

Go be tender, young man!

Go be sweet, young man!

What a way to begin the day: with strangers beholding the potential beauty in us, a beauty that grows as we share it.

Oh, heaven, when strangers call out asking for beauty.

Love,

Noah

Dear Noah,

Which is, Dear Noey, maybe what we're doing when we call for the ball: calling for beauty, for the chance to make our own bit of beauty. I suspect it is, though I didn't put it that way back when I was coaching, and I would compel my kids—I always refer to the kids I have coached as my kids—to call for the ball, to talk, to be constantly chatting and chirping like a flock of sparrows.

I wish we had said it as such: *Ask for beauty! Ask for beauty, David! Open your mouth! Let Ayshon know where you are! Ask for beauty, Stanley. When you're trailing the fast break, you gotta be asking for beauty. C'mon!* Everyone knows that the team that does the most talking usually wins—and, as you've said, the most touching, which is, at its best, also a beckoning for beauty; and maybe here the argument, too, is that talking is touching, and now that I've said it, I realize I do believe it to be true: talk is touch, which makes a poem a kind of touching. The team that chatters more lets each other know where they are on the court. They know how to find one another. They know how to ask for help. They know how to help. And a quiet team refuses to ask for help, refuses to admit having lost track of who they were defending. A quiet team refuses, too, to say, *I'm open. I'm here if you need me.* A quiet team refuses to need and be needed. What is basketball if not the practice of being needed and needy?

How sweet to get old enough, and lucky enough, to start carving out of oneself the old, dumb, bullshit lie of self-sufficiency; to start carving out of oneself the shame of being needy—even the word is a kind of slur. Did you read the piece Rebecca Solnit wrote about Thoreau and how he dropped his laundry off for his sisters and mom to do every week or so? He wouldn't have written *Walden* without their help, just like his beans wouldn't have come up without the rain, without the sun. And the trees gave themselves for his little cabin. And the leaves made shade and air and dirt. And the critters who nibbled his beans eventually made their ways to dying, gave their meager bodies to the good cause of soil and vittles for the littler ones. And sometimes the bigger. And the sun, can you believe it, keeps shining for now. The temperatures we can mostly tolerate, for now. None of it need be, but it is. It is needed, and we are the needy.

Which would make a good name for our intramural team: We the Needy. Imagine the T-shirts! Though, truly, how are we not on our knees kissing the beloved earth all the time in reckless gratitude? And how beautiful that this basketball game, or the final game we're all moving steadily toward, is one of the ways to be kissing the earth in reckless gratitude. How lucky. We the needy.

Love,
Ross

Ross Gay is the author, most recently, of the poetry collections *Be Holding* and *Catalog of Unabashed Gratitude* and the book of essays, *The Book of Delights.* He lives in Bloomington, Indiana.

Noah Davis' manuscript *Of This River* was selected by George Ella Lyon for the 2019 Wheelbarrow Emerging Poet Book Prize from Michigan State University's Center for Poetry, and his poems and prose have appeared in *The Sun, Best New Poets, Orion, North American Review, River Teeth, Sou'wester,* and *Chautauqua,* among others. His work has been nominated for the Pushcart Prize by *Poet Lore* and *Natural Bridge,* and he has been awarded a Katharine Bakeless Nason Fellowship at the Bread Loaf Writers Conference and the 2018 Jean Ritchie Appalachian Literature Fellowship from Lincoln Memorial University. Davis earned an MFA from Indiana University and now lives with his wife, Nikea, in Missoula, Montana.

The Inheritance of Archie Manning

WRIGHT THOMPSON

FROM ESPN • DECEMBER 11, 2020

Archie and Olivia Manning are sitting in gray rocking chairs on their front porch in Oxford. They are a few hundred yards from the Ole Miss campus, where the speed limit is the same as Archie's old jersey number: 18 mph, please. The Mississippi heat is merciful this early in the morning. He's got a hearing aid. When he walks, his knees sound like someone learning to drive a stick shift. If his house caught on fire, he jokes, the first thing he'd grab would be his cane. She is elegant and funny. They've been married for 49 years and smile at each other a lot. Everyone who walks past their condo waves and feels like they've been given an audience when the Mannings wave back.

It's been a busy summer. They tell me they're currently in the process of putting their big house in New Orleans on the market. That's where they raised their three sons, and now they're down-sizing to a condo a few blocks away. Archie is 71, and Olivia's 71st birthday is in a few months. Their children are grown and gone, and that home is cavernous without the noise and dirty laundry and nonstop football games and driveway basketball shootouts. They bought the house when their lives were expanding. That was a long time ago. They said their middle son, Peyton, is particularly upset about the loss of his boyhood home and all the memories they made there, he being the most sentimental of the three. His parents politely told him that yes, they were aware of his immense wealth, and that no, he couldn't buy it, because what would he do with it, and because life is a circle and they are now in the age of shedding things.

This fall is the 50th anniversary of Archie's senior year at Ole Miss—which I know because I am a sentient organism in the state of Mississippi—and of Olivia's senior year too. This is the third time they've been to Oxford during quarantine, helping with Eli and Abby and their kids, who rode out a chunk of the virus time here. In all, Archie and Olivia have nine grandkids, who know him as Red and her as Go-Go. Everyone loves when Red and Go-Go are around. All the Manning grandchildren have had their own moment of realization when they reconcile the sweet doting man they know as Red with the cultural institution named Archie Manning. It's hilarious when they put it together. A few years ago, Eli's oldest child, Ava, was watching *The Book of Manning*, and after a while, Eli explained that the young man throwing bullets and scrambling to keep plays alive was her grandfather.

"That's Red," he said.

She took this new information in for a minute, watching Archie in the fall of 1969 and 1970. It's been 50 years since he played college ball, and even across those decades and generations a 7-year-old could recognize something special.

"Red was good," she said.

RED AND GO-GO are currently off the grandparent clock and enjoying a lazy Saturday morning with a whole day stretched out before them. The quiet is nice but strange. For the first time in 22 years, they don't have any children in the NFL. Eli and Abby are back in New Jersey now, and Archie laughs about an interview Peyton gave to Dan Patrick, in which he said Eli would rather be getting rammed into the ground by 300-pound tackles than homeschooling his kids and joked that Eli would rather go play for the Chargers than tutor math lessons. Cooper is in New Orleans running workouts with his son Arch, the latest Manning quarterback to set the football world abuzz, and Peyton is being Peyton while enjoying the anonymity the required face masks can give him.

I'm wearing a T-shirt from Alpine Camp for Boys, and that's the first thing they notice.

"Did you go to Alpine?" Olivia asks.

I tell her I did. They know it well.

"We have a grandson…," she begins.

"…Heid Manning," he says, finishing her sentence, which happens a lot with them, so much, in fact, that after a while it's hard to tell where one of them ends and the other begins. They aren't Archie and Olivia so much as *ArchieandOlivia*, which is how folks around town pronounce their name. People see them as a team. Archie is militant about his honors being all of their honors. One of his few notes on *The Book of Manning* was to ask that the director show the 10 mph speed limit sign on the campus in honor of Eli, alongside a shot of the 18 mph signs that honor him. When he finally let Drew, the town where he was born, name the stretch of Highway 49 leading into town after him, he quietly made one demand: It must be named Manning Boulevard, not Archie Manning Boulevard, as a way to honor his father, Buddy Manning, who ran the Case dealership on that highway for years.

Seeing that sign now makes him smile, because these days of shedding are also days of remembering, the self-administered anesthesia for loss, and of reckoning too. The last act of famous men is always about closing the gap between the avatar they are in public and the human being they are with the people who love them most. The big anniversaries started three years ago, for Archie's 50th high school reunion in Drew, which Archie attended. Olivia didn't come to this one, although she went to one in Drew a few years before, when they snuck out to eat a steak at Crawdad's in nearby Merigold before returning to the party. The celebrations haven't really stopped, marking 50 years since he played Alabama on prime time or since the Sugar Bowl, and they'll go until next year, when they celebrate five decades of marriage.

"Fifty years in January," she says.

"Who introduced you?" I ask them.

"I think I gave you and Jim Poole a ride somewhere one day," she says, looking over at Archie.

"She had a car," he says, smiling. "I didn't."

"I gave you a ride to Leslie's drug store," she says.

Archie smiles again sheepishly.

"No," he says. "We said Leslie's. We were going to the pool hall."

"We started dating the spring of our freshman year," she says, laughing. "We've been together a long time. I wish I had documented how many football games I've been to."

A few times they've had friends in town for a football weekend and decided to rest Archie's bad knees and watch the game on television. They keep beer iced down in the back, and when Olivia goes out to get one she likes to hear the metallic waves of noise coming from the stadium, the disembodied cheering like a recessional hymn, or maybe just the opposite: a long-lost friend stopping by to say hello.

MY MOTHER'S CONDO BUILDING is next door to theirs, so we catch up about the neighborhood. It's that brief early-morning window when people emerge from the cocoon of air conditioning and walk around town. Archie, Olivia and I talk as a steady stream of people pass on University Avenue. Everyone who walks from the town square to the campus passes their porch. We are close enough to the sidewalk to hear the whispers of the joggers and strollers as they pass: *Holy s---!* Nationally, he's best known as the father of Peyton and Eli. But inside the triangle of, say, Memphis, New Orleans and Destin, Florida, he is as beloved and culturally important as any living athlete.

"It is kind of fun even now," Olivia says, "when you walk on The Square with Archie and people see him and their reaction."

She turns to him and laughs.

"I'm surprised people even recognize you," she says, "but... they know. I've heard people walk by, turn around and kind of come back and go, 'That's Archie Manning!'"

Olivia tells me, as she always does when we are together, how much I look like my late father. I appreciate that. They all went to college together. My dad was in ROTC and felt certain that when law school ended he'd be shipped to Vietnam—he had his post-graduation orders to report to military intelligence school when he jumped at an offer to trade his active duty for many years in the reserves. For my dad and a lot of his classmates, Archie's college career coincided with a desperate need to live in the moment. The students who watched Archie from the stands would miss that feeling once it was gone and would never stop chasing it. My dad and his friends would pass around old cassette tapes of Ole Miss radio calls with the same intensity that I later traded Grateful Dead bootlegs.

Archie gets that. His draft number was 75. A friend-of-the-program doctor down in Jackson did Archie's Army physical and, yes, an All-America quarterback was deemed physically unfit for combat. The strangeness of that time binds him and his fans, and the long tail of his post-career stardom cannot be separated from the moment in which that stardom began. He's always been a kind of vessel. Maybe that's why he is unfailingly generous with liquored-up contemporaries who corner him on the way back from the men's room to tell him where they were when he performed some secular football miracle. It's almost hard to overstate how he exists as a symbol with only a fleeting resemblance to an actual human being. A few years ago, my godfather, Steve Vaught, from Moon Lake, Mississippi, flew up to Washington to see a new Episcopal bishop be ordained in a carnival of incense and liturgy. When he got home, he called my mom. She asked him to describe all that ritual and ceremony. "Mary," he said, pronouncing my mother's name with three drawled syllables, "I haven't seen anything that impressive since Archie Manning's junior year."

The Vaught story is funny to them because they know Steve and can hear it in his almost cartoonish Mississippi Delta accent: *June-yah. Yeee-uhhhh.* I tell them I've been over to Indianola, where incidentally Vaught once ran a John Deere dealership, and that I dug up some funny old clippings from *The Enterprise-Tocsin*, the local paper that covered the tiny farming community of Drew when Archie was a boy. Turns out, long before he became a football star, young Archie Manning was a champion of the Sunflower County 4-H circuit. He and his sister kept their animals out at the small family farm east of town on the Quiver River, and he regularly showed up in the paper. He received a prize for junior public speaking, for a third-place heavyweight Hampshire class fat lamb and for his specialty, the ever competitive and oddly technical subculture of poultry judging.

Olivia knows where this is going and she's already laughing.

"It's Cooper's favorite routine," she says.

"My son just thinks that's the weirdest thing he's ever heard of in his life," Archie says. "That we judged chickens."

He gets into character. Now he's standing up on the condo porch, hands behind his back and his shoulders braced at attention, reciting his speech to Sunflower County's most knowledgeable poultry men. The trick, he says, was you had to check the vents. I don't know what that is, but apparently a sensitive hand can tell a lot from the vents of a chicken.

"You feel these chickens," he says, "then you gotta rate 'em."

Olivia and I are about to fall over. People are walking past, sneaking peeks, as he explains the competition, even down to how they rated eggs both pre- and post-cracking. The three of us spend the morning laughing like this. Archie always seems like he's in a good mood. Cooper says he rarely sees his dad get aggravated, even when he knows Archie doesn't particularly like someone.

Eventually we move inside. There's a new Ole Miss powder blue football helmet with No. 18 on the side and a painting in the kitchen by Mississippi artist Bill Dunlap, who is the Monet of the bespoke shotgun set. The couches are comfortable. I always feel that sitting with Archie and Olivia is like being inside a football snow globe—looking back at the people looking in. That feeling is intensified inside the condo, where all of their family photographs look familiar but slightly askew. It takes a minute to figure out why. There's Eli in street clothes outside Giants Stadium, and there's Cooper and Peyton long after a game. Then it hits me. Their memories often begin just as our memories end. We remember the thunderous noise of a stadium, but they remember the quiet car ride home. They've lived this public-private duality for a half-century now.

Archie occupies a unique place in sports popular culture: Anyone can get him on the phone at any time—a college student at Virginia recently interviewed him for a class project—and he is unfailingly polite and accommodating but lets no one except Olivia inside. He is at once among the most accessible *and* inaccessible people in sports. Few living humans have given as many rubber chicken speeches or held court more at charity golf tournament grill rooms. For 50 years now he's grown expert in the art of being visible and yet invisible, famous and yet private, beloved and yet unknown. He holds his cards close, and his only real tell is silence. Sometimes Archie gets quiet and lost in his memories, and those rare moments when words fail him are when he says the most.

It's 80 miles from their condo to Drew.

Every now and again Archie and Olivia will get into their car and drive out of the hills and into the flatland Delta that starts just outside Marks. They'll take the left to cut across the alluvial cotton fields and the dark green soybean fields nearing harvest. They follow the highway that mirrors the tracks of the old Yellow Dog railroad line. Tutwiler and Rome come and go in a blur of abandoned country stores and shotgun homes. Neither of them needs a GPS to navigate the little towns. They pass through Vance, near where John Lee Hooker was born—and where the brutal landscape makes his droning, hypnotic blues feel created by the dirt and not by human hand. The road signs warn them and all other drivers not to stop within a mile or two of the Gothic Parchman prison farm, where the heavy air of human suffering is an almost physical thing. Summer drives taste like tomatoes, and fall drives smell like thick clouds of defoliant being sprayed on the cotton by low-flying yellow crop-duster pilots, who love to dive under power lines and buzz passing cars. For the Mannings, it's a drive through a world of used to be.

"Drew would have dances," Olivia says. "After you watched Lawrence Welk with your mom and dad."

Archie starts laughing. Did I mention they laugh constantly?

"Oh my, I still watch it," he says.

You can almost hear her eyes rolling. He's getting so nostalgic in his old age—although to be honest he's always wanted to curate his own memories and just pick the good ones. A long time ago he got paired with Welk at a celebrity golf tournament and snuck off to find a pay phone to call his mama back in Drew and tell her. Now 71, he loves that a local New Orleans station still airs reruns.

"At six o'clock," she says.

"Saturday night at six o'clock, and I watch it," he says.

"He has a cocktail and…," she says.

"…I watch it," he finishes.

So when he goes back to Drew now, he always starts the drive by saying that they will only go to the cemetery to visit his mama and daddy and that he won't subject himself to the trauma of seeing his sepia memories stripped away when confronted with the reality of his hometown.

"That's all we've got there is a cemetery," Olivia says.

But he always caves, pulled back into the streets of his youth. He drives around and leaves feeling hollow. It's hard to explain how decayed and ruined Drew looks now, or how much that lives inside former residents like Archie. It's something they carry around, long after they've moved away. There's a store on the main drag through town where the front has just crumbled and fallen, revealing racks of clothes inside. The town can feel abandoned, though the census says 2,000 people still live there. The two most prominent features are burned shells of houses and enormous potholes, some of them as wide as a beach towel and as deep as a quart of milk.

This summer I went to have lunch with Stafford Shurden, my friend from Drew. Stafford is part owner of Archie's old home, and he drove me over. We found it boarded up. Squatters had been living inside or something. Stafford came here with Archie once and, knowing what he knows about the horrible memories Archie might associate with this place, he watched him closely. Archie focused on the good and smiled a little, pointing to the spots in the yard where he'd played. He talked a lot about his mom that day but didn't mention his dad.

"It had to be something he was thinking about," Stafford says.

As I looked over at the abandoned high school, Stafford got a drill out of his truck and unscrewed the plywood over the front door. We stepped into the dark house. The kitchen floor had partially caved in, the stove listing at the back of the room like a doomed ship. We hung close to the walls so we wouldn't fall through. There was an empty pack of Newports on the floor. There were two bedrooms in the back. One of them is where Archie's father died. I didn't know which one. I won't ever ask him.

There was a feeling in the air, unspoken at first, that we were emotionally trespassing. It didn't feel right to me, and we turned to retrace our steps along the sturdier wall joists toward the front door. I tell Stafford what I'm thinking.

"Well, you know," he says, "he says in his book that he felt like his dad set it up for him to find him."

ON AUG. 16, 1969, Archie went to a Delta wedding with his mom and sister. His dad, local tractor dealer Buddy Manning, had made an excuse and stayed home. Dark clouds rolled in from the hurricane gaining speed and power in the Gulf of Mexico. It was the second day of Woodstock in upstate New York. Archie and the guys talked about the coming season, and then he went back home. He walked into the house there on the corner across from the high school, through the kitchen and into the hallway. What he saw from there were his dad's feet dangling off the bed, and something about them felt wrong. That's what made him go into the room.

He saw the shotgun and the stick used on the trigger.

He saw the blood.

One version of Archie disintegrated right there on the spot, and another was born, tougher, more private, wounded, searching. Picture him in these first moments of his new life. It's incredible to consider the reservoirs of courage and resolve he tapped. He summoned the town doctor, called a family friend to make sure not to let his mom and sister come home, and then Archie Manning cleaned up the scene. He wanted to protect Sis and Pam from the horror he would bear wholly himself, locked up deep inside, a pain he would only rarely mention in a life filled with endless opportunities and indeed command performances to talk about himself. He cleaned the floor and walls. He watched an ambulance take his father away. He turned to face the world. He told me not long ago a boy walked into that house and a man walked out.

"When it happened, it was a daze," he says. "I'm rolling along and in this little dream world, a 19-year-old. I'm a starting quarterback for an SEC school and I'm dating a pretty girl and I'm from a nice little hometown and we're gonna play a national night game on TV. Everything was so hunky-dory and then boom…."

A man from the tractor dealership brought Buddy's last check, and when Archie opened it, he understood for the first time how little money his dad made. Archie took responsibility for the arrangements. "I had about 10 days here to help get my daddy buried," he says, "and decide whether I'm going back to Ole Miss. Those 10 days were crucial."

He decided to quit football and get a job in Drew to support his family. But his mother, who would go on to work for a local lawyer until almost the week she died at 81, in 2000, demanded he return to Oxford. Archie would never live in Drew again, and the 4-H small-town life would grow more nostalgically perfect with each passing year. Mayberry, he'd call it. A time before pain. I've often thought that when Archie describes his hometown, he's really describing an innocence before he had to try to rebuild himself and prepare to take the field again. He's not from Drew so much as he's the one citizen of a world his dad's suicide created.

To this day, Archie dreams at night of the life that ended that August day in 1969, always good and happy dreams, of the place where country folks came to town to shop on Saturday night, the rumbling cotton gins, the one stoplight without a yellow for caution, just green for go and red for stop. His future awaited him at Ole Miss, and he reluctantly left his grieving mother and sister and struck out on his own. He rode those 80 miles back into the foothills of Panola and Lafayette counties, leaving behind Drew and his flatland youth, arriving in Oxford a highly touted but still mostly unknown player.

"When I got back," he says, pausing, searching for the words, "...it was really tough. Two-a-days, not really in class, got some time on your hands. Olivia got back on campus. I wouldn't have made it without Olivia."

Thirty-five days after Buddy Manning died, Archie took the field in Oxford as the junior starting quarterback. The Rebels won. Two weeks after that, only 49 days since his father's suicide, he gave one of the greatest performances a quarterback had ever given, accounting for 540 total yards in a hard-fought loss to Alabama in the second-ever prime-time college football broadcast. Archie became a folk hero overnight, and the mania that continues to shadow him even at 71 began. Two moments 49 days apart. That's when both the man and the myth started. If the man Archie Manning is today was born on Aug. 16, 1969, in a small house on Third Street in Drew, and if his legend was born in Birmingham on Oct. 4, then these two closely related but clearly separate people—the private human and the public icon—would have 49 days between them, a separation that the past five decades have closed but never erased.

Archie started getting thousands of letters. Tribute songs hit the radio. This is the season my godfather compared to a religious ceremony: *Archie Manning's Junior Year.* For Ole Miss fans like Steve Vaught and my late father, that was the greatest fall of their lives. For Archie and his family, it was…complicated. "All of a sudden I start having my best year in football," Archie says. "Fifty years later, it's *still* my best year ever. That was a lot—losing my dad and all of a sudden all this success and acclaim."

After a big game, in the quiet moments of a bus or locker room, he raged internally about the unfairness of his dad missing all this by a month and a half. One day not long ago, Archie and I talked about this season on the phone, and I think his voice might have cracked when he talked about the things his father didn't get to see. "He wasn't one of those daddies who always had his nose in it, but he was proud," Archie says, talking slowly. "He would have loved all those games and those wins. He would have loved it."

Archie burrowed himself deep into the team, where a worried head coach John Vaught kept close emotional tabs on his young star. When award season rolled around later, Archie found himself the only one of his peers who traveled with an assistant coach, Vaught wanting to make sure he always had someone nearby. Archie's response to the twin storms of grief and celebrity was to pull the people in his life even closer, especially his girlfriend, Olivia. They'd been dating since freshman year, when her popularity and beauty made her more of a big deal on the campus than just another recruit trying to make the team. I ask if he remembers the first time he saw her after his dad died. He gets quiet. Olivia and her parents came to the funeral, he says. Their support meant so much to Archie that he would later give her dad his Sugar Bowl watch.

I ask if he remembers that first moment of eye contact and the lifetime of promises that lived in it—an understanding that she would share the spotlight with the outward legend but make a real life with the man inside. There is a silence.

"Yeah," he says finally.

Then Archie is gone for a minute, alone for a walk in his memory, his smooth facade down and his tenderest place exposed.

"Yeah," he says.

He is clearly standing again in that cemetery.

"Yeah..." he says.

It's the summer of 1969. Drew is still vibrant, and his stardom is still a month away, and everything remains in front of him, all of it, the Sugar Bowl, the Saints, Cooper, Peyton and Eli, the future unknowable and far, far away. But Olivia is there, and things will somehow work out for the best.

"...yeah...yeah...yeah," he says, six times in all, and then he's quiet again.

ARCHIE'S PHONE IS NEVER SILENT. That familiar Apple alert noise eventually just fades into background noise. It's pretty funny. Cooper, who has quietly become a successful New Orleans businessman while remaining the family comedian, likes to do his impersonation of his dad's pocket.

"Ding, ding, ding, ding, ding, ding," he cracks.

There is a case to be made that Archie Manning has more ongoing text threads than anyone else alive. Olivia's laugh has more than a little side-eye in it.

"He does," she deadpans.

The tentpole thread is named the Dirty 30. That's his freshman teammates at Ole Miss, the recruiting class of 1967. There were 30 of them who survived the brutal winnowing orchestrated by their main coach, a former ass-kicking, island-storming Marine named Wobble Davidson, who regaled his terrified charges with stories of going into caves and killing the enemy. Wobble's wife, Sarah, acted as a kind of den mom to help the boys lick their psychic wounds.

They talk about their grandchildren and what uniforms the Rebels might wear in the upcoming game. They still call football helmets "hats" and make a lot of jokes about being grumpy old men.

"On the thread I'm 18," Archie says. "That's all they call me. They call me 18."

They've lost seven friends in the past 50 years, and Archie was there to eulogize and bury them all except for his right tackle, because a looming back operation kept him from walking—an absence that "killed me," he says. Three years ago, as his season of remembering began, the Dirty 30 had a reunion at Ole Miss.

"Even Sarah Davidson came," Olivia says.

Archie sends out texts every morning to his children and grandchildren and a few of his grandchildren's high school teammates. Sometimes scripture. Sometimes a thought for the day. Sometimes he sends a quote. When Drew Brees decided what the world really needed was his opinion about a protest of social injustice in America, Archie's daily motivational text message the next morning quoted Will Rogers: "Never miss a good chance to shut up."

He checks in on former teammates at all three levels. The fruits of those conversations pepper his daily life: He'll talk about a guy who was on the Saints for two years who has a son who plays college ball out west now, or maybe about a guy from Mississippi who owns a duck-hunting farm or something.

"I'm going, 'Dad, what the hell are you talking about?'" Cooper says.

Sometimes Olivia or the boys will ask him about his day.

"I got a lot of work done," he'll say, and what he means is that he called or wrote about 40 people. It's how Archie chooses to spend his time. Some of this is Archie understanding that a note from him means a lot to people. But he also doesn't want to disappoint. He rarely tries one of the endless and fabulous new restaurants in New Orleans because he feels so guilty.

"The old places have always been so good to me," he explains, "and I feel like if I hadn't been in in six weeks, it's kind of like, 'Where you've been?' So I try to be loyal and faithful."

"I go to the new places with the girls," Olivia says.

"I'm going to Manale's, and I'm going to Clancy's," he says.

He feels a responsibility, to himself, to his mother who endured, to his father who couldn't endure. Sometimes I think about the energy he must spend trying not to let people down. Nearly every person in Oxford has a story, such as the waiters at City Grocery who complained about his table leaving only a 10% tip only to find Archie back in the next day to make it right. My cousin Michael was one of the top people in the athletic department before he took a job at Texas A&M. He told me once about the time he got a phone call from one of Archie's friends. Archie was on crutches from a recent surgery and was trying to figure out how to park close enough to the stadium to get inside. But he would never ask the program for a favor, so his friend was taking matters into his own hands. When Michael called, Archie tried to tell him no until he finally just took the parking pass—which allowed him to park near a building *and* a street bearing his last name. He puts tremendous pressure on himself, it seems, to be the man people expect him to be, which of course is the man he expects himself to be too.

If some kid who attended the Manning Passing Academy eight years ago had a great Arena League game, he could expect a text from Archie. He'll check in with Fran Tarkenton and with former Ole Miss legend Charlie Conerly's widow and still find the time to send NFL general managers gushing texts about his grandson Arch's latest triumph. He checks in with me, for god's sake, giving me an opening to send a picture of my young daughter. "It's constant contact," Cooper says. "His never losing touch with everybody that has been a part of his life has been remarkable. He is really, really, really good at keeping in contact with people."

A lot of people don't know that the summer Buddy Manning took his own life, Archie was up in Oxford working out and taking classes. It was the first summer he hadn't worked on a brick-laying crew in Drew. So in the small window after summer school ended but before two-a-days began, Buddy drove up to Oxford to pick up his son. They rode those 80 miles back out of the hill country into the Delta and went back home. Buddy waited until Archie was home to kill himself, and Archie has spent a lot of time trying to understand why. His best guess is his father knew that Archie could handle it and that he'd shield his mom and sister. In that light, Buddy is a deeply imperfect hero, living in constant inner pain, just hanging on until his special boy was home and would be able to clean up the mess and take up the burden. Archie lives with the fact that he missed the signs, if there were any. He let his father slip through his fingers, and in the five decades since, he hasn't let that happen to anyone else. Once you are in Archie Manning's life, he is fierce in his desire to keep you there.

He never lets anyone go.

ARCHIE KEEPS A LOCKBOX in a bank in New Orleans. Inside are things he inherited from his father. There are more than a dozen pocketknives, including a beautiful green one monogrammed "EAM." His dad always told him a man should carry a pocketknife. His uncle Peyton told him to always carry a handkerchief, and Archie still does. But the real treasures stored in the bank are Buddy Manning's pocket watches. There's one on a silver chain. One is engraved. Another is well worn and scratched. There's one made by the Illinois Watch Company, which was started in 1867 and made it until 1928, the time frozen at 1:54. The Elgin brand is stopped at 12:50, the Bulova at 9:55, the Waltham at 10:32. He doesn't think any of the watches work anymore, which doesn't matter much because their value to him was never about their ability to mark the passage of time. Or rather, because their mere presence in his life tracks the rushing away of days in a more sophisticated and cosmic way than the marriage of springs and gears. The wristwatch my father left me doesn't tell time any longer either, and for reasons I don't fully understand I haven't taken it to get fixed. I think I like it broken. This morning I read a poem by Philip Levine called "Inheritance." It's about an old Bulova watch that "finally threw up its twin baroque arms to surrender to the infinite and quit without a word." That poem unlocked something about the innate human desire to stop time, and about the way that few things are more freighted with meaning and symbolism than a hand-me-down watch that no longer runs. Levine speaks for those timepieces when he writes that heirlooms are merely "amulets against nothing." Archie texted me a dozen photos just now of him holding these watches, turning them over in his hands, the gold and silver and brass cold against his palm.

I, ELISHA ARCHIE MANNING III, being of sound mind and body...

His father died at 59, his grandfather at 79, his great-grandfather at 85. Archie is 71. He's got years and years left, but he is in that glowing final act. What will his children and grandchildren inherit from him?

They will inherit football.

The Manning grandchildren don't really get how rare it is for one family to produce so many professional quarterbacks. Once Eli's daughter, Ava, was trying to sort out the whole situation. She was 8 or so and had questions.

"So you play for the Giants?"

Eli said yes.

"And Uncle Peyton played for the Broncos?"

Eli said yes.

"And Red played for the Saints?"

Eli said yes. Ava considered all this. Her other grandfather, Abby's dad, is called Tom-Tom. You see where this is going.

"Who did Tom-Tom play for?"

Eli tried to explain that Tom-Tom didn't actually play football.
"Why?" she asked.

His family will inherit a lot of stuff. In preparing for their big move, they've been going through a storage unit. Sitting with me one day, Olivia recounts all the stuff that has somehow followed them for all these decades.

"We found Archie's pins from 13 straight years of attending Sunday school," she says, laughing. "Perfect attendance. And his tap shoes."

"Olivia says I'm a hoarder," he says.

They will inherit his deeply ingrained instinct for self-deprecation. Here's a story he loves to tell on himself. The summer before Arch Manning started playing junior high football, he and his dad, Cooper, and Archie traveled to a baseball tournament together. Arch used the time to ask his granddad for advice about the coming season.

"Red," he said, "I'm gonna be playing real football this fall. Do you have any advice?"

This caught Archie off guard.

He thought about all the lessons he'd learned about being a quarterback, and all the lessons he'd taught. With his grandson eagerly awaiting the matrix to be revealed, Archie told him about how important it was for quarterbacks to have total control in the huddle, even if that means standing outside the team for a second to get composure and control.

"You are in charge of your huddle," Archie said.

There was a pause.

"Well, Red," Arch said finally. "We don't ever huddle."

They both laughed.

"I'm old," Archie says.

They will inherit a lot of valuable parenting lessons, as Archie leaned on the men in his life like Coach Vaught and Olivia's dad and his uncle Peyton. Think about his son's names: The oldest is named after Olivia's dad, the middle after his uncle, and not until the baby did he name a child after his own dad. Cooper sometimes wonders how his dad learned how to be a man in the years after Buddy died. It remains something of a beautiful mystery, but he's grateful. At no point in the mania of Eli and Peyton did Archie ever make Cooper feel slighted or somehow inferior, a lesson Cooper leans on now that he has his own superstar in the making. He remembers a moment during one of his brothers' Super Bowl runs when he heard Archie bragging about the youth baseball team Coop had been coaching. "He could talk about that and make it seem just as important as it was when Eli beat Brett Favre at Lambeau Field," he says. "There was never even an ounce of jealousy for me because I felt like Dad and I were in it together."

Archie loves being part of the action. Arch and his Newman teammates have spent the summer doing cruel running workouts texted from Eli to Cooper, while Archie stands to the side and runs the stopwatch and yells encouragement. Long ago he stopped thinking of himself as a quarterback and started thinking of himself as the father of quarterbacks. For years, the last four digits of his cellphone number were a reference to his own pro football career: 0808. A few years ago friends noticed a change. He had four new final digits: 1810.

Now he's the grandparent of a quarterback, and there's some magic at work in the timing. Just as their life of Sundays ended, they found a way back to Friday night. Their children's football careers have ended exactly as their first grandson's career is taking off, just in case they weren't catching enough of the circular vibes being thrown at them by the universe. They are back where all this began, in metal bleachers beneath halogen lights.

"That's a lot more fun," she says.

"High school is so pure," he says.

His grandchildren will inherit a fighting spirit that is sometimes obscured by how friendly Archie is with strangers. Yes, he is a 71-year-old man with an earnest, goofy grin who finds time for everyone. But don't misunderstand. He is also still the young man who found his father's dead body and cleaned it up. He is still the man who won those big football games in college, who won a Sugar Bowl, who endured season after season of beatings in the NFL.

As we talk about all this passage of time, Olivia interrupts us and hands over a photograph that just arrived via text. She seems joyful and proud.

"I just got this from Abby," she says. "Eli and Ava are off to play in a father-daughter golf tournament."

They both look so happy. I wax about how cute they look and what a special bonding experience this will be. Her grandparents know better.

"Ava's competitive," Olivia says with a knowing smile.

THERE IS ONE THING his family will not inherit. They will never experience the darkness Archie battled when his father chose to exit his son's life. Nobody will. He keeps that private. Buddy Manning loved his son. Archie is sure of it. But he never said the words. Not once. Archie says the words to his sons every day. Those three boys, grown men now, live in a world where circles are always whole. The pain that killed Buddy Manning died in that room with him, and not because of luck, and not by random, but because Archie made the decision that he would keep that hurt himself and not pass it on. The public story of the Manning family is famously that his boys followed in his footsteps, a narrative so powerful it leaves little room for a hidden, essential and foundational truth. Archie has chosen the parts of himself and his past that will live on and he has chosen the parts that will not. And the one thing that will die with him, that will not take up hidden residence in his children, or their children, is what that room on Third Street in Drew really *felt* like. That burden is his alone. Carrying it has been the most important job of his 71 years.

LAST YEAR ARCHIE GOT yet another lifetime achievement award, which is as close as a human can get to attending his own funeral. He knows exactly what folks will say when he's gone, which is a weird piece of information to have. This particular ceremony was for being a distinguished American, given out in the Yale gymnasium on the campus in New Haven, Connecticut. Everyone wore tuxedos. The retired Ole Miss sports information director and close family friend Langston Rogers, who used to watch after Cooper, Peyton and Eli at ceremonies just like this one, accompanied Archie to Yale out of love and habit.

A chain of surgeries had left Archie struggling. The walk to the microphone took a far greater toll than he let on. So as Archie started his speech, Rogers looked around for an elevator. He didn't think Archie could make the long trek back up the stairs to the waiting car. Onstage Archie talked about sitting with Buddy Manning on Saturday afternoons and listening to college football on the radio. The memories he shared of that time were light and full of joy. That's a choice he made a long time ago. He indulged his nostalgia for Oxford, talking about the big games and the lifelong friends and how he met Olivia there. He told the crowded room about how Coach Vaught had been like a father to him long after the last play had been called and the last football snapped. Archie talked about visiting his old coach three and four times a week in the last month of Vaught's life.

When the speech ended, to great applause, Langston whispered in Archie's ear that he'd found an elevator and they didn't need to walk. Archie waved him off. With Rogers watching in fear and then admiration and then awe, Archie slowly climbed the stairs by himself, without help or pity, just a man who long ago learned what it took to look at himself in the mirror and be proud.

In the coming years you will be able to find Archie Manning on Friday nights sitting up at the top of the high school bleachers, wearing the green of Newman on his baseball cap, the rare man who has lived a public life of incredible highs and harrowing lows and finds himself content in the glow of the world he created. He presides over a close-knit family whose members haven't let fame or money take the most essential part of themselves. His race is run and he is enjoying the victory parade. That's the energy

Archie puts out when people spend time with him—at a high school game in New Orleans, on his porch in Oxford. You can feel the contentment.

His phone dings and he looks down. More texts from the Dirty 30.

One of them is a link to an interview that young Arch Manning gave to a recruiting website, his first big media moment. The young man talks about the pressure of his last name and how he just wants to be a good teammate and leader. Archie looks at a photograph someone has texted the group. It's of a huge red moon hanging over Deer Island on the gulf coast near Biloxi: a 4-mile sliver of fragile sand that gets smaller by 2 acres a year—literally a piece of Mississippi that is disappearing, a little more with each cycle of that big moon. One day the only thing left of Deer Island will be the memories and stories of those who once enjoyed its shores. Memories and stories, which can withstand even the tide, as long as they are told and retold. Someone else texts a link to an old Elvis Presley video about picking turnip greens. The Dirty 30 are themselves prolific traffickers in the same nostalgia that often ensnares their most famous member. When Archie pulls it up to listen, there's a driving bass line and Elvis is singing on a Las Vegas stage in the summer of 1970, almost 50 years ago to the day. The horns shift into gear, rockabilly trill guitars, then fast bluegrass picking and a funky wah-pedal tone. Archie is transported to that magical time in Oxford, between his junior and senior years, when he and his girlfriend, Olivia, walked hand in hand through a campus that one day would be a shrine to their family name.

Wright Thompson is a senior writer for ESPN. This is his first appearance in *The Year's Best Sports Writing*.

"There Might Be a Family Secret"

JAYSON STARK

FROM The Athletic • SEPTEMBER 11, 2020

On Friday night on the South Side of Chicago, a father and son will sit side by side at a baseball game, like so many fathers and sons before them. But here's what will separate them from all those other fathers and sons:

They've never spoken. They've never met. For more than half a century, by all indications, neither was even aware that the other existed.

And there's more. The father spent 14 seasons pitching in the major leagues—two more than the son he never knew. The father pitched in five All-Star Games. The son pitched in one.

They shared remarkably similar journeys, connected by the same magical allure of the pitcher's mound. Yet they shared virtually nothing else in life.

Even now, as they're about to share a moment that has connected parents and children for generations, they will share it not in the flesh but through cardboard cutouts. Yet there is something special about the presence of those two cardboard figures, seated behind home plate at Guaranteed Rate Field, that makes this the coolest real-life baseball fable of 2020.

The story behind that story—the improbable tale of how former White Sox pitcher Richard Dotson and his mysterious father,

Dick "Turk" Farrell, wound up in this spot, in Section 130-S, row
4, seats 5 and 6—is a saga right out of a Hollywood movie lot.

A family secret, never revealed…a DNA kit that sat in a
drawer for years…a surprise message from a total stranger…a
shocking revelation…a son's pursuit of a never-told story…and
a global pandemic that created a kind of connection that could
never have happened in any other baseball season in history.

Are we sure this isn't a movie?

"There's a lot of this where it feels like that at times," Dotson
says. "And it's funny because I lived my life. I know what went
on. But OK, now here I am, at 60, and it turns out that what you
thought you knew isn't really what you knew."

RICHARD FARRELL WAS BORN in Boston in April 1934. He
was 22 when he first pitched in the big leagues, for the Phillies,
in September 1956. He was 35 when he threw his final major-
league pitch, on a Friday in September 1969—striking out John
Boccabella of the Expos at Parc Jarry in Montreal. Soon thereafter, he moved overseas to work on an oil rig off the British coast.

Richard Dotson was born in Cincinnati in January 1959, six
months after Turk Farrell struck out the great Ted Williams in
the 1958 All-Star Game. Dotson was drafted by the Angels in the
first round in 1977 and traded to the White Sox later that year, in
a deal in which the headliner was Bobby (father of Barry) Bonds.

Dotson was just 31 when he threw his last pitch, which was
lined to right by Luis Polonia for an RBI single. Arm troubles
ended his career. But Dotson has spent the last 19 seasons as a
minor league pitching coach for the White Sox, finding joy in
working with young pitchers and being around a baseball field
every day of every summer.

He grew up in Cincinnati, the son of two loving parents—
James Dotson and Jean Bailiff. Dotson's mom and dad had
enough rocky times that they were married and divorced twice,
but they were still his mom and dad.

"And the biggest thing," he says, "is that I know that I love my parents....I love them, and I was blessed. And the part about not knowing Turk and that part of my family—hell, I'm 60 now. So that doesn't really matter."

Dotson grew up a baseball fan, at a time when Turk Farrell was still pitching, but he has no recollection of any part of Farrell's career. Yet more than 40 years before fate would connect them in any tangible way, their stories would converge via an odd, circle-of-life link to the same life-altering week in June.

On June 7, 1977, the Angels chose Dotson with the seventh overall pick in the baseball draft. Three days later, across the ocean, his biological father died in an automobile crash in England.

Dotson was on his way to Idaho Falls to join his first minor-league team at the time. It would be four decades before he would even become fully aware of what that week would actually represent in his life.

"My mother had mentioned there might be a family secret—and I guess I might be the secret."—Richard Dotson to his newfound cousin, in 2018

There are days Dotson wishes he could build a time machine and ride it back through the years....To April 1958, when his mother apparently met Turk Farrell, while his Phillies team was on a road trip to Cincinnati, during a period when she and Dotson's father were separated....To the 1960s and '70s, when Farrell was still alive and traveling to Cincinnati every year to play baseball....Even just back to a time five or 10 years ago, when Dotson's mother was still alive. (She died in December 2015.)

He wouldn't take that ride to relive the past. He'd merely love to travel back and ask questions, just to know. Was Farrell ever aware he had a son in Ohio? There are no signs that he did. Were Farrell and Dotson's mom ever part of each other's lives again? No signs of that, either.

If only he had taken that DNA test sooner, Dotson wonders. If only he hadn't been the last holdout in his family to explore his genealogical roots.

"Everybody had taken it but me," he says. "I guess there was a reason why, because after the fact it was like, boy, that would have been funny. OK, so now *I'm* the surprise. How the hell did this happen?"

But in truth, those details aren't important anymore. It's the modern-day details that are. And those details begin with a DNA kit that Dotson's sister, Patricia Hicks, gave him as a Christmas gift a decade ago. Dotson tossed it in a drawer and forgot about it.

"Then I think he decided one day, on his own, to do it," Hicks says now. "I mean, I talk about this. I've done a ton of books on our family genealogy. And I think he just heard me talk a lot about it…and decided to do it."

Years before that decision, Dotson's mother had dropped hints to the family that someday there might be a shocker in store for all of them. Maybe it was because she'd already taken one of those genealogy tests herself, at Hicks' suggestion, and had a feeling her 50-year secret might eventually be discovered. Like so much of this story, we'll never know.

"That's true," Hicks says. "She had indicated that there was a secret that she was never going to tell, related to some family member. I had no idea who."

And neither, for that matter, did anyone else…until one day in October 2018, when this message flashed on Dotson's phone:

"Hello Richard. AncestryDNA has you as (my) likely first cousin."

That message, from a stranger in New England named Shannon Kos, piqued Dotson's curiosity. But he didn't respond immediately—until Kos sent a follow-up message a few days later, admitting that *her* family also had a feeling its DNA tests could reveal a big surprise.

Kos is Turk Farrell's niece. They never met, but she'd done enough research and heard enough stories about her uncle to know that he was, well, let's just say a fun character.

So before she even sent off her own Ancestry kit for analysis, she told her family to brace for what might be coming.

"I said to my mother, 'You know, it's very possible that your brother had a child that we don't know about, or that maybe even *he* didn't know about,'" Kos says, "because I never knew my uncle. He died when I was 5 years old. But I hear stories about him. I knew that he had—you know—gotten around. So I knew it was possible."

Then, a month or so later, Kos got her test results back. They revealed the name of a "Richard Dotson" who not only was a first cousin, but had a closer DNA match than any other cousin. She immediately knew what that meant, and began researching who this Richard Dotson was.

"Are you the former White Sox pitcher?" she messaged him. "If so, there are striking similarities."

She apologized for delivering such "shocking" news and told him she would understand if this knowledge would be so upsetting to his family that he didn't want to pursue it. Instead, a little more than an hour later, Dotson wrote her back.

"I'm all in, for all the information you would like to share."

It was then that Shannon Kos delivered the news that would change Richard Dotson's life.

"My uncle was Richard Joseph 'Turk' Farrell. He was an MLB pitcher for the Phillies and Colt 45s/Astros....If I am your first cousin, then he is your biological father."

"And that," Dotson says, "is how this started....So this is the surprise. I'm related to this man who I never met."

HOW COULD THIS BE, REALLY? How could this father and son who never met, who spent not one second in each other's presence, have followed such similar paths?

How could this be, seriously? Was it just coincidence that Turk Farrell would spend all those years pitching in the major leagues—and then the son he never knew would follow and do exactly the same thing? Or was it some force beyond sheer coincidence?

It feels as though baseball has never been more touched by tales of one rising star after another whose dads were also big leaguers. Now what do we make of this tale—of father/son big leaguers who weren't even aware that's what they were?

"That is pretty surreal," Dotson says. "It is. Look, I don't think I was as good a pitcher as he was. At least my career wasn't as long....But still, it's kind of a select group. And the fact that we didn't even have anything to do with each other, and we both ended up in baseball, wow. Maybe there *is* some divine guidance in some of these things."

But if there is divine guidance, that wasn't all that was involved. Study a photo of Turk Farrell when he was in his mid-20s. Then study a photo of Richard Dotson at the same age. DNA is a powerful thing, it turns out.

"It explains a lot of things," Dotson's sister says. "We always assumed my brother just looked like my mom's side of the family, because he doesn't at all resemble my dad....When you see certain pictures of Turk Farrell, it's pretty incredible."

How incredible? Roll back the calendar a little more than a year and a half. Richard Dotson had gone to visit the father he grew up with, then 91 and in the final months of his life. He pulled out a photo and showed it to James Dotson.

"I said, 'Do you know who this is?'" Richard Dotson recalls. "And he pointed at me and said, 'That's you.' And it was Turk Farrell. I covered up the name because I didn't know if he knew or didn't know. And I wasn't gonna tell him...

"So I said, 'No, that's not me,' and I just dropped it. And I didn't bring it up ever again, because to me, I got an answer. If he knew, I mean, you'd know."

For Dotson, this was the moment that essentially completed the circle of knowledge he would need to move forward. The man whom he'd known all his life as his father never knew otherwise. The man who turned out to be his biological father almost certainly never knew, either. And his mother never had any intention of spilling this big, complicated pile of beans.

What he and his family couldn't be totally sure of is whether his mother knew the full story. But about two years ago, Dotson took his family to Nevada to help his sister go through boxes of his mother's most precious keepsakes. The first thing his daughter Claire pulled out of her box? A Turk Farrell baseball card.

"I said, 'You have got to be kidding me,'" Dotson says. "She had his baseball card in all her personal stuff. Which meant maybe she did know that Turk was the father. I don't know. And now I'll never know."

But inside his heart and his mind, it felt to Dotson as if he'd been freed of any of the baggage that could have come along with this staggering revelation. Instead, he was consumed by pride, by exhilaration, by a hunger to learn as much as he could about the father he'd never expected to drop into his life.

He started asking questions, searching for people who knew his father, grateful for the memorabilia Farrell's family sent him, hunting everywhere he could for photos, videos, vignettes.

He began contacting relatives all over the world with connections to Turk Farrell, from Texas to Ireland. He has plans, once this pandemic cloud lifts, to go visit them all and soak up as much knowledge as he can about his new family's past.

"I think it would be cool to see where the parents came from and the grandparents and all that," he says. "It's just that big, long…journey now that I can take later in my life, hopefully, and enjoy it and learn some things."

In reality, though, this is a journey he has been inching toward all his life. He simply didn't know it—until now.

"It's just neat," Dotson says. "It's a very neat thing. I mean, just playing baseball—we're kind of blessed to do what we do, I like to think. And we love it. And now, to have that kind of lineage or heritage, it just makes it that much more important."

BEFORE HE CAN BEGIN that journey to Ireland or anywhere else on this earth, Richard Dotson has one very important place he needs to be first.

At a ballpark in Chicago. On Friday night.

Well, in spirit anyway. Or, to be more specific, in cardboard spirit.

He was watching a White Sox game one night and admiring all the cardboard fans spread out through the empty seats. Then it hit him.

"I thought, wow, that would be cool—to get a cardboard cutout," he says. "Then the next thing I thought was, hey, it would really be cool to have Turk and I in cardboard cutouts. I mean, I had pictures. And there *was* a resemblance. So…"

He contacted Christine O'Reilly-Riordan, the White Sox vice president of community relations and the executive director of White Sox Charities.

"Are you still doing those cardboard cutouts?" he asked. "I'd like to get one of me and my dad."

"Of course," O'Reilly-Riordan said. "We can do that."

He offered not merely to buy the cutouts, but to make a generous donation to White Sox Charities to boot. Then he sent O'Reilly-Riordan something that took her breath away.

"He sent a couple of images, and one of the images was of his dad on a baseball card," she says. "And I replied back to him and said, 'Oh my gosh, Dot. I had no idea your dad was a baseball player.'"

"Well," Dotson told her, "neither did I."

O'Reilly-Riordan was so moved, she tried to pick out a special spot in the ballpark, a few rows up behind home plate, where the TV cameras might happen to capture the sight of these two men, father and son, watching their first ballgame together—in their baseball uniforms.

"It's like a storybook," she says. "You know, there's something unique about baseball, in terms of how people remember their first ballgame. They remember who took them to their first ballgame. There's something about baseball where that's just a really treasured experience.

"So how cool, after all these years, that even with these crazy cardboard cutouts, that Richard is going to be able to have that experience and be at a game with his dad?"

It's an experience that would never have been possible in any other moment in baseball time. After all, there has never been a year like this. There has never been a season like this. And there has never been a time when every ballpark on the continent has nothing but a vast expanse of empty seats—and nothing but cardboard to occupy them.

There's a sadness to that emptiness. But in some ways, there is also opportunity. And this is one of those opportunities. Their likenesses may be in cardboard. But the pounding of the heart—that's real.

O'Reilly-Riordan showered Dotson with heartwarming stories behind so many of those cutouts. "Now," he says, "that'll be us."

For a long, long time, after he first learned this news, he had kept this story to himself and his family, new and old. Finally this spring he began sharing it with his friends in baseball. On Friday night, he will share it with the world.

"Now that I'm more mature, I can handle it," he says. "I don't know how it would have affected me 30 years ago."

Think of all the forces in the universe that had to line up for those two cardboard ballplayers to be sitting in Section 130-S on Friday. Then think of the story of these two men and their eerily parallel paths in life.

If we can't wave them both out of a cornfield, we can at least station them behind home plate, in a spot that allows us to mull the sheer improbability of it all.

"I know there's a lot of stories out there," Richard Dotson says. "But this is just one small story that I just found out. It's interesting that I didn't find it out until later in life. But who knows? Maybe there's a reason for that."

Jayson Stark is the 2019 winner of the BBWAA Career Excellence Award and was honored at the Baseball Hall of Fame during the 2019 Induction Weekend. Jayson has covered baseball for more than 30 years—first at *The Philadelphia Inquirer*, then at ESPN and ESPN.com, and now at The Athletic and MLB Network. He is the author of three books on baseball, has won an Emmy for his work on *Baseball Tonight*, and is a two-time winner of the Pennsylvania Sportswriter of the Year award. In 2017, Topps issued an actual Jayson Stark baseball card.

This Woman Surfed the Biggest Wave of the Year

MAGGIE MERTENS

FROM *The Atlantic* • SEPTEMBER 12, 2020

It's a moment we don't often see in sports: a woman beating a man. But that's exactly what was announced Thursday, when the World Surf League reported that the Brazilian big-wave surfer Maya Gabeira set a new world record. The 73.5-foot wave she surfed on February 11 in Nazaré, Portugal, was the largest wave surfed by anyone this year, earning Gabeira the WSL's 2020 women's XXL Biggest Wave Award. It also broke her own previous record, a 68-foot wave. By contrast, this year's men's XXL Biggest Wave Award winner, Kai Lenny, rode a 70-foot wave.

But Gabeira's historic win was light on fanfare, with the news hampered by an uncharacteristically long delay (about four weeks after the men's announcement), and also because her achievement was subject to a brand-new and completely different set of measuring criteria than was required for the men's waves. The situation highlights a rare and missed opportunity to challenge widespread ideas about women's athletic inferiority.

The WSL's Big Wave Awards are like the Oscars of surfing, usually a live event in May where the men's and women's rides are acknowledged with categories such as Ride of the Year, Biggest Paddle, and even Wipeout of the Year. Because of the coronavirus pandemic, however, this year's awards were given out weekly throughout the summer via social media. The XXL Biggest Wave Award honors the year's biggest waves surfed, many reached via tow-in surfing as opposed to arm paddling. Both the men's and women's awards in this category were due to be doled out together on August 17—but on that date, while Lenny was announced as the winner via video, the WSL said the women's race needed further judging and would be delayed.

Jessi Miley-Dyer, the league's vice president of tours and competition, told me that the women's award was postponed and judged differently than the men's because the waves ridden by the two finalists, Gabeira and Justine Dupont, "were really, really close, and with waves of this size…and such a small margin…it was pretty obvious that this one was too close to call." She said the decision had nothing to do with the fact that the women's waves were so close in size to Lenny's, "as the men's and women's divisions are separate and judged separately." Further, Miley-Dyer said the men's competition was not as close, and did not need further judging because they "did not challenge the current men's XXL record as closely as [the women's waves]."

Wave measuring, historically, has never been fully accurate. WSL judges typically will use photos and videos to estimate the height of nominated waves, Miley-Dyer said. They don't bring complex science into it, a point of consternation for many surfers. Holly Thorpe, a sociologist who studies gender and action sports, told me that the WSL's usual limited methodology has left the league's wave measuring fairly subjective. "And when we have subjective decisions being made," she said, "we've got all the possibilities of gender bias." So on its face, further review of the women's competition would seem to be a good thing, to make this award more data-driven in a year of a tight race and a new potential world record. But doing so now with *just* the women's wave, and at the last minute of judging, has raised questions.

The WSL asked the scientists at Kelly Slater Wave Company, which the league owns, to review the women's waves. Those scientists consulted with others at the Scripps Institution of Oceanography and the University of Southern California's Department of Aerospace and Mechanical Engineering. Michal Pieszka, a research and development engineer at KSWC who helped lead the review, told me that the team calculated the sizes of Gabeira's and Dupont's waves using techniques from photogrammetry. Essentially, they estimated the wave height using equations that measure the size of known objects in the images, like the Jet Skis or the surfers themselves, and triangulate that with the angles and locations of the cameras taking the photos. This analysis determined that Gabeira's wave was "conservatively" 73.5 feet from crest to trough and Dupont's was two to three feet shorter—notably, also larger than Lenny's.

But it's almost impossible to really compare the women's to the men's, because the men's didn't get the same scientific treatment. "It was definitely the first time we've used collinear equations in terms of adjudicating the size of the waves," Miley-Dyer said. "We've never had that kind of real, objective data, scientific data, behind something like this." When Lenny was given the men's XXL Biggest Wave Award on August 17, for instance, the commentator Strider Wasilewski said the league "got the ruler out and the tape measure and we actually measured it out to 70 feet." But that mention of a "ruler and tape measure" is an imprecise reference to the methodology for the men's award—Miley-Dyer told me the typical methods of measurement are "lots of photograph and video analysis"—while the women's extra judging resulted in a 16-page scientific report.

Even though the WSL announced a larger wave measurement for Gabeira's wave than for Lenny's, using a completely different methodology for measuring them just adds to the common perception that women and men athletes are competing in separate worlds. Additionally, delaying the women's award for so long after the men's buried Gabeira's potential recognition for out-surfing all of the men this year. And although the WSL has made some laudable moves recently with regard to gender equality—including toward pay equity in surfing prizes—and the Biggest Wave Award is just one part of the WSL's competition programming, this situation shows that the way we treat women's accomplishments matters.

BIG-WAVE SURFING, like many extreme sports, is seen as masculine to its core. The sport's most recent innovation, towing in athletes via Jet Ski to waves that are 50 to 100 feet tall (sometimes triple the size that surfers can reach by paddling via arm strength alone), ups the macho factor even more. Competing to surf the biggest waves in the world is inherently dangerous and life-threatening. Thorpe, the sociologist, grew up deep in surf culture in New Zealand and points out: "Big-wave surfing is that kind of last bastion of surfing that is still very male-dominated, and it reinforces a particular type of masculinity. So when [women] challenge that, they're really challenging all of those ideas."

Maya Gabeira knows what it means for her existence to challenge preconceived notions. In 2013, her first year chasing the biggest waves in the world in Nazaré, Portugal, she suffered a major crash. The force of the waves broke her right fibula in half and forced her underwater repeatedly, until she was floating facedown in the water for more than a minute. Her surf partner revived her on the beach via CPR. Some prominent male surfers said that she should never have tried to surf such dangerous waves in the first place.

During her recovery time, Gabeira focused not just on healing, but also on becoming a good teammate. With tow-in surfing, athletes go out in teams of two or three, one driving the tow Jet Ski, and one watching to perform rescue when a surfer inevitably crashes out, pounded by the incredible force of those monstrous waves. She learned to drive the Jet Ski and perform rescue, so that when she was healthy enough to surf again, she was seen as a viable surf partner for Sebastian Steudtner, an award-winning big-wave surfer from Germany. After three spinal surgeries,

Gabeira came back. And in 2018, she set the first women's big-wave world record when she rode that 68-foot wave.

Gabeira, who's 33 and began surfing professionally in Hawaii at 17, says a major problem facing women who want to enter big-wave surfing is access. "The loneliness that involves deciding to become a big-wave surfer as a female makes it much more difficult," she told me via phone in August. "It's just harder to establish [yourself as a woman] in a male-dominated community. Guys take other guys under their wing; they travel together. I don't have a group of girlfriends traveling with me chasing huge waves. Men have many different groups to go with."

Gabeira was one of just two women who were invited to the WSL's first big-wave tow-in event this past February. Gabeira and Steudtner participated as the only mixed-gender team, and Dupont surfed while her non-surfing partner drove the Jet Ski. The forecast for February 11 called for huge waves. Though Gabeira won her first Big Wave Award at just 20—for a wave she surfed at 19—she had never participated in a live WSL event before (big tow-in waves are usually judged by video after the fact). So she decided to put it all on the line that day. She knew the record-breaking wave was special. "It was the biggest wave I've ever ridden," she told me.

Gabeira was surprised that the WSL went forward with extra judging in the women's competition this year to measure her wave. She said she welcomed the announcement delay because she didn't want to lose her world record to a subjective decision. Even though she felt sure that her wave was taller than Lenny's and Dupont's before the judging, she wasn't confident that she would be named the women's winner, and she never thought they would measure hers as larger than Lenny's.

She wasn't the only skeptical one. Jorge Leal, a photographer and a videographer based in Nazaré who has filmed nearly every big-wave attempt there since surfers popularized the spot around 2011, was so sure that Gabeira's wave was bigger than Lenny's that he stitched the two videos side by side for comparison and shared it around the surfing community. The caption on the Instagram post where the videos play side by side asks the question point-blank: "Did [Maya Gabeira] or [Kai Lenny] Score the Biggest Wave of the Year at Nazaré?" The comments are almost unanimous: "Maya."

"Maya, on that day, she was really getting different lines…the best I ever saw from her," Leal told me about the event. "She was really committed to do something special. She caught, for me, the biggest wave of the season, not even the contest. And the biggest wave of the season in Nazaré easily represents the biggest wave of the year." But Leal didn't think the WSL would frame things this way. "I feel WSL sometimes, if not every time, doesn't have the guts to say something like that." Of course, WSL did announce her wave as larger than Lenny's, but the league emphasized to me, and in its press release, that men and women compete in separate divisions, not with each other.

Even so, the questionable timing and methodology is reminiscent of another struggle Gabeira went through to have her accomplishments recognized. After her first world-record-setting ride of 68 feet, it took eight months of lobbying by Gabeira (and the pressure of an online petition) to get the WSL to give her wave the approval it needed to be sent to the *Guinness World Records*. Before that, there was no world record for the biggest wave surfed by a woman. Today, Gabeira says she doesn't think the delay was due to outward gender discrimination, just the slow rate of change from surfing as a very male-dominated sport. "I think it was just pure lack of will from the league," she said. "There was no women's world record at the time. So, for them, there was no emergency toward that category being established."

Historically, there were no separate women's categories for WSL surfing awards or records; thus, men held all the world records and won most of the awards. When women didn't have these events of their own, it contributed to the false notion that they couldn't surf big waves. Adding the separate women's-world-record category in 2018 was part of that long march toward more gender equality in the sport, said Miley-Dyer. "You know, it's really an age-old question in sports: Do women have to be better than men? Or better than the best women to be recognized as the best woman ever?" she said to me. "Maya felt very strongly that there should be a separate women's world record, and it turned out that we could do that…and we changed [the Big Wave Awards] platform, to give them the opportunity to win more awards."

Ironically, that gender separation, although important for women athletes in many ways, may be what hurts the perception of Gabeira's accomplishment this time around. Thorpe said certain action sports like surfing often fall into this trap of "reinforcing old-school versions of gender division," which adds to the common perception that women cannot ever outperform men. "Maya, and other women surfers, are sitting out there with the men right next to them, but when we make it a competition… we separate them out, typically," she said. So, Thorpe said, the question becomes: "Do we need to in a sport like that?"

Steudtner wonders, too, why the WSL wouldn't want to capitalize on his surf partner's competitive accomplishments by shouting this moment from the rooftops. Suppose, he said to me, a woman were competing in the X Games in a snowboarding big-air competition with the men. "And you have all the big-name guys pushing themselves, and you have a woman and she is doing bigger airs, and the same size airs as them, and has all the qualities the guys have," he said. "They would put that on their marketing agenda and push that as hard as they could."

In the grand scheme of how women's athletic accomplishments are usually framed, none of this is surprising. Take, for example, skeet shooting in the Olympics, which used to be a mixed-gender competition—until a woman won the gold medal in 1992. The following year, the International Shooting Union, the sport's international federation, barred women from shooting against men. Similar implications are behind the arbitrary rules in many other sports that determine that women simply can't go as far (in bicycling or cross-country skiing, for example, when women's races are shorter), or last as long (as in tennis, in which women play fewer sets, and basketball, which has shorter periods of play in the WNBA than the NBA) in competition. And although many people point to gaps in performance between men and women as the reason for these differences, those gaps in many sports are narrowing as women gain more access to professional training.

Though it is notable that the WSL pays equal prize money to male and female competitors now, and it invited women to participate alongside men in February's tow-in contest, the league seemed to gloss over a moment fans rarely get to celebrate: a woman winning head-to-head in sport with a man. Thorpe thinks this could be a moment that surfing, and other action sports, start to consider how to break out of the gender-binary world we usually see in sports. "They could totally [say] that model doesn't work for us. And revolutionize this completely and offer an amazing alternative that reflects the gender fluidity of our times," she told me. "They could have done something really wonderful here."

Gabeira also believes this moment could signal a new beginning for the league. "Our sport is very male-dominated, with the performances on the male side [being] often much stronger than ours as females," she said. "So to find a way and a place and a certain discipline to shorten that gap, and to conclude this year that a woman did surf the biggest, tallest wave of the year is quite phenomenal. It opens the idea that in other categories and other areas of surfing, this could be accomplished, too."

Maggie Mertens is a freelance writer and editor based in Seattle. Her writing on sports, culture, gender, and the body has appeared in *The Atlantic*, espnW, *Glamour*, *The Guardian*, NPR, VICE, Deadspin, and others. She holds an MFA in creative nonfiction writing from The New School.

Hook Shot Charlie Is Spreading Hope Throughout Charlotte. If You Want Some of It, Just Try The Hook

MICHAEL GRAFF

FROM Axios Charlotte • FEBRUARY 6, 2020

He'll keep shooting until he makes one, then until he misses one, and then…

"Hold on, Michael. I got this one," he tells me.

He's shooting basketball at the Johnston YMCA in NoDa. Actually, he's shooting hook shots. Actually, he's shooting hook shots from half-court. Actually, he's shooting hook shots from half-court at 62 years old.

Another clang.

"Alright, alright," he says. "I'm feeling it *now*."

Then it happens.

Swish.

Swish.

Here we go.

Swish.

Over and over and over. Around the gym, heads start turning. Balls stop bouncing. Kids start hollering and moving closer.

Ohhhhhh!

Hook Shot Charlie is on. He spins the ball on his finger, down his arm and across his back, and lets another one fly.

Swish.

There's something about the sound of a basketball going through a hoop that invites others to join in. But when that sound comes at the other end of a rainbow from half-court, the response is kind of like what happens when "Cha Cha Slide" comes on at a wedding. They all join in.

Every-body shoot your hooks.

Clang. Clang. Clang.

"It's OK," Hookshot Charlie tells the kids. "Keep trying."

Soon the whole floor is hopping with The Hook.

Charlotte's issues are visible just outside the YMCA's doors. Apartments are popping up near the gym, on land once occupied by lovable music venues or family businesses. Parking's gotten worse. Old-timers worry about preserving the neighborhood's artsy character. Old-old-timers still tell stories of when this was a mill village. A block away, the city's highest-profile homicide of 2019, the shooting of Scott Brooks of Brooks' Sandwich House, shattered any sense of safety in the neighborhood.

But in here, with Hook Shot Charlie leading the dance, you're reminded how smiles and kindness can rule the world.

"People just want to be a part of something that's good," Charlie tells me as basketballs fly. "Look, when people do a hook shot, the corner of their mouth turns up. There's something that connects the arm to the mouth."

He's been coming here for a dozen or so years to fire up these shots from the free-throw line, then the three-point line, then half-court. When he makes a bunch, kids want to know how he does it. They want to know what grip he uses, or when his eyes catch the basket. They ask how he makes so many.

They want to know how. Few people, though, ever ask why.

Why is he here? And why would anybody in their 60s become great at something like this?

HOOK SHOT CHARLIE was once a boy named Phillip Currence. His family thought he looked like his uncle Charlie, so they called him that.

Charlie graduated from high school in Gaston County and went off to Wingate College, back in the 1970s when it was a two-year school. He was one of only a few Black men on campus. He didn't drink. Didn't smoke. Just played basketball.

The game became elusive after graduation. He worked in mergers and acquisitions for First Union. He and his wife started a family in the early 1980s. Four kids came: Boy, girl, boy, girl. They lived in north Charlotte, in a neighborhood called Newell that used to be the country but now is very much in the city.

He worked all week, made a mighty fine suburban lawn on Saturdays. On Sundays, he shot basketball to clear his mind.

"I would just feed him rebounds," his son, Jeremy, now 30, tells me.

One summer, he gave his kids a project: Move dirt.

They slumped their shoulders and piled the wheelbarrows high, then dumped the dirt in a designated spot 50 feet away. Pile, dump. Pile, dump. After a few hundred trips, they asked him why—why were they spending their summer hauling one bit of earth to another?

"It builds character," he told them.

One day he told them to stop. They'd done enough. Then he had all that dirt flattened and smoothed, and he built a playground for them on the platform they'd made.

Around 2006, though, something broke in their family. He and his wife weren't getting along anymore. They weren't talking. One weekend while their oldest was off at college, they sat the other three down on a Saturday. Jeremy remembers it well—he was 16 and had his SATs that day. He sat with his two sisters and listened to his parents tell them that their marriage was over. Mom would move into an apartment, and Dad would stay in the home.

They all spent the next few years in a daze.

Charlie felt aimless. First Union had become Wachovia. Each time the company snatched up another smaller bank in his two decades there, he helped make the transition happen. He'd change the letter heads and forms. He'd go into branches and make sure the signs were swapped out. If it's this easy to change the identity of a building, Charlie would think, to take it from one bank to another bank, maybe he could change his own.

One Thursday in November 2007, after 23 years with the company, as the global economy was on the brink of collapsing and not long before Wells Fargo bought Wachovia, he quit.

The next day, Friday, he went to the store and bought a Wilson basketball and started shooting again.

A few years later, in 2010, the kids reserved a room at UNC Charlotte and called a family meeting. They let their parents know the things they'd kept silent. That they'd been sad, confused, all the things kids go through during a divorce but hardly ever say. Everyone had a chance to say how the divorced affected them.

Their parents didn't get back together after that, but on the other side of the unsaid, the family was close again.

"It was just time for us to reconcile," says Jeremy, a web developer and producer. "We were able to start to rebuild with each other."

Charlie usually warms up from the three-point line, then moves back to half-court.

FOR CHARLIE, hook shots are better than therapy.

He lived off savings for some time. Now he finds work through a temp agency, just to pay bills. He downsized. He lives in Brightwalk off of Statesville Road.

His kids take videos and post them online. They built a website for Hook Shot Charlie, through which people can contact him and book him for events. That's how I met him.

A couple years ago, my friend Lewis Donald of Sweet Lew's was serving barbecue at a neighborhood event at St. Paul Baptist

Church in Belmont. Inside the gymnasium, while everybody ate, a skinny man with silver hair was making every hook he shot.

"Is he a Globetrotter?" I asked.

"Nah, that's Hook Shot Charlie," Lewis said. "You don't know Hook Shot Charlie?"

Charlie gets around. He's performed at halftime of high school games and Hornets games. Once, he shot in the Chick-fil-A cow's costume.

He's still never had a drink, he says. Never a cigarette, either. Recently he's found himself drawn to the stories of Mr. Rogers.

"One-four-three," he says, a reference to how Mr. Rogers kept his weight at exactly 143. Then he holds up his fingers to go along with the number of letters in the words. "I l-o-v-e y-o-u."

His friends and family want him to find a way to do this full-time. Harry Workman, a former associate vice president at Wingate, met Charlie a few years ago when Wingate was starting an African American alumni group.

Workman hopes to see Charlie's skills turned into a nonprofit—a hook shot ministry, of sorts.

"It's magic," Workman says. "And maybe you can't bottle it. It may be that he's an artist more than a business. He's the Van Gogh of the court. And he can paint the story over and over and over again from mid-court."

Whatever happens, Charlie doesn't want it to feel like work. That's not how it started. He would never want to lose what's pure about it.

Like when people send him pictures of themselves holding a hook pose, as if they've just released the ball. He keeps a video montage of folks doing that, one after the other, telling him how much they love the shot, and him.

Charlie hopes it spreads, hopes to be tagged in more posts for The Hook. It's not a nod to basketball, or athleticism, or even about him going viral. No, in each picture, Charlie sees a person who's been through something and persevered.

THE HOOK IS MORE THAN A POSE. It's a statement of hope. "It's not even about the hook shot anymore," he says. "It's about uniting people in a way to say we have more in common than we do that's different."

In the gym that day with all the kids around, I wonder if we'll ever leave. Musicians can't end with missed notes and golfers can't end on bad swings, but Hook Shot Charlie can't end on a good note or a bad note. He can't stop, either way.

Jeremy says his father will "miss 'til he hits, and hit 'til he misses," and when that's your mantra, there is no beginning and there is no end, no good and no bad.

There is only next.

Michael Graff is a writer and editor based in North Carolina. He's co-author of Axios Charlotte, a daily newsletter with more than 110,000 subscribers. His first book, co-authored with Nick Ochsner, on the characters and circumstances that contributed to the largest case of election fraud in U.S. history, is scheduled to be published in November 2021. His work has appeared in ESPN, *Garden & Gun*, *The Guardian*, the *Oxford American*, POLITICO, and *Success*. He was the editor of *Charlotte* magazine, and senior editor at *Our State*. Before that he worked in newspapers—the *Fayetteville Observer*, *Rocky Mount Telegram*, *Winchester* (Virginia) *Star*, and *High Point Enterprise*. He lives in Charlotte with his wife, Laura, son, George, and mutt, Gizmo.

The Most Magical Place on Earth

TAYLOR ROOKS

FROM *GQ* • NOVEMBER 20, 2020

Prologue: Before the Bubble

Rudy Gobert felt panicked and scared. And so he did what you do when you feel panicked and scared: He tried to call his mother, Corinne, but he was having trouble reaching her. "She was sleeping because it was about 4 a.m. in France at the time," says Gobert. "But I was calling her every 10 minutes to make sure I was the first person she talked to, before she saw the news on Facebook."

It was early March, and Gobert hadn't been feeling well. He'd been in bed at the 21c Museum Hotel in Oklahoma City, getting ready to watch his Jazz teammates face the Thunder. He was showing symptoms that he says he's had "a thousand times" in his life, symptoms he believed he could just sweat out, drink some ginger tea, and be right back healthy. Only this time, that wasn't quite the case. When the game was about to start, someone came out onto the court to talk to the officials. "I was like, *Oh, shit,*" Gobert recalls. "Thirty seconds later they called me and said I was positive for COVID-19." Gobert, as it turns out, learned that he had the coronavirus at the same time that the rest of the world did.

Which is why he was frantically calling his mother, especially since there was a humiliating viral video circulating that night of him touching a bunch of reporters' microphones as a joke earlier in the week—a video he says does not accurately portray who he is. "I had to tell her that I was okay," he recalls. "I would always tell her that I'm good even when I'm not, because me not being good would hurt her literally more than me." Gobert wound up being the first NBA domino to topple, and within hours commissioner Adam Silver would announce that the rest of the season was suspended indefinitely. Basketball would not officially resume until 141 days later, on July 30, inside what would come to be called the NBA bubble, in Orlando, Florida: the daring, temporary, artificial home of the world's greatest basketball players.

Chapter I: This Must Be the Place
In early July, 22 NBA teams descended on Disney World in central Florida to take part in a once-in-a-lifetime experiment. More than 300 athletes boarded a series of repurposed Mickey Mouse tour buses and were scattered among three different hotels—the Gran Destino, the Yacht Club, and the Grand Floridian—each designed to cater to the needs and wishes of the kinds of people who travel vast distances for the immersive family fun of the Magic Kingdom.

It was a strange time for the NBA to be restarting. The George Floyd protests were still going strong across the country, and a lot of people—including players—were questioning whether we even needed basketball. I flew into Orlando on July 12 from New York, a city that, at the time, appeared to be on its way to successfully containing the spread of the virus. I was there to cover the NBA for Bleacher Report and Turner Sports, and was one of the few media members granted "Tier 1" clearance, meaning we were to be tested every single day and, once we completed a seven-day quarantine, were allowed to inhabit the same spaces as the players themselves.

But my experience inside got off to a rocky start. I was assigned a fourth-floor room next door to the Gran Destino, a vaguely Southwest-themed space with lots of natural light and pictures of cacti on the walls. I was tested the night I arrived, and by the following afternoon, a doctor had called and told me I had tested positive for the virus. I was shocked and scared but mostly confused, because I had rarely left my apartment and had tested negative a few days prior. So I got retested and spent the next two days incredibly worried. (This time, it was me calling *my* mom crying.) After more tests, the doctor called again to tell me that the initial result was a false positive.

After quarantining for a week and passing all the required medical exams, I was cleared to finally enter the bubble—ostensibly the safest place on the planet, thanks to daily testing, mandated masks, and strictly enforced social distancing from the outside world.

When people ask me what the bubble was like, I tell them it felt like summer camp, except most of the campers were multimillionaires and a considerable percentage of them were seven feet tall. There were times I'd be heading to the Maya Grill for lunch (my go-to was the chicken nuggets, vegetable pasta, and a strawberry-lemonade Popsicle) and I'd see the Lakers' LeBron James and Anthony Davis casually ride past me on their bikes. Or I'd spy Kyle Lowry of the Raptors, walking alone across the same bridge every morning to go grab breakfast. In a surreal way, the campus granted athletes the rare freedom to move through the world unbothered. No security details, no fans stopping them for photos. It's something I imagine a lot of them haven't been able to experience since they were teenagers.

Inside, we devised all kinds of ways to pass the time. Once, I played Heads Up! (the charades-like game where you hold your phone up to your forehead) with Kemba Walker of the Boston Celtics at the end of an interview. The answer on the screen was "*Harry Potter and the Sorcerer's Stone*," and the clue he gave me was "They be flying on brooms and shit." Ja Morant of the Grizzlies and I would play Connect Four on the iPhone (he still hasn't beaten me), and Chris Paul and Russell Westbrook—who were traded for each other before the season began—would team up and play spades on their phones against Chris's brother, C.J., and his mom, Robin. Westbrook in particular was a model bubble citizen. He always made sure his hotel room was "clean and in good shape," and he reportedly left an $8,000 tip for the housekeepers. (When we spoke, Westbrook confirmed he wrote a thank-you note and left a good tip, but wouldn't confirm the amount: "The money doesn't matter. I just like to do the right thing. That's it.")

Perhaps because of the strange environment, a few of the players seemed to relax and let down their guard. George Hill of the Milwaukee Bucks said he missed the national anthem before a game against the Magic because he was busy taking "a shit," something he tells me he does every pregame when there's six minutes left on the clock. He joins the layup line, shoots a single layup, and then, like clockwork, sprints off to the bathroom.

All the actual basketball took place about 10 minutes away. After games and practices, the players would race to the bus in order to get back to their hotels first. (Bam Adebayo was always dejected when he was late to the first bus and had to wait for the second one.) Once back at the hotels, the guys would mostly spend the nights playing cards (after Heat practices, I'd sometimes hear Jimmy Butler yell, "We playing Phase 10 tonight?!") or drinking together at the hotel bar.

Like a lot of people in lockdown in the outside world, players spent their free time inside the bubble drinking. And seemingly at the center of it all was CJ McCollum of the Portland Trail Blazers, who became something of the NBA's unofficial source for wine. McCollum stacked his hotel room with cases of his own Pinot Noir blend, McCollum Heritage 91, keeping the thermostat at a cool 65 degrees. He gifted dozens of bottles to players, and CJ's wine became a hot-ticket item—a bubble grail. Kawhi Leonard once stopped CJ to ask questions about the Pinot Noir and say he was a huge fan. ("I got the endorsement from Mr. Leonard!") As was Anthony Davis, who, according to McCollum, stood next to him at the free-throw line during a Round 1 playoff game to tell him: "Thanks for that wine. That shit was good."

But no one was a bigger fan than Damian Lillard. McCollum's backcourt running mate said Heritage 91 was a magic elixir, the good-luck charm behind his historic bubble hot streak. Every time Lillard drank some, he'd go out and drop 50 on the other team, so he made it a point to incorporate McCollum Heritage 91 into his nightly routine. According to CJ, Dame was like, "'Don't bring me nothing besides that Heritage—I only want to drink the Heritage!' So I was bringing him it, and we was drinking it for, like, a streak."

This being central Florida in the summer, players would spend a lot of their free time poolside. The Houston Rockets would ritually gather at the Grand Floridian pool to eat and drink, and James Harden would rave about how good the hotel's hot dogs were. (Teammate Austin Rivers offered a similar review: "That shit almost changed my life.") One night at the pool, players from the Rockets and the Trail Blazers—two longtime rivals—both happened to be watching the Clippers play the Mavericks on their iPads. The Blazers' stream was a couple of seconds ahead, and the Portland guys were shouting and hollering before the Rockets players knew what was happening. "So we turned off our iPad and went over to where they were at," says Rivers. "We're all talking like, *Nah, this guy's going to take that. Oh, no, they can't leave him open....* You can see guys, like, delving into the game. It wasn't about, you know, Dame versus Russ. Like everybody's just cool, you know what I mean?"

The collegial atmosphere made it easy for the guys to bond, and friendships new and old blossomed in Orlando. Some of the O.G.s used it as an opportunity to connect with the next generation: like Carmelo Anthony, a 17-year veteran, who said his most memorable conversation took place over drinks at the Yacht Club with younger players Kyle Kuzma and Devin Booker. Melo told them that they were the "future of the NBA" and to "start using your voices more and stop relying on us to do all the talking while y'all sit back." When Lakers guard Danny Green won his third championship, he says, his old coach Gregg Popovich sent him a text: "Tell LeBron and AD I said congrats as well, but tell them to play a little more defense." Meanwhile, a few players used the new proximity to let go of old grudges. Raptors president Masai Ujiri said his favorite moment off the court happened while he was on the sidelines, watching his team play the Lakers, and one of his former players came up to him. "I'm sitting down there, and I see this person walking straight to me with a blue tracksuit," says Ujiri. It was DeMar DeRozan, who had spent nine seasons with the Raptors before he was traded to the Spurs for Kawhi Leonard. The trade had left DeRozan feeling "extremely hurt" and betrayed but earned the Raptors the franchise's first championship. "And he walks up to me," Ujiri continues, "and he gives me a big, big hug. This was really the first time that we've really had that kind of contact since the trade. I left the game and I felt that we had crossed a certain…we'd reached a new place."

My whole time in the bubble, I never once saw Jayson Tatum of the Celtics without his teammates Kemba Walker and Javonte Green. It was natural for players to form cliques, but the trio were inseparable. Tatum says his favorite night in the bubble was when he was sipping a drink (he rotated between a Hennessy and pineapple, a Crown Royal Apple, and a Moscato) and Walker said he had a confession, something that he had to get off his chest. It was a revelation that brought the already close teammates even closer, according to Tatum: "Kemba was like, 'Yo, before I met you, I thought you were just…like, the epitome of a light-skinned dude with good hair who went to Duke. But being around you, you're just a country dude from St. Louis!'"

Chapter II: Groundhog Day
Pro athletes are already creatures of habit, but the limitations of the bubble forced a lot of the people inside it to adopt routines in order to preserve their sanity.

For example, every day at 5 a.m., inside room 950 in the Gran Destino (where all the top-seeded teams stayed), Masai Ujiri would wake up, read his book, hop on the Peloton, and work out before heading down for breakfast. He thought nothing of his daily ritual until one morning, several weeks into the bubble, when he got a text from another former player of his: "Morning boss, you good up there?"

The text was from Kawhi Leonard—Finals MVP with the Raptors, now a star on the Clippers—who was staying in room 850, directly below his old boss. Ujiri had been waking Kawhi up with his noisy workouts for weeks, but Kawhi was reluctant to say anything.

Ujiri told Kawhi that he would stop for the time being and joked that he would continue again when the Raptors met the Clippers in the Finals, messing with Kawhi's sleep. Kawhi responded with the kind of trash talk that's best read aloud in Kawhi's dry monotone: "Haha, you know the saying 'Don't poke the bear'? I'm gonna call the NBA on you…get you out the bubble."

Everyone coped with the monotony as best they could. One small way George Hill managed it was by eating the same exact breakfast every morning: a bacon-egg-and-cheese croissant with a hash brown casserole; a double serving of bacon; a coffee; and a tangerine juice. Doc Rivers, who was head coach of the Clippers, put the endless repetition to me this way: "It was Groundhog Day, I swear to God it was. Every morning I woke up, I did the [COVID-19 check-in] app, ran downstairs, did the testing. Went to watch film with my coaches, watch film with the players, practice, and rode my bike. And then I was back in the room. Every day."

"You really just had to accept the fact that, man, I'm going to see these four walls every day," says Tatum.

The isolation also took a toll on players mentally, especially with everything going on in the outside world—and here they were, hermetically sealed inside a Disney resort. Many of them had an especially hard time being away from their families. "I didn't tell anybody, but I was going through mental problems," says Ja Morant. He says his daughter, Kaari, is the joy of his life, all "light and energy," and he missed her first birthday while inside the bubble. ("I wanted to just sit in a room that day by myself.") The first time he heard her clearly say the word "Dada," he was talking to her on FaceTime. Her mom would ask, "Where's Dada?" and Kaari would point at the screen: "Dada!"

The moment broke him.

"Some don't really know how serious that can be," Morant says when I ask him how hard it was to be confined in the bubble. "And, you know, a lot of people want to make jokes and stuff until they actually go through it."

Chris Paul, the head of the NBA players' association and a 15-year veteran, said he similarly struggled with being away from his family, especially when he missed his daughter's eighth birthday. "You ever seen on social media the thing that says, 'Make sure you check on your strong friends'?" Paul asks me. "A lot of times, it's the guys who may seem like they got everything together, you know? For me, shoot—*I* needed somebody to talk to at times."

But for all the loneliness, for all the outside life that the players missed, there were some moments of real joy inside the bubble, memories they say they'll never forget. There was Morant, taking his first legal drink—a bottle of Don Julio 1942 tequila—when his teammates and coaches threw him a surprise party for his 21st birthday. There was LeBron and AD, rushing back to the hotel after a win so they could celebrate their victory with a big glass of red. There were the Houston Rockets and how, after practice, they'd all look at one another and shout, "Lil Yachty! Lil Yachty!"—which meant they were going to the boat to drink. "There were a lot of really good times in the bubble," Paul adds. "As much as people talk about how tough it was to be away from their families and stuff, to me there were probably a lot of better times than not."

A few players took the isolation in stride and just appreciated the quietude. Around 7:30 every night Austin Rivers says he
would sit out on his balcony, put on some headphones, and take
a moment for himself. "My room had a view of the little magic
castle or whatever," he says. "It was nice."

Whenever the sun went down, Bam Adebayo would take a
left out of the back lobby of the Gran Destino and go for a long
walk along the perimeter of the hotel's campus to clear his head
and "get a somewhat different look from Groundhog Day," he
says. He went on his walk after losing Game 6 of the NBA Finals,
even though the route took him past the Three Bridges restaurant, where the Lakers were celebrating their championship win
over the Heat. "At that point you realize the season's over," says
Adebayo. "That was part of what was going through my mind:
This is the last walk for my routine. Of being in the bubble."

Chapter III: Everything but Basketball

I remember being at Fred VanVleet's post-practice press conference after Jacob Blake was shot in Kenosha, Wisconsin. VanVleet's
eyes were glazed, and he didn't want to take any questions about
basketball. When it was my turn to speak, I simply asked him how
he was doing; the games just didn't feel important in the moment.
VanVleet collected himself and gave an answer that was at once
raw and multidimensional: He said he was heartbroken and had
survivor's remorse. That he felt isolated in the bubble. That people
can't underestimate the trauma that comes from watching videos
on their phones of Black men dying and seeing comments that
argued they should have just listened to the police. He told me
about his father, who was killed when VanVleet was young.

It was a heavy moment for all of us, and when that press
conference was over, I looked down at my phone and saw I had
a text from Fred asking me how I was doing. My answer was the
same as his: I was heartbroken too.

Most of the players felt the same way. On August 26, a few
days after Blake's shooting, George Hill asked for a breakfast

meeting with head coach Mike Budenholzer and the rest of the coaching staff. Hill ordered the same breakfast he always did, with his double serving of bacon and a tangerine juice, and told them that he "didn't feel comfortable playing" and wasn't going to.

"That was the last thing on my mind," says Hill. "I didn't want to do it." It wasn't just Blake who sparked his decision to sit out: It was Kyle Rittenhouse, a white 17-year-old who crossed state lines into Wisconsin and shot three protesters, leaving two dead and one seriously injured. "We let that kid go all the way back home," Hill tells me. "They didn't slam him on the ground. They didn't put him in handcuffs. They didn't do anything. They let him go all the way back to Illinois and arrested him the next day. If it was the other way around, would that have happened? I don't think so."

Hill had seen enough, and his coaches informed the Bucks of his decision to sit out. One of those players was Sterling Brown, who was tased and arrested by Milwaukee police in 2018 over an alleged parking violation. For Brown, this was personal. It wasn't long before the Milwaukee Bucks organization collectively made the unprecedented decision not to play in Game 5 against the Orlando Magic, effectively bringing the NBA to a halt.

And if George Hill hadn't sat out, there was a strong possibility that a league-wide strike still would have taken place. The Raptors were set to play the Celtics the day after the Bucks decided to stay in the locker room. While the Bucks were deliberating, Raptors players Fred VanVleet and Kyle Lowry quietly met with members of the Celtics to discuss what they should do, and Masai Ujiri ran into Celtics coach Brad Stevens, and the two talked about not playing. "It was *going* to happen, to be honest," says Ujiri. If it hadn't been the Bucks who initiated the strike, it probably would have been the Raptors and the Celtics.

Meanwhile, players inside the bubble were all wondering the same thing: *What can we do?* A few wanted to end the season then and there. They all had a decision to make, and so later that evening, the remaining teams agreed to convene at the Gran Destino for a historic meeting to discuss what was next.

Chapter IV: The Meeting
The players all gathered in what was described to me as "a big-ass room." Media weren't present; it was players and coaching staff only. "It was a bunch of circles—each team was in a circle," says Austin Rivers. "And then other players started going to other circles."

"I was worried that night because it was more emotional than it was anything else," Doc Rivers says. "It was great to see, because I don't think people feel like guys who are millionaires care. But I saw guys with tears in their eyes, guys with anger, guys who were mad. Guys who wanted to do something. And then I also saw a bunch of us not knowing what to do."

"It was like chaos," says Austin.

"We were just throwing ideas back and forth off of each other," says George Hill. "Why we should play, why we shouldn't. What's going on in the world? What are we standing for?"

At some point, money became a point of contention. The fact of the matter was there were guys in the bubble in different financial situations, and not everyone could afford to forgo the season. A few of them were max players, with multiyear contracts in the hundreds of millions, while other guys were just trying to carve out a career for themselves. "It definitely felt that a lot of what was talked about was the social injustice part," says Hill. "And then there was a handful that would talk about the financial loss. A lot of us were saying, 'What does money mean if you have no humanity?' And a lot of [other people] were saying, 'We want the money.' So sometimes money trumps humanity, I guess. But that's what it was, and I don't fault anybody. Everyone has a different life, and everyone has different values." Carmelo Anthony put it another way: "We want change around the world, but then you start talking about money? Money is the root of all evil."

Pretty much the whole room was upset that the Bucks decided not to play without informing the other teams. Multiple players told me that everyone felt like one team made the decision for the rest of the league. "Then Jaylen [Brown of the Celtics] stood up and said that the Milwaukee Bucks don't owe anybody no apology," Hill recalls. "They did what they thought was right, and that's what it was. It was very special. As a young man himself, to stand up and say that? It meant a lot."

Everyone was looking for leadership. The Clippers and the Lakers were so adamant about doing something that at one point they just walked right out. "We were just willing to make a stand, willing to put it all on the line," says Lakers guard Danny Green, "even though we knew we had a really good chance at being the last team standing."

Tensions were high, and with teams storming out, the night ended without any real resolution.

The following morning, members of the NBPA executive committee had a phone call with owners and executives across the league. Some of the most powerful people in sports were on that call, including Charlotte Hornets owner Michael Jordan. "Michael was a calming influence," Mavericks owner Mark Cuban tells me. "I think that was really impactful. Because in the back of everybody's minds, people think, 'Republicans buy sneakers too.' And here was Michael Jordan stepping out and really connecting to players and really saying, 'Okay, we're all in this together. What do we need to do?'"

It was LeBron James who had the final statement on the call. "I thought [LeBron] was really compelling," Cuban recalls. "He talked about how we need to be able to connect to young African American kids. What really stuck with me was when he said a lot of kids where he grew up can't afford cable and that the only way to watch our games is on cable. And we have a challenge [in addressing] those types of issues and lifting people up, so that it's not about cable or watching the NBA on cable but more about: How do we help these kids improve where they are in life?"

The players and owners landed on a plan. Not only would the league commit to making social justice a cornerstone of its mission going forward, but it would form an official coalition within the NBA that, per a joint press release, focused on "a broad range of issues, including increasing access to voting, promoting civic engagement, and advocating for meaningful police and criminal justice reform." This coalition would be composed of players and owners, with hundreds of millions of dollars behind it.

And it was the players who made it all happen. They were fighting for real change, something they could point back to, something that would have a lasting impact beyond their time in Orlando. And once they had that plan in place, the games resumed.

Chapter V: The Right Space at the Right Time
By the end of August, basketball had resumed and continued at a high level—and a few breakout stars were playing out of their minds, including Jamal Murray, who competed in a custom pair of Adidas sneakers painted with the faces of George Floyd and Breonna Taylor that he wore into the ground. ("I think the bubble just showed who the real hoopers were," says Murray.) But I was beginning to feel a sense of exhaustion creep in. Guys seem fatigued. Fewer players lingered in the common areas after practices or games. "It was a lot tougher than I ever thought it would be," says Doc Rivers of his time inside.

Doc's Clippers came into the postseason with lofty aspirations, and it seemed like a foregone conclusion that we'd get a groundbreaking L.A. vs. L.A. Western Conference Finals. But the bubble was not kind to the Clippers, and Paul George in particular was heavily criticized for his playoff struggles. A press conference following a win over the Mavericks provided a little clarity: George said he was feeling "anxiety" and "a little bit of depression from being locked in here." It was notable because it was the first time any of us had witnessed George be vulnerable. "PG, clearly [the bubble] was bothering him," says Doc Rivers. "And because he's such a quiet guy to begin with, I honestly didn't see it until I heard about it and I saw it. And then it was real for me."

It was up to the players to be there for one another. During the Finals, when Danny Green missed an open three at the top of the key to clinch a Lakers championship at the end of Game 5, he and his fiancée started to receive death threats online, which made an already difficult situation even harder. "It was one of those nights that you don't sleep much," Green tells me. He was thankful for the brotherhood of players who had his back, including George, who reached out to Green directly and also posted a message to his Instagram Stories: *Stay blessed bro...One of the best guns out there.*

That realness hit us all at different times. You're in a place that's safe from the coronavirus, doing the exact same thing every day, and it's easy to feel like you aren't a part of the outside world. The problem with that feeling is that everyone you love is in the outside world and their lives are moving at a pace that yours is not.

That realness hit me when I learned about my great-uncle, Lou Brock, who played for the St. Louis Cardinals. He passed away back home in Missouri. The day after he died, Jayson Tatum—St. Louis's very own and someone I've known since he was 15—wore his Cardinals-colorway Jordan 34 shoes and wrote "R.I.P. Lou Brock" on the side. After the game, he found me to make sure I was okay, and it was one of the few times inside the bubble I remember feeling at home.

A couple of players said one of the rawest moments happened during that big meeting, when Houston Rockets assistant coach John Lucas launched into a speech and talked about how stressful the bubble was for everybody. It had been particularly stressful for him, as someone who's struggled with alcoholism. "I know most people in here are just drinking every night because there's nothing else to do," he said. "And at some point a lot of people are going to turn into alcoholics."

The moment hit hard for a lot of the players. "We're [in the bubble] going crazy, the testosterone levels are through the roof, no one's significant other is there, and the single men are probably *really* going crazy because they're used to just doing what they want," says McCollum. "So it was just like a lot of tension and stress. And then [John] just comes out and starts saying what everybody was thinking." When his speech concluded, the players all erupted and gave Lucas a standing ovation.

For me, there was one moment in the bubble that sticks out above all the others. It was the week that Jacob Blake was shot, and I was sitting outside the Coronado Springs convention center ballroom waiting for the Raptors' practice to end. Masai Ujiri walked up to me and another reporter unprompted and said, "We should have never come to the bubble."

Ujiri was emotional. He is intimately familiar with how it feels to be wronged by police just because you're a Black man. The week prior, body cam footage from the 2019 NBA Finals had surfaced, showing a white police officer grabbing and shoving Masai as he tried to step on the court after his Raptors beat the Warriors for the championship. There it was, plain as day: Even a powerful Black man, the president of an NBA team, wasn't safe from being brutalized by the police.

Ujiri knew he had to show his players before they saw it elsewhere. "I cried when I showed the players my video," he says. "And I cried when I got the video from the lawyer. And when my wife watched it [with me]… That was emotional, and I cried again." In hindsight, Ujiri says he doesn't regret returning to the bubble: "Honestly, Taylor, sports brings us all together. We have the ability to address these issues head-on and galvanize and hope for change and try to create that change. We have to be in that space, and the bubble was that space at that time."

I left the bubble for good right before the Conference Finals to attend my uncle's funeral. As I passed the cartoon signs on the ride to the airport, the sense that I was there for a moment in history finally hit me. Here were these players fighting for equality, fighting with each other for a championship while fighting for each other. These were men who were constantly checking on each other, who showed us all that while being great is impressive, being good can be just as meaningful.

"When I first got out and got home, I'm like, 'Damn, what am I supposed to do now?'" Jayson Tatum tells me. "I got no plans. I've got nowhere to go. I'm not waking up to get tested every morning and check my heart monitor and take my temperature. The first couple days were weird.

"I was like, 'Damn, do I miss the bubble?'"

Taylor Rooks is an Emmy-nominated sports journalist and interviewer who probes some of today's most pressing discussions beyond the game. She hosts the *Take It There with Taylor Rooks* interview show for Bleacher Report, among other duties for Turner Sports. Previously, she worked as a host, reporter, and correspondent for the Big Ten Network, SNY, and as a sideline reporter for CBS Sports Network. Taylor is from Gwinnett County, Georgia, and currently lives in New York City.

Is College Football Making the Pandemic Worse?

LOUISA THOMAS

FROM *The New Yorker* • NOVEMBER 25, 2020

For four quarters, at least, Graham Mertz, the quarterback for the University of Wisconsin, lived as if dreaming. A lanky redshirt freshman, Mertz took the field for his first start as a Badger, in the Big Ten Conference's season opener, on Friday, October 23rd, against the University of Illinois, and completed his first pass attempt, a gain of three yards. His second attempt gained twelve. His third, a pretty touch pass, went for a touchdown. Mertz completed his fourth attempt, his fifth, his sixth. He followed a conservative strategy, mostly screens and short passes, but grew more daring. He rolled out on a play fake and threw a touchdown off his back foot. He whipped another over the middle, a precise dart into the end zone. With less than a minute to go in the first half, he launched a fifty-three-yard touchdown pass to a streaking wide receiver. By then, he was fourteen for fourteen, with four touchdowns—he threw the ball seventeen times before he missed a target, and only then because the ball was dropped. (Graciously, he blamed himself.) He finished the game twenty for twenty-one, with five touchdowns. Patrick Mahomes, the best quarterback in the world, tweeted his amazement. J.J. Watt, the three-time N.F.L. defensive player of the year, posted a video of a man using a flamethrower, in tribute. Wisconsin won, 45–7.

In a normal season, the freshman quarterback would have looked up to see eighty thousand people cheering for him, chanting and singing and calling his name. But this was not a normal season. The cold metal bleachers were bare, and the cheers that followed each of his touchdowns were fake. When the song "Jump Around" played before the fourth quarter, the small cluster of cardboard cutouts that had been installed in the stands did not jump. When it's empty, Wisconsin's Camp Randall Stadium has about as much charm as an old airport concourse. But a touchdown is still a touchdown, even if no crowd makes a sound. "He was smiling cheek to cheek after the first touchdown," the tight end Jake Ferguson said of Mertz afterward. "He knew, and everyone in that huddle knew, that we were rolling."

Two days later, Mertz tested positive for the coronavirus. Then it was reported that Wisconsin's backup quarterback had tested positive as well. By midweek, the number of positive tests within the football program was up to twelve, and included the head coach—and the team's next game, against the University of Nebraska, was cancelled. A week later, the number of cases on the team was up to twenty-seven. Two players for Illinois also tested positive, although it was unclear if they were infected during the game or somewhere else entirely. Wisconsin's next game, against Purdue, was called off.

Purdue vs. Wisconsin was one of ten top-tier college-football games that was postponed or cancelled that weekend. The Badgers returned to the field a week later, on November 14th, routing Michigan, but fifteen other games were not played as originally scheduled that weekend, including four of seven games that were to have featured teams from the powerhouse Southeastern Conference (S.E.C.). So far, more than eighty games have been cancelled, and several conferences are only a few weeks into their schedules. But the season has rolled on, even as coronavirus cases have skyrocketed across the country. If we could say definitively, in precise and dramatic detail, that the former was connected to the latter, then presumably universities would face public pressure to stop the games. But this is probably the wrong way to think about life during a pandemic. And the approach that we have taken to college football likely reflects our broader failure to grasp what it takes to shut down the virus.

BACK IN AUGUST, the Big Ten announced that it was postponing its football season until the spring. Players had begun returning for workouts in June, and team after team around the country had suffered outbreaks of SARS-CoV-2. There were reports of athletes suffering serious long-term effects—an anguished Facebook post written by the mother of one player, which described her son's struggle with myocarditis, an inflammation of the heart muscle that can follow a viral infection, shook many within the sport.

The Big Ten is the oldest conference in the country and includes some of the largest and most respected universities in the world. The decision to call off the season was hugely costly—the conference was in the middle of a multi-billion-dollar television deal—and hugely unpopular. But the concerns prompting it were grave, and many people expected the rest of the so-called Power Five conferences to follow suit, as the Pac-12 did, just hours later. The season appeared to be on the brink of cancellation.

It turned out that there is no more unity in college football than there is in the rest of the country. Not all medical experts agreed about the riskiness of playing. Some parents of players protested the Big Ten's decision. Players sued. Commentators railed about the decision on sports radio. A player labor movement merged with, and then morphed into, a movement to play the season. The President of the United States mocked the conference on Twitter. The rest of the Power Five—the Big 12, the Atlantic Coast Conference, and the S.E.C., which, collectively, are home to fourteen of the last fifteen national champions— were not inclined to defer to the Big Ten, and announced that they were going ahead with games. Football brings in more than a hundred million dollars in revenue to top schools, and, although the financial impact for smaller programs is less clear, athletic departments generally depend on money from football. Programs had not stashed away revenue for a rainy day or a pandemic. They had spent it—on other sports, expensive coaches, and lavish facilities.

The season began without the Big Ten. Some players got sick, others tested positive without showing symptoms, and still others were held out while contact tracing was being conducted. Several big games were cancelled, but enough were played to make it appear that something like a full season would eventually be completed. A couple of weeks after the nation's first game had been played, the commissioner of the Big Ten, Kevin Warren, announced that the conference's member schools had taken another vote: the Big Ten would resume playing football at the end of October. The Pac-12 soon released a similar statement, as did smaller conferences that had also put off playing. All but a handful of teams across the country would participate in the season.

Big Ten university presidents said that the reversal was prompted by new medical advice. The conference had enlisted a private company to provide daily rapid tests to all teams; experts had provided stringent health and safety guidelines. There was evidence that heart complications might be rarer in athletes than had been feared—and doctors and researchers had developed a screening protocol for detecting myocarditis.

There was truth to all of this, but it was not the whole story. While some medical experts believed that you could find a safe-enough way to play, most epidemiologists and public-health professors I spoke to were not in favor of it. What had really changed between August and September was that college football had come back without the Big Ten, outbreaks had happened, and there had been little outcry. By the time that the Big Ten resumed play, in late October, Notre Dame, Florida, Cincinnati, and several other ranked teams had all had coronavirus clusters. The L.S.U. head coach, Ed Orgeron, casually mentioned that "most" of his players had contracted it during the summer. (He seemed to frame this as a plus, because the team presumably wouldn't need to worry as much about the virus as the season went on; two months later, the team's game against Alabama was postponed after more members of the program tested positive.) Jamain Stephens, a defensive tackle at a Division II school outside of Pittsburgh, died of complications from COVID-19. But football fans kept tuning in. Teams are not generally forthcoming about infections, both out of concern for the privacy of their players, and, at least according to the University of Oklahoma football coach Lincoln Riley, because it gives them a competitive advantage. Only rarely did stories of players struggling with the illness, or even being hospitalized, appear in the press. COVID cases and mandatory quarantines were described by coaches and analysts as an annoyance or a misfortune roughly on par with a sprained ankle. Television contracts were being honored. Money flowed to schools and to coaches, if not to players. The playoffs were on the horizon. Fans went to bars. Families and friends gathered for game day. The lower stands of stadiums at many schools were filled with people. You could turn on the television every weekend and see some semblance of normalcy.

The introduction of daily rapid testing had seemed like a real advance—and it was loudly touted by the Big Ten. The argument was that widespread, frequent use of tests with quick turnaround times could allow for a return to more or less normal activity, even if those tests were not as accurate as those that take longer to produce results. The tests wouldn't stop people from catching the virus, but, theoretically, they could identify infected people before they'd interacted much with others. (The Pac-12 is also using daily rapid testing. Players in other Power Five conferences are tested less often, typically using the more accurate P.C.R. tests, while teams in less prestigious conferences have differing—and sometimes less stringent—testing regimes.) The results of the approach would potentially have ramifications far beyond football. "This is one of the first really high-quality, real-world tests of that concept," Dave O'Connor, a professor of pathology and laboratory medicine at the University of Wisconsin, told me.

It didn't quite work. For the first month, testing went smoothly, but Wisconsin's outbreak occurred anyway—and other programs conducting daily antigen testing had outbreaks, too. At the University of Maryland, twenty-three players tested positive in a two-week span; several Pac-12 teams had to cancel games because they did not have the minimum number of scholarship players available.

When I spoke to O'Connor, in early November, his lab—in collaboration with county and state public-health officials and the C.D.C.—was trying to figure out how the disease had spread within the Badgers football program. The lab was looking for genetic signatures in the team's positive samples, and was using what O'Connor's colleague, Thomas Friedrich, called shoe-leather epidemiology to find clues about where the virus had originated. Had there been lapses in social-distancing protocols? Would a more sensitive test have made a difference? Could the outbreak be traced to one source, or was there more than one simultaneous infection? Did the efficacy of daily rapid testing depend on lower rates of community transmission?

O'Connor told me that he'd been partial to the view that, with "really fast turnaround testing, even with lower sensitivity tests, you could enable a safer reopening of schools, a safer reopening of the economy." And yet, he said, "You can still have an outbreak." The rash of positive tests on the football team had reminded O'Connor and Friedrich of the need both for data and for humility. When I asked them, over Zoom, if the investigation had changed their views on whether it was advisable to play football this year, Friedrich gave me a wry smile. "My personal view is that it wasn't advisable in the first place," he said.

"I started a little more optimistic than Tom on the ability of testing to make it safe," O'Connor said. "I didn't think it was advisable, but for another reason. We are in a state where there's an entire culture around football." Friedrich chimed in to agree. That culture is intensely social. The bigger problem, as they saw it, wasn't whether the protocols could protect the players. It was that those protocols wouldn't protect the rest of us.

THIS PAST SUMMER, a group of researchers at Washington State University started thinking about what a football season might mean for the city of Pullman, where the university is based. At that point, Washington State, which plays in the Pac-12, planned to begin its season in September; the question was whether fans would be allowed to attend the games. The perils were obvious: every public-health expert was advising against large gatherings. But what was the precise level of risk? Washington State's athletic department was running an operating deficit of nearly a hundred million dollars, and around half of its usual revenue came from football, including ticket sales—but the considerations weren't only financial. Although Washington State has one of the smallest stadiums in big-time college football, its fan base is passionate. Game days are big days in Pullman.

The researchers used mathematical modelling to simulate how visitors coming to a campus community very much like Washington State's to attend a football game would affect the levels of the virus in the community. The scope of their inquiry was relatively narrow: they did not have anything to say, for instance, about whether a visitor might become infected and bring the virus back to her own community—a risk that "could lead to multiple outbreaks around the country," as Jill Weatherhead, a professor of infectious diseases at the Baylor College of Medicine, told me. The Washington State paper has yet to be peer-reviewed, but what the researchers found was sobering. In simulations in which a small number of visitors with COVID-19 mixed lightly with a campus community experiencing an uncontrolled outbreak, cases rose in the community by twenty-five per cent. When visitors with a high prevalence of the coronavirus mixed heavily with a campus community where the virus was previously under control, the local increase was more than eight hundred per cent.

The Pac-12 and the Big Ten ultimately decided not to let fans—with the exception of players' families—into stadiums at all. But the rest of the Power Five, along with several smaller conferences, did. On those campuses, and in those college towns, we don't yet know whether things played out the way the researchers' model projected—for one thing, most of the schools are admitting fewer fans than the model estimated. And we may never precisely learn the results of these gambles. Two weeks before the S.E.C. football season began, Oxford, Mississippi, where Ole Miss is situated, had the highest daily infection rate—eighty-five per one hundred thousand people—of any college town whose school was playing football. (Health officials generally recommend the suspension of nonessential activities at anything above twenty-five.) When the team kicked off the season, nearly fifteen thousand fans were in the stands; more than two and a half million people watched on television, many of them doubtless gathering to watch at bars or inside homes. Katie Taylor, an epidemiologist with Mississippi's department of health, told me, in an email, that the department had not "at this time directly tied cases to outbreaks or clusters associated with football-related activities." She added, "However, we know that many of these settings, especially gatherings for football watching, can lead to transmission." The University of Alabama saw a massive surge in cases when students returned to campus. The number of cases had dropped by the time the football season began, and it has not risen precipitously since. But cases in Alabama as a whole have been rising steadily all fall. Karen Landers, an officer in Alabama's public-health department, told me, "Attendance at sporting events and also attendance at parties relating to sporting events has contributed to outbreaks." Department policy prevented her from providing specifics, she said.

The Texas Department of State Health Services maintains a database of investigations conducted by local health departments.

The database is not comprehensive, but, for what it's worth, earlier this month, it included only eighteen cases indicating in-person college-football attendance. Eric Lofgren, one of the Washington State researchers, told me that, as far as predicting outbreaks goes, "I would really like to be wrong." It's possible that students and visitors don't mix in the way the researchers' model assumes. It's also possible, Lofgren noted, that people going to games are taking the virus more seriously than they sometimes get credit for. It may help that people at football games are captive audiences for public-health messages about mask-wearing and other precautions. The games are played in large, outdoor stadiums where fans have been required to wear masks: these factors, too, may have reduced the risk of widespread transmission. And with such uncontrolled community transmission across the country, it's hard to say where infections are occurring.

Some football programs are using in-person attendance as an opportunity to identify positive cases. The University of Texas at Austin requires proof of a negative test in order for students to pick up their tickets; of the twelve hundred students tested before the first game of the season, ninety-six tested positive, and the seventy-five who had not previously had the virus were then isolated. "It was an incentive for folks to come and get tested, which is great," Amy Young, the vice-dean of professional practice at the university's medical school and the chief clinical officer for UT Health Austin, said.

And yet, viewed another way, that data simply illustrates what a risky experiment schools are undertaking. At most of these schools, no test is required before a fan may enter the stadium— and even at the University of Texas, only twelve hundred out of the fifteen thousand people who attended were tested. That nearly a hundred people tested positive out of this small sample suggests that, across the state, thousands of people infected with the coronavirus are going to games, where they shout, use bathrooms, and grab beers from concession stands. The city of Lubbock, where Texas Tech is situated, has permitted some tailgating. A month into the season, Lubbock had one of the highest coronavirus-infection rates in the country.

Darlene Bhavnani, the head of the University of Texas's contact-tracing program, told me, "Looking at the data we've collected, there doesn't seem to be transmission at the game, at the stadium." But contact tracing is an imperfect art, and, as a general rule, it is more focussed on preventing further spread than on determining the specific activity that led to an infection. The point is "primarily to establish an infectious period and then to identify contacts," Sam Jarvis, a Community Health Manager at Johnson County Public Health, in Iowa, wrote in an email.

What's more, as Lofgren pointed out to me, "The majority of people's engagement with sports is not actually in the stands." The Washington State study includes transmission from any event surrounding a game, such as an out-of-town visitor catching the virus while going out to dinner near campus the night before. "Does the contact tracer identify that as because of football?" Lofgren asked. "I don't know. I think there's ambiguity." In places like Iowa City, where the University of Iowa is situated, they probably wouldn't, Jarvis told me. "We don't have the capacity to pinpoint single events like that," he said. "It's frustrating, for sure, because we know it's happening, but it's difficult to pinpoint like that with all the noise." Tracing has only become harder as the pandemic has entered its third wave. "With overwhelming spread, public-health resources are going to have a much harder time tracing back where infection happened," Jill Weatherhead told me.

And there may be another reason that no college football game has been confirmed as a superspreader event: luck. The Washington State model is stochastic—it involves randomness. "There are many examples in the data where you don't have anything bad happen," Lofgren explained. That doesn't mean that holding mass gatherings is a good idea, just that it's possible schools have taken chances but have not been burned—yet. In that case, the more transmission there is within communities, and the more games that are played, the more likely our luck, such as it may be, will end.

D URING A NORMAL YEAR, in the lead-up to a Michigan State home game, Aaron Stephens, the mayor of East Lansing, would be worrying about traffic. This year, he was focussed on a public-messaging blitz: don't go to the stadium; don't tailgate in the parking lot; do wear a mask. Indoor gatherings in East Lansing were capped at ten people, and outdoor gatherings were limited to twenty-five. Violators could face fines of up to five hundred dollars, but Stephens tried to emphasize the carrot rather than the stick: "If we want to have football, we have to adhere to these rules."

Stephens, who became the mayor this summer, is twenty-four years old, and a recent graduate of Michigan State. "I understand the reality of being in college," he said. He was at game-day parties himself not so long ago. This year, during the season-opener, people crammed inside apartments off campus, with the game on television in the background and the kegs tapped. "I saw a couple of parties that were probably above a hundred people," Stephens told me later that week. There was only so much the city could do. "By the time we get there and break up the event, the spread has already happened," he noted. We spoke the day before Halloween, when Michigan State was set to play its rival, the University of Michigan. Stephens was dreading it, expecting mayhem if the Spartans won. "In a weird way, it got me rooting against my own team," he said. Michigan State beat Michigan, 27–24, and fans flooded the streets. Some wore masks. Many did not. They headed toward the apartment complexes in Cedar Village, where they partook in a time-honored tradition of setting couches on fire.

I asked Linda Vail, the head of the health department for Ingham County, which includes East Lansing, if there was evidence that the game had contributed to the spread of the virus in the area. She told me that, in the two weeks after the game, there was a significant increase in cases. "That said, we're seeing a significant increase across our community, too," she said. "So, yes. But who knows."

The cities where Big Ten universities are situated form a kind of consortium. In early October, Stephens's office started contacting the other mayors, and a Zoom call was arranged. Stephens proposed writing a letter to the Big Ten executives, requesting that, when they decided whether or not to hold games, they take into account the prevalence of the virus not only among players and coaches but within the local community. The mayors had other suggestions, too, such as scheduling games earlier in the day—night games are often preceded by hours of drinking, which can lead to more reckless behavior. The final version of the letter was signed by eleven of the fourteen Big Ten mayors. It was carefully worded—almost painfully so. The mayors "humbly" requested that the Big Ten determine "defined metrics for overall community population positivity rates and test positivity" when deciding whether to play. Every mayor I spoke to emphasized the strong relationship that he or she had with the local university. Some said that they were glad to have football back. All of them were in an impossible position.

Football helped put East Lansing, a city with a population under fifty thousand, on the map. Ohio State has a phenomenal veterinary program, but that is not what brings most visitors to Columbus. The economic impact that football has on these local economies is tremendous, and so is its effect on the morale of many people who live there. The mayors understand this. Still, they had watched the virus spread on campuses, and they knew that the social buffer between students and locals, which had helped contain the virus during earlier outbreaks, was likely to break down when football arrived. Several of them described what took place after games like scenes out of a COVID-19 nightmare: students pouring into downtown, spewing the virus with drunken screams.

Such behavior isn't wise, but it is predictable. Fans, especially young fans, play their roles as well as any defensive line. It is possible that the enduring image of the 2020 season will be the strange and stupid sight of hundreds of Notre Dame students flooding the field after their team upset No. 1 Clemson. (It was a somewhat fluky result: Clemson's star quarterback, Trevor Lawrence, missed the game because he had contracted the coronavirus.) Afterward, the university's president, who had contracted the virus after attending a gathering at the White House for Justice Amy Coney Barrett without wearing a mask, admonished the students, in a letter, for their poor decision-making. The letter did not offer any reflection on the institutional decisions that had led to the students being in the stadium in the first place.

After the mayors sent their letter, Jim Borchers, Ohio State's team physician and the chair of the Big Ten's return-to-play medical subcommittee, told the *Wall Street Journal* that the university did monitor "other metrics from the university, local communities and states where the teams are participating." He added, "I don't know that the student athletes should be punished for the inability of the general public to get their minds around how to prevent this." Many of the arguments in favor of having college-football games come down to the idea that players deserve to chase their dreams. Football always involves some risk, and every decision we make during a pandemic involves trade-offs and risk assessments. But those who criticize the schools can make a similar argument. College athletes are not more deserving of their dreams than those who have postponed weddings, or attempted remote learning for their kids, or held virtual funerals rather than gathering in person.

"Every step we take back toward normality has a risk and a benefit associated with it," Zach Binney, a professor at Emory with a degree in epidemiology, told me. "Establish the level of risk that you're O.K. with. And that's going to vary based on the benefits. This is not some crazy theory. We never closed grocery stores. Why not? Because the benefit of having them open was too high." Other activities, though, lead inevitably to arguments. How much risk is acceptable when marching for social justice? Or celebrating a political victory? With college football, the calculation is even more complicated, because much of the risk is connected with associated behaviors—those watch parties, for instance—that don't have to happen but should probably be expected. The sport provides a welcome, and some would even say necessary, distraction, at a moment social ties are under strain. But at what cost? "If you have to ask the question, should people be able to party during Badgers games or have first graders in school, you should choose first graders in school," O'Connor, the University of Wisconsin epidemiologist, said.

Part of the issue, perhaps, is that the focus on the safety of players and on fans in stadiums has obscured the risks of game-day rituals and the ripple effects whenever infections spread. "All those other activities," O'Connor said, "conspire to make it more difficult to bring the virus under control."

IF THERE IS A SINGLE UNDERLYING FALLACY that has led to the persistence of college football during the worst pandemic the country has seen in a century, it is the idea that football is a discrete activity that can be considered separately from all the other things that we do. College athletes are young and generally healthy; even if they contract the coronavirus, they are unlikely to face its severest consequences. When the Wisconsin Badgers resumed the season after a few weeks of cancellations, Graham Mertz was back on the field and threw two touchdowns. (He threw three interceptions in a loss a week later.) For the most part, the students who were cheering him on at home or at watch parties probably do not belong to the most vulnerable population when it comes to the virus, either. But many other college football fans are older. Some have underlying health conditions. And those with asymptomatic cases can and do spread the virus to others. The people they spread it to can then spread it further.

The real danger that college football poses during the pandemic may not be in the mass gatherings and dramatic outpourings of enthusiasm but in the ordinary and suddenly unsafe behaviors of small groups of people trying to find, in football, the refuge of their remembered lives. Millions watch the games every weekend, and many are watching in groups that include people from outside their household. Public-health officials have made numerous statements warning of the dangers of viral spread when people gather to watch football, but it's hard to get such messages across when events are being held as if little has changed. Kathleen Bachynski, a professor of public health at Muhlenberg College, asked me, rhetorically, "If football is proceeding, what does that signal to people about where we're at with our pandemic response?"

Football, particularly college football, is an occasion, a communal event. The ecosystem around the sport is vast. It starts with the players, but it extends to their classmates and to their coaches. It branches out to athletic trainers and their partners and kids. It extends to journalists, and camera operators, and photographers, and stadium workers, and bus drivers, and their families. It includes alumni scattered all over the world, and their children, and other children in other places who root for the teams with the uniforms they like. It brings together grandfathers and granddaughters, and aunts and cousins, and their spouses, and their friends. This is the majesty of college football: it connects people in a great web of affection. These are the filaments along which the virus can spread.

Louisa Thomas is a staff writer at *The New Yorker*. She is the author of *Louisa: The Extraordinary Life of Mrs. Adams*, and *Conscience: Two Soldiers, Two Pacifists, One Family—A Test of Will and Faith in World War I*. She is also the co-author, with John Urschel, of *Mind and Matter: A Life in Math and Football*, and the co-editor, with Mary Pilon, of *Losers: Dispatches from the Other Side of the Scoreboard*. She lives in Boston.

The Confederate Flag Is Finally Gone at NASCAR Races, and I Won't Miss It for a Second

RYAN McGEE

FROM ESPN • JUNE 10, 2020

The stars and bars have been banned from NASCAR racetracks.
Finally.

On Wednesday afternoon, three days after the Cup Series showed a unified front against racism at Atlanta Motor Speedway, and only a few hours before Bubba Wallace's No. 43 Chevy hit the track at Martinsville Speedway adorned with an image of black and white hands embraced, NASCAR announced it was officially pulling the battle banner of a nation long gone off of its racetrack properties. It's the culmination of a one-man campaign by Wallace, who this week appeared across major news outlets and called for NASCAR to finally do what it has wanted to for years. Now it finally is.

Good.

In its statement, NASCAR wrote: "The presence of the Confederate flag at NASCAR events runs contrary to our commitment to providing a welcoming and inclusive environment for all fans, our competitors and our industry. Bringing people together around a love for racing and the community it creates is what makes fans and sport special. The display of the Confederate flag will be prohibited from all NASCAR events and properties."

Damn right.

The Confederate flag is gone. I will not miss it for one single second.

Because gone with it is the perpetual need for me to apologize to my coworkers of color, who politely winced whenever we entered a speedway infield to be greeted by a line of Confederate flags. Gone is the instant evidence always used against me by friends and colleagues who refused to accept my pleas of "NASCAR has changed, really!" because they only had to point over my shoulder at the flags whipping in the wind in HDTV every Sunday afternoon. Gone are the skeptical rolled eyes that Wallace has had to combat his entire life. Same for NBA All-Star-turned-NASCAR team owner Brad Daugherty, or NASCAR official Kirk Price, or the family of NASCAR Hall of Famer Wendell Scott, the only other Black driver to make his living as a Cup Series driver. All of them have spent their lives going to the racetrack, having achieved their dream of working at the highest level of stock car racing, only to have to explain over and over again why they chose to work at a place where multiple symbols of hate are displayed out in the open.

Before we go any further, I want to address the "Heritage Not Hate" crowd. I'm talking about those who sound like me and look like me and, like me, have a deep-rooted Southern upbringing. Let's be totally clear here: By agreeing with NASCAR's decision, I'm not betraying anyone or anything. And don't start lecturing me on history, either. You don't have a boot to stand in when it comes to teaching me what that flag means. You go tale-of-the-tape with me on our Confederate DNA, and you're going to go down harder than Pickett's Charge.

I am a direct descendant of slave owners. My family still owns the home where my forefathers lived while the human beings they owned worked all around them. As I write this, I am sitting on the North Carolina coast just south of Fort Fisher, the would-be protector of the port of Wilmington that was overrun by Union forces during the winter of 1865. My great-great-great grandfather and uncle were taken prisoner after fighting under that flag and were shipped off to a prison camp in Elmira, New York—a.k.a., "Hell-mira"—and when the Civil War ended, they walked home, 600 miles, to Rockingham, North Carolina. I have a photo of myself as a newborn, being held in the arms of my great aunt, who, as a child, talked to those men about what they fought for and lost. In the end, they were buried as citizens of the United States of America, with their nation's real flag, the Stars and Stripes, displayed over the gate to the cemetery.

So, don't come at me with claims that I don't understand what the flags of the Confederate States of America stood for, or what it stands for now.

My forefathers lost that war. I'm glad they lost it. They were on the wrong side of history. They've all been dead for more than a century and yet I've found myself still working to correct their wrongs. My brother has stood in the same field where the slaves once worked for my family. The man with the deed on the house, holding hands and weeping with the descendants of the people of whom my family once held the deed.

Bubba Wallace, NASCAR's only Black full-time driver, said Wednesday he knows some will not be happy about the decision to ban the Confederate flag: "We should not be able to have an argument over that. It is a thick line we cannot cross anymore."

So, yeah, spare me the arguments about what that flag really means. I know exactly what it means. It means pain. It means anguish. It means embarrassment. It means the most shameful blight on the pages of the history of the United States, and that's no small achievement.

Even if there had ever been a stitch of honor left in that flag after the Civil War was over, that was wrung out when hate groups chose the stars and bars as their go-to banner, under which they set fire to crosses, lynched Black Americans, and held aloft as they stood at the doors of desegregated schools and screamed at innocent children, schoolbooks in hand, who did nothing more than be born.

There was a time when the swastika meant nothing, too. It first appeared in Asia 5,000 years ago. It was meant to signify the sun. But then someone came along and turned it into the symbol of one of the greatest evil forces that Earth has ever known.

You wouldn't fly that over Talladega, would you? Because to millions upon millions of Americans, that's what they see and what they feel when they see that Confederate flag. I am 100 percent confident that a real NASCAR fan has the ability to enjoy a weekend in the infield just as much while flying an American flag as they do under the flag of a misguided, defeated nation that hasn't existed for 155 years. If they can't, then they've never loved NASCAR as much they have always claimed. They certainly have never loved it as much as I do.

No, the only place where we should see the stars and bars now is displayed in a museum, encased in glass and context. You really want to teach someone about heritage versus hate? You really want to have a debate with someone about what those flags mean? Go to the Smithsonian. Go to the National Civil Rights Museum in Memphis, at the Lorraine Motel where Dr. Martin Luther King was assassinated. Go to Gettysburg, Appomattox, or meet me down at Fort Fisher. We can talk about it all day. At the right places.

But not at the racetrack. Not anymore.

ESPN senior writer **Ryan McGee** is a regular contributor to ESPN.com, *SportsCenter*, and *E:60*, as well as co-host of *Marty and McGee* on SEC Network and ESPN Radio. His four books include the *New York Times* bestseller *Racing to the Finish* with Dale Earnhardt Jr. and the 2020 memoir *Sidelines and Bloodlines*, written with his father and brother. McGee is a five-time Sports Emmy winner, six-time National Motorsports Press Association Writer of the Year, and National Sports Media Association board member. In addition to listing career achievements, McGee also enjoys race cars, pulled pork BBQ, and playing Madden '92 on Sega Genesis.

Twelve Minutes and a Life

MITCHELL S. JACKSON

FROM *Runner's World* • JUNE 18, 2020

Imagine young Ahmaud "Maud" Arbery, a junior varsity scat-back turned undersized varsity linebacker on a practice field of the Brunswick High Pirates. The head coach has divided the squad into offense and defense and has his offense running the plays of their next opponent. The coach, as is his habit, has been taunting his defense. "Y'all ain't ready," he says. "You can't stop us," he says. "What y'all gone do?" The next play, Maud, all 5 feet 10 inches and 165 pounds of him, bursts between blockers and—BOOM!—lays a hit that makes the sound of cars crashing, that echoes across the field and into the stands, that just might reach the locker room. It's a feat that teenage Maud also intends as a message to his coaches, his teammates, and all else that ain't hitherto hipped: Don't test my heart. Some of those teammates smash their fist to their mouth and oooh. Others slap one another's pads and point. An assistant coach winces and runs to the aid of the tackled teammate. And the head coach, well, he trumpets his whistle. "Why'd you hit him like that?" he hollers. "Save that for Friday. Let's see you do that on Friday."

That Friday, in Glynn County Stadium (one of the largest high school stadiums in all of gridiron-loving Georgia) the Pirates, clad in their home white jerseys with blue and gold trim, huddle in the locker room. Maud, who wears high shoulder pads, a 2x4 face mask, and number 21 in honor of his brother, Buck, and his idol, famed NFL safety Sean Taylor, swaggers into the center of his teammates and begins the chant he's christened into a pre-game ritual.

"Y'all ready!" he shouts.

"Hell yeah!" they shout.

"Y'all ready!" he shouts.

"Hell yeah!" they shout.

"Y'all ain't ready?!" he shouts.

"Sheeeeeit!" they shout.

To applause that could be thunder, the team stampedes out of the fog-filled mouth of a blow-up tunnel onto the field. The school band plays the fight song and cheerleaders shake pom-poms from a row in front of the band. There's a raucous sea of blue and gold in the stands, including plenty of Maud's people. Game time, the opposing team calls the play that Maud put the fierce kaput on in practice, and beneath a metal-halide glare that's also a gauntlet, Maud barrels towards the running back and—BOOM!—lays a hit that sounds like trucks colliding. It's a noise that resounds across the field and into the stands, that just might ring all over Brunswick. The fans send up a roar but Maud trots to the sidelines almost insouciant. Jason Vaughn, an assistant coach who also coached Maud on JV, grabs him by his face mask. "Now that's how you hit," he says, tamping astonishment that a boy his size could hit that hard.

But that's young Maud, undersized in the physical sense, super-sized in heart.

Sunday, February 23, 2020 | 1:04 pm

Time-stamped security footage from an adjacent home shows Maud, who's out for a run in Brunswick's Satilla Shores subdivision, wandering up a sunny patch of narrow road and stopping on the spotty lawn of a sand-colored under-construction bungalow addressed 220 Satilla Drive. There's a red portable toilet in the front yard. The garage is wide open.

Ahmaud, dressed in light-colored low-top Nikes, a white t-shirt, and khaki cargo shorts, loafs on the lawn for a moment before drifting into the building. The security camera records him inside the home, a brightened skeleton of beams and plywood and stacks of sheetrock and piping and wire. There are boxes of materials scattered about and a small forklift pushed in a corner. Maud doesn't touch any of those things. He looks around, gazes beyond the frame of the camera toward the river behind the house. Maybe he wonders what the home will look like when it's finished. Maybe he conjures an image of a family who could afford to live in a place so close to water.

Maud ain't the first person to wander onto the site. Its security cameras have recorded others including a white couple one evening and a pair of white boys one day. On four occasions, it also recorded what appears to be the same person: a slim young Black man with wild natural hair and tattoos on his shoulders and arms, a dude, that by my eye, don't resemble Maud. Let me add that the homeowner will confirm that nothing was stolen or damaged during any of the visits.

Meanwhile, a coveralled neighbor spies Maud roaming the site and calls 9-1-1. "There's a guy in the house right now," he reports. "It's a house under construction. 219 or 220 Satilla Drive." The man waits near the corner of Jones Road and Satilla Drive. "I just need to know what he's doing wrong," says the dispatcher. "He's been caught on the camera a bunch before. It's kind of an ongoing thing out here," says the caller. It's a statement of which he can't be sure, though he does get right Maud's physical description: "Black guy, white t-shirt."

TO FATHOM WHAT IT MEANT for Maud to be out for a run in Glynn County, you need to know a thing or two about the pastime of recreational running. Before the 1960s, the idea of jogging for almost everybody save serious athletes was this: Now why would I do that? But in 1962, legendary track coach and Nike co-founder Bill Bowerman visited New Zealand and met with fellow coach Arthur Lydiard who'd developed a cross-country training program. Bowerman returned to the States excited by what he'd seen. He launched a similar program in Eugene (home of his alma mater and employer, the University of Oregon), wrote a pamphlet on the subject in 1966, and the next year, published a co-written book titled *Jogging: A Medically-Approved Physical Fitness Program for all Ages*. That book became a bestseller and kickstarted jogging as an American pastime.

Let me acknowledge that I am one of the rarest of Americans, one otherwise known as a Black Oregonian. As such, I feel compelled to share a truth about my home state: It's white. I'm talking banned-Blacks-in-its-state-constitution white. At the time that Bowerman was inspiring Eugene residents to trot miles around their neighborhoods in sweatpants and running shoes, Eugene was a stark 97 percent white. One could argue that the overwhelming whiteness of jogging today may be, in part, a product of Eugene's demographics. But if we're keeping it 100, the monolithic character of running can be credited to the ways in which it's been marketed and to the systemic forces that have placed it somewhere on a continuum between impractical extravagance and unaffordable hazard for scores of people who ain't white.

Matter of truth, around the time Bowerman visited New Zealand and published a bestselling book, millions of Blacks were living in the Jim Crow South; by 1968, Blacks diaspora-wide had mourned the assassinations of Medgar Evers, Malcolm X, and Martin Luther King Jr. And by the late '60s and beyond, the Blacks of the Great Migration were redlined into ever more depressed sections of northern and western cities, areas where the streets were less and less safe to walk, much less run. Forces aplenty discouraged Blacks from reaping the manifold benefits of jogging. And though the demographics of runners have become more diverse over the last 50 years, jogging, by and large, remains a sport and pastime pitched to privileged whites.

Peoples, I invite you to ask yourself, just what is a runner's world? Ask yourself who deserves to run? Who has the right?

Ask who's a runner? What's their so-called race? Their gender? Their class? Ask yourself where do they live, where do they run? Where can't they live and run? Ask what are the sanctions for asserting their right to live and run—shit—to exist in the world. Ask why? Ask why? Ask why?

Ahmaud Arbery, by all accounts, loved to run but didn't call himself a runner. That is a shortcoming of the culture of running. That Maud's jogging made him the target of hegemonic white forces is a certain failure of America. Check the books—slave passes, vagrancy laws, Harvard's Skip Gates arrested outside his own crib—Blacks ain't never owned the same freedom of movement as whites.

Sunday, February 23, 2020 | 1:08 pm

Maud strolls out the house and in just a few steps, begins to jog. He's unaware of the witness who called 9-1-1, a man still surveilling him. "He's running right now. There he goes right now," says the witness to dispatch. "Okay, what is he doing?" says the dispatcher. "He's running down the street," says the man. The footage shows Maud jogging past the Satilla Drive home of Gregory and Travis McMichael—a father and son. Gregory McMichael, an ex-cop stripped of his power to arrest for failure to attend use-of-force training, notices Maud passing his house and deems him suspicious. "Travis, the guy is running down the street," he hollers. "Let's go." For reasons the McMichaels must now account for in court (both have been indicted on nine counts, including felony murder and aggravated assault), they arm themselves—the son with a Remington 870 shotgun and the father with a .357 Magnum—and hop in a white Ford pickup truck.

THE GOLDEN ISLES lie along Georgia's Atlantic coast between Savannah and Jacksonville, Florida. The region encompasses the barrier islands of St. Simons, Sea Island, Little St. Simons, and Jekyll, as well as the mainland cities of Darien and Brunswick. Satilla Shores, part of the Golden Isles, is an unincorporated neighborhood of upper- and middle-class families; of blue- and white-collar retirees; of seasonal vacation-home owners and lifelong denizens; of fresh transplants. The small neighborhood features narrow roads canopied by moss-draped live oaks, tall Southern Pines, and crepe myrtle; and one- and two-story homes with landscaped lawns and driveways parked with late-model vehicles and boats. Homes on one side of Satilla Drive—the neighborhood's main street—boast as a backyard amenity the sediment-colored Little Satilla River, replete with its miles-wide spartina salt marshes.

Maud's family home in Brunswick, the one where he lived at the time he was murdered, is a mere two miles from Satilla Shores, but in meaningful ways, it's almost another country. The median household income for all of Glynn County is $51,000; in Brunswick that figure is $26,000. The poverty rate of what young Black residents call "The Wick" is a staggering 38 percent.

"The Wick" is where Ahmaud Marquez Arbery was born on May 8, 1994. He was the third beloved child of Wanda Cooper-Jones and Marcus Arbery Sr. Their working-class family included his older brother Marcus "Buck" Jr. and sister Jasmine. The family called Ahmaud "Quez," a shortened version of his middle name, while his friends called him Maud. Maud had a slight gap in his front teeth and dark skin forever burnished by hours outside. He and his stair-step siblings attended Altama Elementary School. Around that time, Maud met his best friend Akeem "Keem" Baker, a fellow resident of the Leeswood Circle apartment complex. Keem, who in those days was a chubby introvert, recalls Maud being one of the popular kids in the neighborhood, someone he won over by bringing him snacks. The "sandlock brothers" were soon inseparable: sitting together on the bus ride to school, scouting the neighborhood in search of basketball rims, playing a football game called "Hot Ball" or a basketball-shooting game they christened "Curb Ball."

In those days, Maud's brother, Buck, just three years older, was a hovering protector. Buck also introduced Maud to the sport he grew to love. It happened during the 2002 BCS National Championship game. Buck's favorite player at the time was Sean Taylor, and despite the Ohio State Buckeyes upsetting Taylor's Miami Hurricanes, he became Maud's favorite player too. The next year Maud began playing peewee football, ultralight beaming as a running back and linebacker.

Maud also began playing tackle football with Buck's friends, boys who were two and three years older or more. During an early neighborhood contest, one of those friends tackled Maud so hard that Buck thought his brother was injured and moved to defend him. Before he did, Maud sprang to his feet and shook it off. "I knew then he was tough," says Buck. "That he was going to be able to take care of himself."

Around that time, Maud's parents gifted his sister a Yorkshire terrier she named Flav. Maud might've been hard-nosed on the field, but he spent hours frolicking with Flav outside and helping his sister with caretaking duties. Their bond was such that Flav would sleep at the foot of Maud's bed when Jasmine was gone.

The family moved to a small white house on Brunswick's Boykin Ridge Drive when Maud was in middle school, and in the new place Maud continued to share a room with his brother. "I was a neat freak," says Buck. "But Maud would have his shoes scattered everywhere. Have his t-shirts where his boxers go. His polos with his socks."

In high school Maud got a job working at McDonald's, to keep some scratch in his pocket, but also to help his mother, who often worked two jobs. By then Maud had experienced a first-crush transformation, had adopted some of his brother's tidiness, had become fashion conscious. He favored slim jeans and bright-colored polo shirts and rugbys, and kept his hair shorn low with a sharp hairline. Some days Keem—he was the first with transpo—would swoop Maud, wheel to the Golden Isles YMCA, and play basketball and/or work out for six or seven hours straight, jaunt across to street to Glynn Place Mall for the fries and wings combo at America Deli, and head right back for hours more of playing/training. Or else they'd roll as long as their gas needle allowed with Lil Wayne or Lil' Boosie or Webbie or Gucci Mane (Maud's favorite artists) cranking from the speakers.

Brunswick High JV coach Jason Vaughn met Maud his sophomore year when a fellow coach promised him a tough linebacker for his squad. When Maud, always-ever slim and undersized, walked out, Vaughn was quick to doubt him. "Are you forreal?" he said. "What's this little guy gone do?" He soon had his answer. Team workouts often included a drill called Oklahoma where two players would stand three to five yards apart and go heads up like. Keem remembers Maud excelling at the drill, not from cock-diesel strength, but because "he was fearless on that field."

Maud tore his ACL and meniscus in a game sophomore year. A less dedicated player might've given up, but he completed an arduous rehab. He reinjured his leg the following summer and committed again to a tough rehabilitation. "Our parents used to tell us, if you start something, don't quit," says his sister, Jasmine. Maud wore a leg brace during junior year, which hampered him and no doubt limited his prospects of playing in college. Still, the fact that he played at all is further proof of strong character. This was South Georgia football, and Maud played in a league that included a number of future pros as well as a game against Valdosta High School, the winningest high school football team in all the land.

Sunday, February 23, 2020 | 1:10 pm

The McMichaels, both strapped, tear off after Maud in their pickup, stalk him down Burford Road, another narrow street shaded by lush oaks, pines, and magnolias. From his front yard, William "Roddie" Bryan sees his neighbors hounding Maud, and for reasons he'll have to answer for in court (he's been indicted on nine counts, including felony murder and criminal attempt to commit false imprisonment), jumps in his pickup and joins them. The McMichaels race ahead of Maud and try to cut him off, but Maud doubles back—maybe recalling all the times he's eluded a would-be tackler—only to find himself facing down Bryan's pickup. Bryan tries to block Maud, but he skirts the truck, and huffs around a bend onto Holmes Road. The elder McMichael, Gregory, climbs from the cab to the bed of his son's truck, the one with a Confederate flag on its toolbox, armed with his .357. They track Maud as he sprints down Holmes Road.

MAUD PLAYED in the ballyhooed Florida-Georgia War of the Border All-Star game after his senior season but didn't land a football scholarship. After graduating, he enrolled in South Georgia Technical College (SGTC), in Americus, and set his sights on becoming an electrician.

Like Maud, I was a passionate high school athlete (my sport was hoop) who was not recruited to a major college program. And like Maud, I attended a small school (mine a community college) in my home state. Both Maud and I witnessed friends reap scholarships, float off to towns or cities elsewhere, and continue playing the sports we loved. Maud quit SGTC after a year and returned to Brunswick and his mother's home. I, too, quit my first community college. But unlike Maud, I didn't have to return to my mother's apartment because I already lived there. James "J.T." Trimmings, another one of Maud's day-one homeboys, believes homesickness was the root cause of Maud's premature return from college. But I suspect that Maud also doubled back because his life as an athlete was over and disappointment can grind on even the toughest of us.

The year after he graduated, Maud was arrested for carrying a gun and sentenced to five years of probation, which he violated by shoplifting. A few years after I graduated high school, I was arrested with drugs and a gun and spent 16 months in a state prison.

Maud—dear God, whhhyyy?—is dead, and I, by grace, am a writer-professor hurtling toward middle age.

If Maud nursed thoughts of re-enrolling in SGTC, that idea lost appeal once he met his first serious girlfriend in 2013. Shenice

Johnson first saw Maud when he strolled into McDonald's one day and convinced the manager to give him his old job back. The pair, both shy, were soon google-eyeing each other on their shifts. It's a little unclear who made the first move. Keem says Maud talked for weeks about the beautiful girl at his job, and how he was nervous about approaching her, that is, until Keem hyped him. "Man, you Maud," he said. "Just walk up to her and introduce yourself." Per Shenice's story, their five-plus year relationship began when she offered the handsome boy on her job a free McFlurry.

Their first date, Maud swooped her in the gold Camry ("The Cam") that his mother had bought him and that J.T. says he treated like a Mercedes. Decked in a white-collared shirt and sparkling Air Force 1s, he treated Shenice to a seafood feast and opened doors and pulled out her chair and paid the full bill without hesitance. "When I was with him, I didn't have to worry about anything," she says, a smile in her voice. On the couple's first Valentine's Day, Maud drove all the way to Savannah, bought Shenice a Build-A-Bear he named Quez, and delivered it to her along with a gold heart-shaped promise ring.

Sunday, February 23, 2020 | 1:14 pm
Cell phone footage captures Maud on Holmes Road, bolting away from Bryan's pickup but toward the McMichaels' white pickup. Bryan, about this time, pulls out his cell phone and starts to film. Meanwhile, Gregory McMichael calls 9-1-1. "Uh, I'm out here at Satilla Shores," he tells dispatch. "There's a Black male running down the street." The dispatcher asks where. "I don't know what street we're on," he says. "Stop right there. Dammit. Stop!" the tape records him yelling at Maud.

Maud, fleeing now for no less than six minutes, runs toward a red-faced Travis McMichael who stands inside the door of his truck with his shotgun aimed, toward Gregory McMichael perched in the truck bed with his gun in hand, runs into what must feel like a trap, but perhaps feels like another time his courage has been tested. Maud zags one way and the other. He darts around the right side of the truck and crosses in front of the hood. Travis McMichael heads him off at the nose of the truck and shoots Maud in no more than a heartbeat. The blast cracks over Bryan's cell footage. "Travis!" screams Gregory McMichael and he drops his phone in the truck bed.

The buckshot blast hits Maud in the chest, puncturing his right lung, ribs, and sternum. And yet somehow, he wrestles with Travis McMichael for the shotgun, and yet somehow, he manages to punch at him. Gregory watches for a moment from his roost. Meanwhile, Bryan continues to film. Travis fires his shotgun again, a blast that occurs outside the view of Bryan's phone, but sends a spray of dust billowing into the frame. Maud, an island of blood now staining his white t-shirt, continues to tussle with Travis McMichael, fighting now for what he must know is his life. In the midst of the scuffle, Travis McMichael blasts Maud again point blank, piercing him in his upper chest. Maud whiffs a weak swing, staggers a couple of steps, and falls face down near the traffic stripes. Travis, shotgun in hand, backs away, watches Maud collapse, and makes not the slightest effort to tend him. His father, still clutching his revolver, runs to where Maud lies facedown, blood leaking out of his wounds.

MAUD JOGGED ALONE on the day he was killed. No one can know for sure the route he took before reaching Satilla Shores, but he'd set off from his home, which means there's a strong chance that on his run he encountered homes flying a Confederate flag or a Gadsden flag ("Don't Tread on Me"), homes tacked with No Trespassing signs. To reach Satilla Shores from Boykin Ridge, he would've also had to cross US Route 17, a highway that for years served as a de facto county border between the area's Blacks and whites.

Maud had been running for years, but the origin of his practice lacks consensus. According to his sister, Jasmine, who was once an avid runner, sometime in 2017 Maud asked her how many miles a day she ran and soon after, began doing it himself. She says it was natural for her brother since he loved the outdoors and "wanted a release." Akeem agrees that Maud used running as a kind of therapy, but thinks his main motivation was staying fit after football. This theory would locate the timing of when he began running to a few years before 2017.

Maud would run in a white t-shirt and khaki shorts. He'd run shirtless in basketball shorts. He'd run in a tank top and basketball shoes. Or as Keem sums it, "He could run in anything." Sometimes Maud would persuade his boy J.T. who "doesn't like running all like that," and a couple of other homeboys to ride out to the North Glynn Country Recreational Complex and run miles around the park's freshwater lake. Other times, when Keem was home from college, he and Maud would cruise to one end of the Sidney Lanier Bridge—the longest spanning bridge in all of Georgia—do some warm-up stretching and run back and forth across it, a distance of just under three miles. The pair would keep a steady pace. "But sometimes he'd push me," Akeem says.

There's no evidence of Maud training for 10Ks or full or half marathons or obsessing over his miles or PR times. And yet it's obvious that he was a young man who loved to run and who by all accounts was a gifted runner. It's also clear to me that the same forces that transformed running from a fledgling pastime in my white-ass home state into a billion-dollar global industry also circumscribed a culture that was at best, unwelcoming, and at worse, restrictive to him.

Sunday, February 23, 2020 | 1:15 pm

Per the police report, Gregory McMichael rolls Maud from prostrate to his back to check for a weapon. He checks despite the fact that Maud hasn't brandished or fired a gun during any part of his flight, not even when caught between two armed white men and what he couldn't have known was an unarmed white man behind him. Glynn County police officers will arrive within seconds of the shooting, their sirens screaming along Satilla Drive.

But before those squad cars reach the scene, Travis McMichael—per Bryan's statement to investigators in May—will call Maud a "f*cking [n-word]."

THE BRIDGE THAT MAUD AND KEEM USED TO JOG is named for 19th century poet and Confederate Sidney Lanier. It's hard to imagine a Georgian with honorifics on par with Lanier. Not only is he the namesake of that bridge, there's also the eponymous Lanier County in southern Georgia, and Lake Lanier, a reservoir in northern Georgia. Keem seems surprised when I mention Lanier's Confederate ties, which makes me wonder how much Maud knew about the history of his home. Whether the young men were aware of Lanier's hagiography or not (who stops to read the plaque on a bridge?) every single jog across that bridge was insult, an insidious means of humiliating them and their/our people. Yeah, the tiki-torch toting bald-face racists menace a spectacle. But what about the legions of bigoted invisible men and their myriad symbols?

Lanier died in 1881, which is to say near the end of Reconstruction and the outset of Jim Crow. In 1964, a few months after the Civil Rights Act ushered the de jure end to Jim Crow, a documentary film crew from National Educational Television (the precursor to PBS) profiled Brunswick because it was managing to integrate without the bloodshed that was occurring almost everywhere else in the South. *The Quiet Conflict* won numerous awards and was a key reason for Brunswick's reputation as a "model southern city."

While Brunswick might not have equaled the bloodletting of its southern counterparts, its segregationists still put up stern resistance. In one example, the KKK was called in to threaten Blacks attempting to integrate a local bowling alley. In another, whites filled a public pool with dirt rather than let Black kids swim in it. Several residents have gone on record to proclaim their surprise at Maud's slaying and to downplay the significance of race. And for those who would argue that the spirit of Sidney

Lanier and the segregationists is bygone, or that the younger McMichael might not have said what Bryan claimed in his statement to police, recent evidence—including McMichael's own social media posts cited by investigators—I submit, as another example, this Facebook post from Chris Putnam, a former high school classmate of Travis McMichael:

> "I'm not going to be one of the classmates of Travis McMichael's that sat here saying nothing. He was always the very definition of a racist gun-loving redneck, and we all knew something like this was going to happen one day. I remember plenty of people that were themselves very openly racist and joked about how 'at least [they weren't] Travis.'"

THE NAACP ONCE DEFINED LYNCHING as a death in which 1) There was evidence that a person was killed 2) The death was illegal 3) A group of at least three actors participated in the killing. According to "Lynching in America," a report by the Equal Justice Initiative, there were 4,084 southern-state lynchings between 1877 and 1950. Of the 594 reported in Georgia during that period—one of only four states yet to pass a law on hate crimes—three occurred in Glynn County.

Between 1920 and 1938, the NAACP New York headquarters flew a flag that announced "A Man Was Lynched Yesterday" to mark a murder that fit their criteria.

A boy was lynched today: for walking hooded down a street and refusing the command of an overzealous neighborhood watchman. A man was lynched today: for selling loosies outside a bodega. A teen was lynched today: for a disputed exchange of cigarillos. A child was lynched today: for holding a toy outside a rec center. A man was lynched today: for fleeing a traffic stop unarmed. For hawking CDs outside a convenience store. For announcing a legal gun and reaching for his license. A woman was lynched today: for sleeping. And yet another man was lynched today: for suspicion of passing a fake twenty. D-e-a-t-h!

In Florida, New York, Missouri, Ohio, South Carolina, Louisiana, Minnesota, Kentucky, and again in Minnesota.

Sunday, February 23, 2020 | 1:16 pm
"Two subjects on Holmes Road. Shots fired. Male on ground, bleeding out," radios an officer. Maud musters his last breath near the intersection of Holmes Road and Satilla Drive, a mere 300 yards from where, not 10 minutes prior, he wandered inside a construction site. The officers will cordon the scene and investigate. They will question the McMichaels—Gregory's hands bloody from rolling Maud onto his back—and William Bryan. And in an act that is itself another violence, they will let all three go about their merry way as free men—for almost three months.

On February 23, 2020, a young man out for a run was lynched in Glynn County, Georgia.

His name was Ahmaud Marquez Arbery, called "Quez" by his beloveds and "Maud" by most others. And what I want you to know about Maud is that he had a gift for impressions and a special knack for mimicking Martin Lawrence. What I want you to know about Maud is that he was fond of sweets and requested his mother's fudge cake for the birthday parties he often shared with his big sister. What I want you to know about Maud is that he signed the cards he bought for his mother "Baby Boy." What I want you to know about Maud is that he and his brother would don the helmets they used for go-carting and go heads-up on their trampoline, and that he never backed down from his big brother. What I want you to know about Maud is that he jammed his pinkie playing hoop in high school and instead of getting it treated like Jasmine advised, he let it heal on its own—forever crooked. What I want you know about Maud is that he didn't like seeing his day-ones whining, that when they did, he'd chide, "Don't cry about it, man. Do what you gotta do to handle your business." What I want you to know about Maud is that Shenice told me he sometimes recorded their conversations so he could listen to her voice when they were apart. What you should know about Maud is that he adored his nephews Marcus III and Micah Arbery, that when they were colicky as babies, he'd take them for long walks in their stroller until they calmed. What you should know about Maud is that when a college friend asked Jasmine which parent she'd call first if ever in serious trouble, she said neither, that she'd call him. What I want you to know about Maud is that he was an avid connoisseur of the McChicken sandwich with cheese. What I want you know about Maud is that he and Keem were so close that the universe coerced each of them into breaking a foot on the same damn day in separate freak weight-room accidents, and that when they were getting treated in the trainer's office, Maud joked about it. You should know that Maud dreamed of a career as an electrician and of owning a construction company. You should know that Maud gushed often of his desire to be a great husband and father. You should know that he told his boys that he wanted them all to buy a huge plot of land, build houses on it, and live in a gated community with their families. You should know that Maud never flew on a plane, but wanderlusted for trips to Jamaica, Japan, Africa. What you must know about Maud was that when Travis McMichael, Gregory McMichael, and William "Roddie" Bryan stalked and murdered him less than three months shy of his 26th birthday, he left behind his mother Wanda, his father Marcus Sr., his brother Buck, his sister Jasmine, his maternal grandmother Ella, his nephews, six uncles, 10 aunts, a host of cousins, all of whom are unimaginably, irrevocably, incontrovertibly poorer from his absence.

Ahmaud Marquez Arbery was more than a viral video. He was more than a hashtag or a name on a list of tragic victims. He was more than an article or an essay or posthumous profile. He was more than a headline or an op-ed or a news package or the news cycle. He was more than a retweet or shared post. He, doubtless, was more than our likes or emoji tears or hearts or praying hands. He was more than an R.I.P. t-shirt or placard. He was more than an autopsy or a transcript or a police report or a live-streamed hearing. He, for damn sure, was more than the latest reason for your liberal white friend's ephemeral outrage. He was more than a rally or a march. He was more than a symbol, more than a movement, more than a cause. He. Was. *Loved.*

SOME OF THOSE LOVED ONES got to see Maud play the last game of his senior season, a play-in [playoff] away game at Lakeside-Evans High School. In the locker room, the coach delivers a passionate pep talk, and Maud, accessorized in school-color blue high socks and a sparkling white wrist band, leads the team in the pre-game chant. "Y'all ain't ready," he shouts. "Sheeeeeeeeit!" they say, and ramble out of the locker room, cleats clattering against the concrete, and onto the field. Maud's a team captain, so he swanks onto the 50-yard line to help call the coin toss.

Rare is an athlete that ends a season on a win. Maud, who'll earn the team award for most tackles that season, blazes around the field stopping play after play, and still his Pirates commit four turnovers in the first half and trail by 20 points. But the team—hooray, hooray—mounts a second-half comeback, one no more promising than when Maud leaps to snatch an interception in the middle of the fourth, zags here, jukes there, and bursts down the field, wind whispering through his helmet, his lithe legs floating him across the 50, the 40, the 30, and oh so close but not into the end zone. The Pirates don't score on the preceding drives. They lose the game and miss the playoffs for the first time in half a decade. While their opponents celebrate and fans mill out of the stands, Maud and some of his senior teammates circle in the middle of the field. There they stand, hand in hand, grass stains in their tights, tears running into their eye-black strips. Boys who will soon be young men mourning a season-ending loss, boys in thrall of youth mourning the eternal end of their football seasons. Maud could use his gift for humor to lighten the mood, but this time, he concedes to the moment's gravity. Yes, some will play on in college. Indeed, others will attend as students alone. And sure, some will forsake a campus altogether for work. But here's the truth, a whole truth, so help me: Under that final gleam of Friday night lights, neither Maud nor any of his teammates can be sure of what lies ahead.

Mitchell S. Jackson's debut novel *The Residue Years* received wide critical praise. Jackson is the winner of a Whiting Award and the Ernest J. Gaines Prize for Literary Excellence. Jackson's honors include fellowships, grants, and awards from Creative Capital, the NYPL's Cullman Center, the Lannan Foundation, the Ford Foundation, PEN America, and TED. His writing has appeared in *The New York Times Book Review*, *Time*, *The New Yorker*, *Harper's*, *The Paris Review*, *The Guardian*, *Harper's Bazaar*, and elsewhere. His nonfiction book *Survival Math: Notes on an All-American Family* was named a best book of the year by 15 publications. Jackson's next novel—*John of Watts*—will be published by Farrar, Straus, and Giroux. He covers race and culture as the first Black columnist for *Esquire* and teaches creative writing at the University of Chicago. "Twelve Minutes and a Life" was awarded both the Pulitzer Prize and the National Magazine Award in the Feature Writing category in 2021.

Kobe Always Showed His Work. So We Have to in Remembering Him, Too

BRIAN PHILLIPS

FROM The Ringer • JANUARY 30, 2020

There was that sickening hour when you knew it was true but you still thought it must be a mistake. No, Kobe Bryant wasn't dead. Kobe Bryant couldn't be dead. Fans were already turning up at L.A. Live with bouquets and tearful faces, and tributes were starting to roll in from players and coaches who knew him, but the story wasn't right, it didn't add up; there had to be some other explanation. One after another, news outlets confirmed *TMZ*'s original report, and the details, vague at first, turned hideously specific. The fact that it was Kobe's private helicopter. The brush fire, on a hillside in Calabasas, that kept rescue personnel from getting to the wreckage. The five, no, nine people on board, including his 13-year-old daughter, Gianna. Some of this information might be wrong, but *all* of it? The oddsmaker in your brain looked up from its calculator and said: *no chance.* Still, still, you waited for the increasingly unlikely but necessary twist, the new revelation that would put the world back to normal.

I heard the news sometime before 3 p.m. ET Sunday. "Wait, Kobe Bryant died?" my wife said. She'd gotten a text from her college roommate and was still looking down at her phone. We'd just come in from the dog park. I was hanging up collars and leashes. "No," I said. "That can't be right." Kobe was 41 years old, healthy, seemingly in not just a good but an excellent place. He was the rare athlete who appeared genuinely energized by life after retirement. He relished family life, loved raising his four daughters. He was at the start of what every indication said would be a long and impressive second act. Why would he die right after winning an Oscar? He wouldn't. You can know theoretically that death is arbitrary and irrational. In the actual presence of death, you still think you're entitled to an explanation.

Death, please state your reasons for claiming this human being. I'm sorry, but that's one of the dumbest arguments I've ever heard. I'm rejecting your application. Return this man to his life.

I looked at the home page of ESPN.com and *The New York Times*. Neither one said anything about Kobe. "See?" I said. "If he'd died, it would be all over the news." Then I looked at Twitter. "Oh, shit." And for the next hour and a half, maybe two hours, I watched the tragedy grow more and more certain while still expecting Kobe to appear and clear up the mistake. *We're fine, folks! Death had an unpersuasive argument.* And even at the end of all doubt, when it was clear what was coming—NBA stars taking the court in tears, grizzled coaches breaking down in interviews, Grammy presenters in open shock, throngs of fans gathering to share the awful burden of the moment—my brain was still picturing a different future. Kobe on late-night shows assuring everyone that he and Gianna and all the other passengers were fine. Jokes and memes about how we'd all gotten it so wrong. An anecdote to tell our kids someday. A trivia question.

That day, or maybe the next day, I thought of something I wrote about him years ago, before he retired. I never published it. What I wrote was that he played basketball like he was determined to be the word *but* in the great sentence of the game. There's no word more competitive than *but*. There's also no word more transformative. It opposes everything. It refuses to compromise. It's dramatic, heroic, annoying. It goes it alone, and it changes everything that follows—but changes it equivocally, imperfectly, without erasing the contrary idea.

No one can consistently hit 20-foot jump shots against a dou-ble-team—and then here's Kobe, pulling up with the ball on his forehead—*but...*

Michael Jordan and LeBron James are the greatest basketball players of the past 25 years—and then here's Kobe, hoisting his fifth championship trophy—*but...*

But creates two realities and then stands between them, forcing you to pick a side. That's how it always was with Kobe. Whatever happened, there was the fan's version and the hater's version, or there was the pragmatist's version (you can't come back from an Achilles rupture in your mid-30s) and the version that existed in his head (I can come back from an Achilles rupture faster than anyone dreams is possible).

It was the same with his death. You believed it, but you didn't believe it. Or you believed it, but you didn't want to believe it. Or you didn't believe it, but deep down you knew you should.

I remember when he first entered the league, right out of high school. I was in my freshman year of college. I didn't believe it then because he was my age, and I still saw professional athletes as grown-ups, people appreciably (and therefore, at that age, infinitely) older than me. Tiger Woods hadn't yet won his first Masters. People our age didn't suddenly become sports stars, much less arrive in the NBA dripping with undisguised ambition to surpass Michael Jordan. (Who was at the peak of his career with the Bulls, don't forget. He was the Finals MVP that year.) Yet here was Kobe. One of my college friends had actually gone to high school with him at Lower Merion, which only heightened the strangeness. From now on, there would be an NBA superstar I could plausibly imagine having grown up with.

"Did you know him?" I asked Andy.

He arched an eyebrow. "We were aware of each other," he said.

I always remembered that sentence—the dry, slightly pomp-
ous reserve of the phrasing—because I could so easily imagine
Kobe himself using it under different circumstances.

*Kobe, were you friends with the hero Achilles, the greatest
warrior who ever lived, before he was slain by an archer's arrow
during the Trojan War?*

Kobe, not smiling: "We were aware of each other."

I think it was like that for a lot of people my age. Kobe was the
athlete who separated our childhood love of sports from our adult
love. In that way, too, he was a word in the middle of a sentence,
though when you're 19 or 20 or 21, it's a sentence whose second
half you can't quite read. *You're young, but.* As time passed, we
could measure our lives as sports fans by whatever was happening
in his career. He got older and his relationship to the league and
its players gradually changed. We got older, and ours changed too.

He was singular from the beginning. For all his preoccu-
pation with Being Like Mike, right down to copying Jordan's
physical mannerisms on the court, Kobe never resembled anyone
else. Even the obsessive drive with which he Belmondoed MJ's
Bogart showed that he represented a break. It was hard to believe
in a player with so much talent but (but!) so fierce a reverence
for technique. Jordan valued hard work, but hard work for him
was something that happened off-screen, something notional.
He wanted the commentators to tell you he got up at 3 a.m. to
lift weights, but with one second on the clock and the ball in his
hands, he wanted you to believe in magic. At his core, Kobe had
no patience for anything so childish. He was the chooser, not the
chosen one. His version of the game was something too hard and
too pure to be swayed by anything as arbitrary as fate.

For Kobe, it was the 1,000 repetitions that won basketball
games, the 10,000 footwork drills you kept running long after
your opponents had collapsed. He had too much respect for excellence—both his own and in the abstract—to want to hide his work.
(*Kobe Doin' Work* was the title of Spike Lee's 2009 documentary
about him.) Years before he was drafted, at a moment when youth

basketball in the United States was veering toward AAU flairball, Kobe learned the game in Italy, under last-gen coaches, running sets drawn up by Red Auerbach. He was a cutting-edge player, but he never lost that old-school sense that you did the job properly or not at all. *Hollywood, but make it discipline.* Late in his career, with his shooting percentage falling, he was still complaining about the league's tightened hand-checking rules. They made it too easy for lesser players to score. Kobe never wanted the game to be easy. That was why you could just about put up with his phenomenal, at times bordering on absurdist, arrogance, if you were one of the people who could. It wasn't based on what he was born with. It was based on what he was willing to do. Leave it to Jordan to sell the glamour of destiny. Kobe sold the glamour of craft.

It was easy to see why a player like that would be divisive, why he'd turn half the world into die-hards and drive the other half to despair. It was harder, at least early on, to imagine he'd even be functional. You expected him to psych himself into oblivion from the word go, or take a Björn Borg–like swerve into prima donna nihilism. A 20-year career at the highest level, for someone that relentless? Could he really be everything he seemed?

Outer boundaries of the basketball imagination, not smiling: "We were aware of each other."

You believed it, but you didn't believe it. Or you believed it, but you didn't want to believe it. Or you didn't believe it, but deep down, you knew you should.

What does basketball know about death? I'm tempted to say nothing, because the whole point of basketball, the beautiful trick of it, is to convince you that the human body has no limits. Basketball at its best makes you feel a sympathetic echo of what it's like to run that fast, jump that high, fly. Those are not feelings that encourage the strict contemplation of mortality. (Even as I type that, though, I'm thinking that Kobe's game was a pointed rebuke to that assumption—that he also taught you how it felt to hurt, to get hit, to fall down.) I'm also tempted to say basketball knows nothing about death because basketball is a game almost all of whose icons are still alive. Wilt Chamberlain is dead, of course, but then you have to go a long way down the greatest-ever list, back to the era of black-and-white photos and spider-limbed white centers in short shorts, to find even an approximate comparison for Kobe. Bill Russell, George Gervin, Jerry West, Elvin Hayes, Elgin Baylor—all still alive. Magic Johnson was diagnosed with HIV in 1991, which was taken at the time as a death sentence, but Magic is still a thriving chaos-imp almost 30 years later. The winner of the first-ever NBA MVP award, Bob Pettit, is 87 and living in Louisiana.

There are young players who have died without warning, but they (Len Bias, Reggie Lewis, Dražen Petrović) hadn't played a whole career, as Kobe had. They hadn't lived an intense relationship with fans going back almost a quarter-century. Pete Maravich was retired and around Kobe's age in 1988, when he collapsed and died during a pick-up game in Pasadena. Pete Maravich was a delightful player. But neither his cultural significance nor his on-court legacy was equal to Kobe Bryant's.

For basketball fans, nothing quite like this has happened before. When a beloved actor or musician dies suddenly, part of the pain comes from the "oh God, not again" sensation, the history-repeats-itself aspect. It's the ache of pattern recognition: We've lost great actors and musicians prematurely too many times before. In this case, though, there's no pattern, and if many of us feel a little lost this week, it's because we're actually lost. We're grieving without a template. (When Prince died, you could go in your room and blast "Purple Rain." What are you supposed to do now, stream NBA highlights?) We're coming to terms not just with the knowledge that this has happened, but that it *could* happen—that killing Kobe Bryant was something the world was allowed to do.

You want to turn away from the meaninglessness of it, the stupid sloppy accidental randomness. They seem unworthy of him. But then there's Kobe, demanding that you do the hard work, demanding rigor to the bone. There's Kobe, saying: *Don't turn away from hard truths.*

So: hard truths. There was the day in 2003 when the news broke that he'd been arrested. A 19-year-old hotel worker in Colorado told police he had raped her. One after another, news sources filled in their reports, and the details became hideously specific. The bruise on the woman's neck, revealed in a hospital exam. The vaginal lacerations. The blood on Kobe's shirt. At first he told the police he hadn't had sex with the woman, then he changed his story and said the sex was consensual. He was charged with felony sexual assault. We followed along as his lawyer revealed the woman's full name in court, exposing her to threats and hatred. We watched as they questioned her character, turning her sexual history into a national headline: "Could it be that [her] injuries were caused by having sex with three men in three days?" (One study later found that more than 42 percent of news articles included statements questioning the woman's honesty, while only 7 percent included statements questioning Kobe's.) The woman backed out of testifying; the prosecutors, left without their witness, dropped the charges. Kobe settled a civil case with the woman, at the end of which he issued an apology: "I now understand how she feels that she did not consent to this encounter," he wrote. The settlement included an NDA, preventing her from speaking publicly about what had happened.

Kobe didn't exactly receive a free pass in the years that followed—he lost some sponsors—but the rape charge didn't have the effect on his life or reputation that similar cases against other men have had post-#MeToo. He won titles. An MVP in 2008. We know the statistics on how few women lie about sexual assault. But it was easier, with Kobe, to sort of half-forget the hovering question mark. This week, even mentioning the allegations has been a supercharged decision. *The Washington Post* suspended a reporter after she tweeted a link to a four-year-old story about them. (She was later reinstated.) Many people have felt that it's "disrespectful" or "too soon" to talk about anything negative in the aftermath of Kobe's death.

I'm going to sound like a drive-time radio host for a second. Disrespectful? Are you *kidding me*? We're talking about Kobe Bryant. You don't respect someone by ducking the hard work of understanding their lives. You face it. You reckon with human character properly or you don't reckon with it at all.

In any case, not everyone was so circumspect. In his book *The Last Season*, Kobe's longtime coach Phil Jackson talked about learning of the arrest. "Was I surprised?" he wrote. "Yes, but not entirely. Kobe can be consumed with surprising anger, which he's displayed toward me and toward his teammates."

There we are again. Two realities.

Yes, but.

You believed it, but you didn't believe it. Or you believed it, but you didn't want to believe it. Or you didn't believe it, but deep down you knew you should.

Watching basketball highlights might not be a sensible response to tragedy, but I've been watching his for days. I love watching him play basketball—I think we can still use the present tense; when you're as good as Kobe was, your jump shot outlives you—because he was a beautiful player but not a pretty one. Steph Curry, at his best, is a pretty player; he's putting on a show for you, recruiting you into a little conspiracy of happiness. I love that, too. But Kobe is something else. He's not playing for you at all. His game was spectacularly inefficient by today's standards, and he notoriously loathed the statistical revolution that transformed basketball in the mid-2010s, but he still conveys the sense that he's solving the game, playing against a mathematical ideal. It's abstract, fiercely unsentimental. He dribbles into a crowd of defenders, and the court separates into planes and angles. He pulls up for a shot and the arc of gravity reveals itself.

Somewhere in the middle of all this highlight viewing, I found a supercut, obviously made by someone with more time and a larger hard drive than I have, of every play on which he suffered an injury. He played for two decades; the video lasts more than 10 minutes. I don't know why, because it showcases very little of his brilliance, but (but!) I found it intensely comforting. It's honest, I guess. Kobe was, God knows, an unbelievably high-bullshit human being in many ways—this was the player who once filed a lawsuit to prevent his own mother from selling some memorabilia of his—but there was something about the nakedness of his ambition and the excruciating psychological stakes it imposed that seemed to cut through a great deal of feel-good sports bullshit. Even at what turned out to be the end of his life, when he'd mellowed a little, when he was having so much fun going to games and sitting courtside with his daughters, he seems like he'd have hated false comfort. And whatever watching him twist his ankle and then hobble to the foul line for 10 straight minutes is, it's not that. (Kobe is also, of course, the player who ruptured his Achilles and then sank two free throws.)

So he'll be playing who even knows—the Clippers or the Spurs or the Rockets, doesn't matter; in most of the clips you can only tell what year it is through context clues. (Shaq or no Shaq, Pau or no Pau, hair or no hair.) He'll have the ball usually, because he usually had the ball. He'll attack the basket, the thing he was put on Earth to do, and right away everything starts to snap into place; he's got one man beat, only one more to go; you can see what he sees, you can see what's about to happen. But then, before it does, there's a lurch. Something cracks in the middle of the thought. Draymond sticks a thumb in his eye, or his knee buckles, and he goes down holding the injured part. You see the play turning into what it was supposed to be, and then he falls. I mean the future is right there. He just falls.

Brian Phillips is the author of *Impossible Owls: Essays*, a *New York Times* best-seller and finalist for the 2019 PEN/Diamondstein-Spielvogel Award for the Art of the Essay. He is a staff writer at The Ringer, and has previously written for Grantland, *The New York Times Magazine*, *The New Yorker*, and the *Los Angeles Review of Books*. He lives in Carlisle, Pennsylvania, with his wife and two whippets.

How Kobe Bryant's Death Brought Bobby McIlvaine—an Athlete, a Scholar, the Friend I Should've Known Better—Back to Life

MIKE SIELSKI

FROM *The Philadelphia Inquirer* • APRIL 9, 2020

On the day after Kobe Bryant died, a friend and high school classmate of mine sent me an email that carried the force of a punch I couldn't see coming. "Thought you'd find this interesting," Ben Relles wrote. Embedded in the message was a link to a 36-second video. I clicked on the link, then gasped.

On the right side of the video's split-screen shot was Kobe, wearing a charcoal scoop-neck sweater, sitting at an expansive cherry desk, riveted to flickering images on a laptop. He was in the executive offices of YouTube, where Ben was working to find original content for the platform. Kobe had gone to the company's Southern California headquarters in January 2018 to pitch a show based on Wizenard, a series of children's books he had created that combined the themes of sports, fantasy, and magic. As it turned out, YouTube wasn't funding children's programming at the time and didn't buy the show, but "it was genuinely one of the most impressive pitches I've heard," Ben said. "He was incredibly passionate about the idea and clearly hands-on in every aspect of it."

On the video's left side were the images that had grabbed Kobe's attention: footage of a high school basketball game from 1992, Lower Merion vs. my alma mater, Upper Dublin. Ben and I were seniors then. He was a backup forward on the team. I was an editor of the student newspaper and lacked the skills and athleticism to play organized ball beyond intramurals. Kobe Bryant was a freshman at Lower Merion. It was the second game of his high school career.

In those 36 seconds, an Upper Dublin player close to the camera, the No. 24 gigantic on the back of his red jersey, whipped a crosscourt pass to a teammate, Ari Greis, who caught the ball on the right wing, used a left-handed dribble to surge past Kobe, and banked in a floater from the lane. A family friend of Ben's had filmed the game, and Ben, having kept the tape all these years and knowing he would be sitting down with Kobe, had converted the recording to a digital file. Then, once the YouTube meeting had ended, Ben had played the footage on the laptop, and one of his coworkers had taken care to capture Kobe's reaction to it. There it all was, in cosmic juxtaposition. You could watch Kobe, as a 39-year-old, watch himself, as a 14-year-old, in real time.

"That is hilarious," he said. "Great defense, Kob.... That's horrible defense.... You can replay that all f---ing day.... Oh. My. God.... Nawwwww!... That's funny.... We only won four games that year."

Memory is a gift often hidden away within a box locked tight, and that game film was the gliding, turning key, allowing Kobe access to sights, sounds, places, and people made tactile and intimate again, allowing me the same. I posted the link on my Facebook page immediately. I posted it because Kobe was in it, but mostly because someone else was, too.

A brain who could play ball
God, look at him. You wouldn't know it from that clip, from that pass that set up Kobe's moment of embarrassment, but Bobby

McIlvaine came to kill you on the basketball court. He was all bones and acute angles and stiletto elbows. He wasn't dirty, but he let you know he was there. It was great if he was on your team, provided you played as hard as he did, but it was a b---- if he wasn't or you didn't.

When I met him, in ninth grade, he was as close to a fully formed adult as a 14-year-old kid could be. His parents were special-education teachers, and in retrospect, it's clear how much his milieu shaped him. His father, Bob, had been a star running back at Springfield High School in Montgomery County, but the family bloodline didn't account completely for Bobby's rabid desire to win; something deeper seemed to drive him. He had been so competitive as a boy that Bob would cut short their one-on-one battles at the playground court down the street from the McIlvaines' home in Oreland. Bobby was that intense, that much of a pain: Even his sports-hero dad had to walk away sometimes. During a backyard football game, his brother, Jeff, three years younger, might end up shoved face down into an ice puddle or tackled headfirst into the concrete stairs if he dared to beat Bobby for a touchdown.

His mother, Helen, had grown up in Chester, watching her town decay throughout the 1950s and '60s amid redlining, riots, and block-busting. Through her, Bobby developed a less parochial, more empathetic view of the world, a recognition that his life and experiences in middle-class suburbia were not everyone's. At a high school as diverse as Upper Dublin, where one's group of friends could include white kids, Black kids, Korean kids, Chinese kids, Eastern Indian kids, Protestant kids, Jewish kids, and Catholic kids (like Bobby and me), his upbringing and perspective enabled him to be comfortable among the jocks and the brains and everyone in between. He played varsity basketball and soccer, was one of the two top-ranked male students in our class, and aspired to become an author. He could speak with equal knowledge and insight about Charles Barkley and Geoffrey Chaucer. Rumor was, he already had begun writing a novel.

We were friends, though not particularly close. His competitiveness seemed cut with an edgy perfectionism—the insecurity found in every teenager cranked up to a higher level because Bobby expected more from himself than most teenagers do. That insecurity, to me, could manifest itself as arrogance—in my senior yearbook, Bobby scribbled in black ink a single word big enough to take up an entire page, COCKY—and it kept me at arm's length. Still, it was impossible not to respect his intelligence, his ambition, his achievements, and not to seek or hope for his respect in return. He was someone against whom I measured myself, even in those aspects of our lives where I knew I couldn't keep up with him.

Basketball was one. He was taller, stronger, more diligent about the sport's fundamentals. He taught himself what he regarded as the single proper way to shoot a jump shot—keep your body ramrod straight, snap your wrist at the apex of your rise—and was so zealous about his technique that he insisted his friends follow it themselves. Once, during a pickup game, I hit a couple of long jumpers, and he whispered to me as we ran down the court, *You're playing well, Siel.* Two conflicting reactions smacked me at once: *Wow, it's cool that Bobby, of all people, would say that* and *Who the hell does he think he is? My coach? My dad?* Maybe he believed he had earned the right to say it. Maybe, in our stratified little social order, he had.

On Dec. 7, 1992, as part of its high school boys' basketball preview package, *The Inquirer* published a pair of brief articles, one about Upper Dublin, one about Lower Merion. Both teams were green and were expected to struggle, but two players represented slivers of hope. In the Upper Dublin story, correspondent Joe Fite wrote: "Any one of 11 players...could end up starting, with senior Bob McIlvaine the only player with perhaps a better shot than most of grabbing one of the starting slots." In the Lower Merion story, correspondent Jeremy Treatman wrote: "Remember this name: Kobe Bryant."

The following week, the teams squared off in the consolation game of a four-team tournament at Lower Merion. Kobe scored 19 points in a 74–57 victory, and in the video, his recall of that season was perfect: The Aces won just three more times, finishing 4–20. Somehow, the 1992–93 Upper Dublin Flying Cardinals were worse. They won three games all season, though Jeff Huddleston regarded them as one of his most enjoyable teams during his 25-year tenure as the school's head coach. "Nobody ever came late to practice," he said. "I never had any worries with them, and Bobby was a great part of that team, a silent leader. He could shoot the ball, and in the huddle, he would look at me intently for what I was going to say. He would almost be shaking, excitedly shaking. He couldn't wait to get going."

The game against Lower Merion was one of Bobby's best of the season. He scored 16 points, hitting two three-pointers, and after he began his freshman year at Princeton University, in the fall of 1993, the game grew into a family legend for the McIlvaines, a fond remember-when as Kobe, over time, became Kobe. Jeff scissored the box score out of *The Inquirer* and kept it. Bob had attended the game, had watched it from beginning to end, but he was unaware that someone had been recording it, and he himself took no photos and didn't document the game in any manner. There were no smartphones then, of course, and the family didn't own a video camera. "I wasn't big on video," Bob said. Helen once had borrowed a camcorder and toted it to one of Bobby's summer-league games, but it had been so cumbersome to hoist the machine onto her shoulder and track the action that neither she nor Bob bothered to bring it again.

A better version of Bobby

When we graduated from high school, Bobby and I made no point of saying to each other, *Let's keep in touch.* So we didn't. We saw each other twice thereafter, and neither occasion offered us much of an opportunity to talk in depth. The first was in the winter of 1998, at a class reunion, and he revealed none of the granular details of his college years that I learned later.

How, for instance, during a pickup game his first week at Princeton, he caught an accidental but hellacious elbow in the mouth from his new roommate, Ken Senior, then kept up such aggressive defense that Ken asked himself, *Why is he playing like this in a friendly game with guys he doesn't know?* How he majored in English but minored in African American studies, diving into courses taught by a powerhouse group of professors—Cornel West, Arnold Rampersad, Nell Irvin Painter, more—winning the department's Ruth J. Simmons Thesis Prize for his analysis of the stereotypes that white authors fell into, the mistakes that they made, when depicting Black characters. How he took up yo-yoing. How he earned an A in a dance elective by devising a routine in which his moves spelled the name of his girlfriend, V-A-N-E-S-S-A. How he told his college friends who were unfamiliar with Philadelphia-area high school basketball, *Keep an eye on this kid Kobe. I played against him. He's going to be great.*

I saw Bobby again, and for the last time, on Sunday, April 15, 2001, at Easter Mass. There, with Bob, Helen, and Jeff, he looked sharp in a navy-blue blazer and light blue button-down, his brown hair closely cropped, his upper body having filled out with muscle. He appeared sure of himself, less anxious. Outside the church, we chatted about the 76ers, who were finishing their regular season and were about to begin an exhilarating run to the NBA Finals, where they lost in five games to Kobe and the Lakers.

Bobby lived in Battery Park and had been working in publishing, as a public-relations executive, since college—a whiz kid who had booked an appearance on *The Oprah Winfrey Show* for one of his writers and soon enough would be searching for a new mountain to climb. He didn't mention that he also had taken a job as an usher at the Metropolitan Opera House, just because he knew little about opera and wanted to learn more. He didn't mention that he planned to accept a position in July with Merrill Lynch, as an assistant vice president of media relations. And he couldn't possibly have known then, as we shook hands and said goodbye on that gorgeous spring morning, that this new position would require him to represent the company at a conference, held high inside the North Tower of the World Trade Center, on the gorgeous late-summer morning of Tuesday, Sept. 11, 2001.

The "absence of his person"

The phone chain, linking our shared high school friends, finally snaked its way to me the day after the terrorist attacks. Bobby was dead. His body had been among the first identified at the site. Soon I was back at the same church to say goodbye to him again, this time two months before his 27th birthday, this time forever.

More than 1,200 people filled the pews. In one of the eulogies, Ken Senior described Bobby as "charming and engaging, special in the way that world leaders are special." Those who had kept in touch with him told me that Bobby had developed into a terrific listener, someone you could talk to anytime about anything. As the pallbearers led the coffin away and the organist played "How Great Thou Art," mourners mouthing the words through their tears, the music of the hymn rising into the night, I buried my face in my hands and bawled—not over the kid I had known, but over the young man I had failed to know.

In the days and months and years thereafter, there were attempts to memorialize Bobby, to console his family. Upper Dublin High School erected a bench with Bobby's name etched on it, with a clear view of the school's athletic fields, and every year on Sept. 11, one of our classmates and her father would return to campus, make themselves comfortable on Bobby's bench, and crack open a couple of beers for a toast in his honor. The basketball team held a ceremony at the gymnasium, with a plaque. One of Bobby's professors at Princeton, before sending the McIlvaines a handwritten note of condolence, dug up a copy of one of his term papers.

"Rereading it brought immediately into focus my recollections: his intelligent curiosity, his candor, and his infectious good humor," Toni Morrison wrote. "You will never stop missing him, of course, but when your memories of his vivid life overtake the absence of his person—it will be better."

The McIlvaines appreciated the kind words, the soft hands on their shoulders, but the gestures did little to help them heal. Bobby's presence had loomed so large in their lives, and it continued to, because the horror of Sept. 11 seemed to have no end.

How would you handle having millions of people bow their heads on your behalf every year, having the entire nation commemorate the day that you lost your son, your brother? One counselor put it this way to them: *Hold a silver dollar in front of your eyes. The dollar represents Bobby and his death. It will be huge at first, then shrink as you get distance from the day, but it will always be there in your line of sight.*

Helen and Bob kept a black-and-white photo of Bobby, her favorite photo of him, that showed him in a dark turtleneck, sitting forward at his desk, working on whatever project or vocation happened to be filling his mind and heart in that instant. "I'd always be behind him," she said. "If I wanted to talk to Bobby, I had to talk to his back." Jeff became a biology teacher and track coach at Sterling High School in Somerdale, N.J., and he and his wife, Kelly, had two boys and two girls—had a big family on purpose so that Bob and Helen could dote on grandchildren, so that the siblings always would have a web of support among themselves. But the silver dollar was fading to a speck in Jeff's peripheral vision, so small that he couldn't make out many of the details anymore. Bobby's bearing, his tics and mannerisms, his vocal inflections in joy or anger—to Jeff and his parents, those moments when Bobby's body and spirit had harmonized to make him *Bobby* were becoming wisps of vapor, too weak and fleeting to grab and hold. Jeff found himself wishing he could go back to Sept. 11, because he and his brother had gone out for drinks two nights earlier, because at least Bobby was fresh in his mind's eye then.

Now all they had were photos of Bobby, still pictures, and they assumed they had collected every temporal piece of him there was to collect. They had no reason to believe that another memento, anything that might jog their memories, was still out there, unseen, and as the distance from Bobby's death grew to five years, 10 years, 18, Jeff started to ask himself a haunting question. *Am I remembering my brother and all his dimensions, flesh and blood and breath, or am I remembering a picture?*

The connections between two young men

The game footage had surprised and overwhelmed me. It had sent Kobe and me hurtling deep into our pasts, but to different places for different reasons. He was seeing himself anew, as the prodigy he no longer was. I was seeing a friend who had influenced me and others in ways I had begun to appreciate only after he was gone. In Kobe and Bobby, I was seeing two young men whose similarities were obvious—both so driven and inquisitive and raw, their interests so varied—but only after the passage of time, only after I had cause to connect them.

Jeff McIlvaine drew the parallel immediately. He had kept a photo of the Lower Merion-Upper Dublin box score on his phone, and when that helicopter crashed into that ravine in Calabasas on Jan. 26, the perspective that had taken so long for him and Helen and Bob to gain swept over him in a wave.

"When Bobby died, it was hard to think, 'I feel bad for him that he doesn't get to do all the things he wanted to do,'" Jeff said. "You're so overcome by his loss, that he's not in your life anymore. But when Kobe died, that was the emotion I was feeling: I'm not just sad that he's gone. I'm sad that someone like that, who worked so hard to set up his life a certain way, was gone."

On the day after Kobe Bryant died, Pat Brady, a friend and high school classmate of Jeff's, logged on to Facebook. The video of Kobe and Bobby, trailing a string of delighted comments and heart emojis from fellow Upper Dublin alumni, appeared on his feed. He copied the link, then called Jeff, who was coaching at an indoor track meet in Toms River. Jeff—standing on the infield, his attention on the meet, the whole place loud—didn't answer until Pat dialed him a third time.

"Dude," Jeff said, "I'm at a meet."

"Look at the text I sent you," Pat replied.

The text was the link. For 20 minutes, Jeff remained frozen on that infield...except for his hands, which trembled as he held his phone. There was no meet, no sound, nothing but that video. He played it over and over, all the little things that he feared he had forgotten about his brother rushing back to him. "I was elated. I was completely elated," he said. "It was like Christmas morning. I didn't have any sad feelings. I had only happy feelings."

He sent the video to Helen, and she and Bob saw their son again, for the first time in more than 18 years. "It was like he was still alive," Helen said, "almost like he was going to walk through the door later with his gym bag." Then Jeff sent it to Ken Senior and Bobby's circle of friends from Princeton. "I got chills," Ken said. "It was incredible. It was not something I experience on a regular basis. I'm not confronted with a moving Bobby. That was more meaningful than seeing a young Kobe Bryant."

A few days later, Jeff emailed me to ask if there was more video available from the Lower Merion-Upper Dublin game. I suggested that he reach out to Ben Relles, who had preserved that precious 36-second, 27-year-old piece of footage. On Feb. 11, he did.

Hey Ben,

I can't tell you what a thrill that video was for me and my family. We don't have any video of Bobby, so seeing him in live action was emotional and very therapeutic.

Later that day, Ben wrote back.

Hey Jeff,

Great to hear from you! I do believe there's about 15 minutes of that game that needs to come off an old VHS tape. Will get right back to you on that. I think about Bobby all the time. He was such a great guy.

Ben did not have 15 minutes of that game, but he did have five. He saved the clip as a multimedia file and forwarded it to Jeff. Though he hadn't known that the McIlvaines had no video of Bobby, Ben regretted that he hadn't sent them the footage years earlier. "It feels like everyday moments are captured on video constantly now," he said, "and maybe we're taking their value for granted."

One family doesn't. Bob McIlvaine recently met several of his high school buddies for lunch, and the day before the get-together, he looked forward to cueing up the video and passing his phone around the table. "I can't wait to tell them the story," he said. "I tell it to everyone." Helen has heard from distant friends who had seen the video on Facebook, people she hadn't spoken to in years, and the conversations are warm and sweet. Jeff's oldest child, Bobby, 11 years old, now has seen his namesake, the uncle he heard stories about but never met, play basketball.

Early in that longer, five-minute excerpt from the game, Kobe drives into the lane and scores. Kobe pulls up for two. Kobe frees himself on an inbounds play and rattles in a wide-open shot from the left baseline. It seems a highlight reel of Kobe and Kobe alone. But then 90 seconds in, Bobby throws that pass to set up the basket that started Kobe cursing and snickering at himself. And two minutes later, the Upper Dublin players take off on a fast break, and someone finds Bobby on the left wing. He catches the pass in rhythm, releases the ball at just the right time, at the peak of his jump, and swishes a three-pointer. He will never miss again. Out of death had come a renewal of memory and love. Out of tragedy had come a miracle.

Mike Sielski has been a sports columnist for *The Philadelphia Inquirer* and Inquirer.com since 2013 and is the author of three books, including a forthcoming biography of Kobe Bryant. He lives in Bucks County, Pennsylvania, with his wife, Kate, and their sons, Evan and Gabe.

Andrew Giuliani, Official Sports Guy of the White House, Sees a Score in Big Ten's Return

KENT BABB

FROM *The Washington Post* • OCTOBER 23, 2020

About midway through the first presidential debate, President Trump reminded viewers of a recent accomplishment.

"I brought back Big Ten football," Trump said as part of an answer about reopening businesses and schools amid the novel coronavirus pandemic. "It was me, and I'm very happy to do it."

Earlier in the summer, one of college football's most prestigious conferences had voted to postpone its fall season, endangering another major sport in an already chaotic year. Then, Trump kept saying, the White House got involved. The president spoke with Big Ten Commissioner Kevin Warren. Meanwhile, the story went, a cluster of emissaries worked tirelessly behind the scenes to broker the safe return of college football.

On the front lines was 34-year-old Andrew Giuliani. Officially, he's the White House's "sports liaison." But his path to this political fight was unusual: He's the son of "America's Mayor," a scratch golfer who played (until he didn't) at Duke, a savvy and ambitious staffer who can navigate sports as a political measuring stick. Perhaps most important, he's a Trump loyalist who has earned the president's trust.

So when the presidents of the Big Ten schools reversed course last month and voted to play, targeting this weekend for a conference-wide kickoff, the White House put its sports expert on a conference call with reporters to explain. And Giuliani, still baby-faced nearly three decades after upstaging Rudolph W. Giuliani's inauguration as New York's mayor in 1994, was booked for interviews on right-leaning and local news shows. Again and again, he lauded the administration's role in rescuing this important symbol of Americana.

"I was happy to play a small role in it," a smiling Giuliani said after a Newsmax TV host called him "instrumental" to the effort. "And obviously I don't think we're celebrating today—I know we're not celebrating today—if the president doesn't call Commissioner Kevin Warren."

Giuliani posted on Twitter that he was "in the room for these discussions" with the Big Ten. He said in a different interview that the White House was "in constant communication" with the conference and indeed leveraged football's return with "hundreds of phone calls."

It was quite a story, and the timing couldn't be beat. Seven months after the coronavirus shut down the sports calendar, football would return to the Big Ten—and return a sense of normalcy to the Midwest, including four key swing states—just in time for Election Day.

There was only one problem: It wasn't precisely true.

Listening to Giuliani's Sept. 16 briefing call with reporters, a Big Ten official who was directly involved in discussions to resume play "was just rolling my eyes," the official said. Though Trump and Warren had spoken for 20 minutes, there had been no follow-up with the White House. If anything, the official said, bringing politics into an already overheated negotiation threatened to scare away some members of the Big Ten Council of Presidents and Chancellors, each of whom oversees an anxious—and highly polarized—community.

"The more that you grandstand," the official said, "the more they'll push back. They don't want to be seen as bullied."

Giuliani's profile was nonetheless rising, compelling him to ponder his own political career. But it's unclear what he actually did. In an email exchange with *The Washington Post*, Giuliani referred an interview request to a senior White House official. That official declined the request but provided statements of praise for Giuliani's work ethic and a list of his accomplishments, including that he had engaged with Big Ten athletic directors, football coaches and players.

The Post contacted each of the Big Ten's 14 schools to ask about Giuliani's specific role in these discussions. Twelve representatives replied, and each offered a variation of the same response.

"We are not familiar with the individual you referenced," one wrote.

"No contact with Athletics," wrote another.

"I have confirmed we have no knowledge of this at all."

Throughout the conference, there was a consistent theme when it came to Giuliani.

"From a Big Ten standpoint," the official said, "we've never heard of him."

"A father figure"

When Brett Favre traveled to Bedminster, N.J., in July to play golf with the president, three others tagged along. Two were golf pros: Jim Herman and Jason Gore. The third, to Favre, was something of a mystery.

The legendary NFL quarterback recognized Giuliani's last name and thought he was built like a former college football player. He could bomb it off the tee and proved capable of both amazing shots and unfortunate ones.

"Kind of like me playing football," Favre said. "There's a little bit of good, a little bit of bad. But the good is like: 'Are you kidding me?'"

What most struck Favre, though, was Giuliani's willingness to needle Trump and their obvious comfort with each other. Giuliani knew Trump was joking when he suggested playing for $25 a hole, and he okayed the group to play on when Trump stepped aside for a phone call. It was clear the two had known each other a long time, Favre said, and had played a lot of golf together.

In fact, they have been golf buddies for decades. Rudy Giuliani was friendly with Trump when Andrew was a kid, but father and son were estranged for much of Andrew's youth. Andrew and Trump both like golf and bonded on the course. During one round several years ago, according to *Newsday*, they were on the course when Andrew wanted to call figure skater Sarah Hughes to ask her to the movies. But he lost his nerve and instead had Trump ask Hughes out.

"I find him to be similar to an uncle," Andrew said of Trump in a 2018 interview with *The Post*.

Others saw a different dynamic.

"A father figure," Herschel Walker, the former football star who has known Trump for four decades, said in an interview.

If that's the origin story, it helps explain why Giuliani, who had no government experience, now has a $95,000-a-year job in the White House's Office of Public Liaison and Intergovernmental Affairs. It also suggests a reason, in an administration defined by frequent turnover—unless you're a member of the family—Giuliani still has it. He even had West Wing access, unusual for a mid-level staffer, until then-chief of staff John F. Kelly revoked it. Then Trump ordered that access restored and Giuliani promoted to special assistant to the president.

"One of the hardest-working, respected, and well-liked members of President Trump's team at the White House," deputy press secretary Brian Morgenstern wrote of Giuliani in an email.

His job is ostensibly to act as a go-between when politics and sports collide, though for the first three years that didn't give him much to do. He set up calls between the White House and professional sports executives, but, according to a senior staffer in a major league office, Giuliani doesn't participate. He occasionally helps coordinate championship teams' visits to the White House. But those have become increasingly rare during Trump's presidency, and Giuliani is often one of several staffers copied on correspondence. When North Dakota State's football team visited the White House in 2019, Athletic Director Matt Larsen never met or spoke directly with Giuliani.

If Walker wants to speak to Trump about the President's Council on Sports, Fitness and Nutrition, which Walker co-chairs, he calls Giuliani.

"I don't just call the president like it used to be," said Walker, who once bypassed the NFL to play for Trump's ill-fated New Jersey Generals of the United States Football League. "Andrew is the one who can get me in whenever I need him."

Giuliani also tags along when Trump golfs with senators, world leaders and sports luminaries: John Daly, Peyton Manning, Augusta National Chairman Fred Ridley. Unlike Favre, Giuliani is used to it when Trump wants to switch partners after a few holes—as he did when Gore went birdie-eagle to start their round at Bedminster.

"It seemed like every time somebody made a birdie," Favre said, "he somehow fell onto the president's team."

Some suspect Giuliani's ability on the course is the real reason he was hired.

"He's obviously an amazing golfer, and you have a president who loves to golf," said a former senior White House official who, like several people interviewed for this story, spoke on the condition of anonymity to talk honestly about a staffer's role. "I don't think this is shocking."

But then the virus hit, sports ground to a halt, and the nation was divided on when and how games should come back. With sides being taken, that meant there were votes to be won. According to the White House, Giuliani hosted calls with pro sports leagues, commissioners and medical staffs. He worked with the U.S. Tennis Association before the U.S. Open in New York to help override quarantine guidelines for international players.

"He treated it like it was a big thing to him," said Daniel Zausner, the USTA National Tennis Center's chief operating officer. Was it partly related to Giuliani being a native New Yorker? Or because his father actually detested the U.S. Open, refusing to attend during his eight years as mayor?

Amid a rise in virus cases this summer, alongside nationwide protests and the removal of outdated statues and problematic symbols, Giuliani went on the radio to accept credit for bringing back major league baseball—and to extol its return as a sign that the nation's problems were dissolving.

"As we see our America's history being questioned," he said, "to see baseball, America's pastime, being back out there, I think that's going to be a big boost to the psyche of all Americans."

Favre said his round at Bedminster was casual, fun, apolitical. It was also two weeks after SEC athletic directors met to discuss whether its schools should press forward. So, at one point, Trump gathered the fivesome, Favre said, and polled them: What did they think? Should there be college football in 2020?

A Blue Devil sees red

Fifteen years ago, the newest member of the Duke golf team didn't introduce himself as Andrew Giuliani. He was "G." He didn't say much about his past. And he never talked about his dad.

Still, he made a strong first impression. "A brat," former teammate Brian Kim said.

Now he feels guilty about that. He had no idea then how broken Giuliani's relationship was with his father. He couldn't have known that the elder Giuliani had blown off Andrew's high school graduation and never attended younger sister Caroline's plays. He would never visit Andrew at Duke, and Rudy learned Caroline was accepted to Harvard by reading about it in the newspaper.

Caroline rejected her dad's politics, supporting Barack Obama over her father in 2008 and recently endorsing Democratic nominee Joe Biden. Andrew seemed intent on making his own name.

At Duke, he became known as quiet, sullen, occasionally explosive. In February 2008, he attacked his golf bag with a putter, destroying his driver. He replaced it during an event, breaking the rules, but lied about it to Duke's coach, O.D. Vincent.

According to a legal document filed later on Duke's behalf, Giuliani "consistently violated the rules and integrity of the game of golf." He tackled a teammate during a flag football game meant to promote team-building, became confrontational with one of Duke's coaches, peeled out of a crowded parking lot in his car. After a particularly windy day on the course, Giuliani snapped at Kim, and the two brawled in the locker room. Andrew picked up an apple and hurled it at Kim's face, causing the apple to explode.

"He's got a pretty good arm," Kim said. "I'll give him that."

Vincent, who declined an interview request, kicked Giuliani off the team. Giuliani sued the school, asking for reinstatement or, failing that, lifetime access to the school's golf facilities. In the suit, Giuliani suggested Vincent conspired to "secretly expel" him and compared the program to "Lord of the Flies." A U.S. magistrate judge didn't just recommend the suit be dismissed, which would happen in March 2010; he ridiculed it, peppering his opinion with golf references—"Plaintiff attempts to take a mulligan with this argument; however, this shot also lands in the drink"—and at one point quoting *Caddyshack*.

Giuliani turned pro and won the Metropolitan Open championship, pocketing $27,500 and "a step onto even greater things in the future," he said then. But again and again, he missed advancing to the PGA Tour's qualifying school. He appeared on *Big Break*, a Golf Channel show in which the winner receives exemptions to certain tour events, leaning into the character of a spoiled, rich New York snob.

"I can be one of the best players in the world," Giuliani told the *New York Post* in 2009, during an interview conducted on the condition he not be asked about his father.

Years passed, and Giuliani found himself toiling in golf's minor leagues. He represented Trump National Westchester, where he was a member and wore hats with "TRUMP" on them. Eventually, he seemed to grow up. Acquaintances describe the Giuliani they know not as the pretentious competitor from *Big Break* or the golfer who threw tantrums at Duke or the cherubic kid who repeated his father's words as he was sworn in 26 years ago. In fact, they say, he's intelligent, savvy, outgoing.

"I don't think it's a fair characterization to say he's the same kid he always was," said someone who has known Giuliani for more than a decade.

But when he turned 30, he was just another golfer without a plan. In August 2016, with only a handful of career victories, Giuliani announced he was giving up the dream and applying to regain his amateur status. He had a wedding to plan and a future to figure out. Though he had a marketing degree and had applied for jobs in real estate and finance, Giuliani told a reporter he had no idea what to do with the rest of his life.

Three months later, his old golf buddy got elected president.

Giuliani's next swing

This is a White House where the survivors are convincing avatars of the president. After three years, there may be no one more committed to his role than Andrew Giuliani. He plays Trump's game, literally and figuratively, from willing golf partner to breathless hype man.

"An incredibly clutch putter," Giuliani said during a July radio appearance when asked to analyze the president's solid-if-self-inflated golf game. "He lets his clubs do the work."

Giuliani is also a prolific user of Twitter, Trump's favorite medium, and has posted more than 1,100 times since April. At times he seems to be directly impersonating the words and style of his boss: criticizing the media, bringing up Hillary Clinton's emails, praising allies such as Walker and Lou Holtz but suggesting that LeBron James, in winning his fourth NBA championship, "DID IT FOR CHINA!"

It has given Giuliani job security and relevance. It also seems to have helped him patch things up with his dad. Rudy Giuliani, now Trump's personal attorney, did not reply to messages requesting an interview. Last year he told the *Washington Examiner* that he's "very close" with his kids.

"And I'm going to tell you one of the people that helped me with that: the president of the United States," the elder Giuliani said then. "He became very close with my son. He played golf with him all the time."

The two won a father-son golf championship in New Jersey in July, and a few days later Rudy invited his son to appear on his radio show. They talked about the New York Yankees, whose players—along with those from the Washington Nationals—took a knee during a moment of silence before MLB's season opener as part of a pregame ceremony against racial injustice.

"Americans don't kneel down," Rudy said.

"Very disappointing," Andrew said, pointing out that Trump's edict is to kneel only before God.

A few days after that, Favre flew to New Jersey and Trump made college football his next crusade. Andrew Giuliani was supportive, of course, and he retweeted players who indicated a desire to play on. Beyond that, there's not a lot of evidence Giuliani did much.

But he and his boss said they did, and it gave the Trump campaign one more thing to pitch.

It also gave Giuliani a hit of publicity he will need in his apparent next career. Recently he started hinting that he had finally decided what to do with his life. Whenever Trump's presidency ended, Giuliani was thinking of going home to New York to run for mayor.

Kent Babb is a member of the sports enterprise team at *The Washington Post* and is the author of two books, including the recently published *Across the River: Life, Death, and Football in an American City.* He lives in the Washington, D.C., area with his wife and daughter.

Baseball's Fight to Reclaim Its Soul

TOM VERDUCCI

FROM *Sports Illustrated* • MARCH 3, 2020

The enormous fallout from the Houston Astros' sign-stealing scandal has pushed baseball into a moment of crisis. The root cause of the scandal is embedded in the nine-page report by commissioner Rob Manfred: technocrats gaining power in how the game is played.

Amid all the outrage and the reviews of press conferences and interviews as if they were performance art, union chief Tony Clark issued the most important words in a statement last week that should have received more attention:

"How the parties handle the next several weeks will significantly affect what our game looks like for the next several decades. The opportunity is now to forge a new path forward."

Manfred has vowed to reduce the live video available in and around clubhouses. It's a start toward winning back trust. "That's a joint obligation," Manfred said. "It's something we have to do and something the players have to us help us do."

Discussions with the union have included an all-out blackout: video rooms closed, clubhouse televisions off, no more running inside to look at video during a game. Managers overwhelmingly favor the blackout. Several of them briefed by Manfred last week expect it to happen. It is the first step toward re-balancing baseball to be more of a player-driven game than a front office-driven one.

"Get rid of it," said Arizona catcher Stephen Vogt. "Get rid of the in-game video. It's hard because sometimes you want to study your swing and go back and look at a pitch and see what it's doing.

"But I'm all for removing all in-game technology. Let's go back to six, seven years ago when we just didn't have this instant feedback from all these cameras. Technology has really enhanced our game in a lot of ways, but it's also created opportunities for people to take advantage of it, to take it further than it should have. If you want to work on that in between games, yes. It's called preparation."

Baseball is in a fight to reclaim its soul. That soul of the game must be found in its aspirational value: players of all sizes playing a simple kids' game. The conceit we like to keep is that this is *our* game writ slightly bigger.

Baseball lost its soul under a growing technocracy. Brutish efficiency and cold, inarguable algorithms guide searches for the smallest of advantages. To be abundantly clear, the Astros are not evidence that this embrace of information and technology is wrong. It's provided much good for the game, especially as a training tool. The Astros are the warning shot of what happens when it goes too far.

Games are being decided in real time, not just on the field but also in front of computers, often in clubhouses. Analysts overlay in-game video of the opposing pitcher to see if he is tipping his pitches, replacing human craft. Others monitor thousands of real-time data points to watch if their pitcher is dropping his elbow by an inch or two. Why do clubhouses look like start-up labs *during games*? Why is the replay monitor even in the clubhouse and not in a press box booth or TV trailer?

"The Houston Astros are a product of their environment," said agent Scott Boras. "When fans go to games, they don't want to know that the manager is not the one making the moves. You've got to create theatre, drama. I don't care about efficiency. I care about the audience to help our game grow.

"My biggest problem with this thing is it came from the front office. Jeff Luhnow buried the memo from Rob."

Baseball is borrowing ethos from Wall Street. Banking and stock trading are not spectator sports. Brewers manager Craig Counsell said the biggest change over his five years managing is the population of the room in staff meetings to plan spring training: it swelled from about 10 people to 45. The Dodgers last week introduced their R&D staff to their players: 12 of them, or about one analyst for every two players on the 25-man roster.

The Astros' scandal was not wholly "player-driven" any more than is the game itself. We have a game so driven by metrics that players choose not to run from first base on a full count and less than two outs because they know a caught stealing hurts their Wins Above Replacement. (Yes, it happens.) We have a game in which 35% of all plate appearances end in a strikeout, walk or home run, when athleticism is moot. We have a game that saw a decline in attendance even with a spike in offense—the first time in 50 years that tried-and-true correlation didn't work in tandem. We have a game that takes longer than ever: three hours, 10 minutes on average.

This is the game we get when knowledge is valued over wisdom.

What the Astros did, layered over what the Padres did (fuzzy medical records), what the Cardinals did (hacking) and what the Braves did (cheating on international signings), demands a deep examination of how the game is played and where it is going.

"A lot of front offices are going away from hiring former baseball players," Dodgers ace Clayton Kershaw said. "I'm not saying it's right or wrong. A lot of teams almost alienate the former player, saying they don't want that in their front office. They don't want that in their clubhouse. They don't want that influence of old school baseball.

"They want a lot of guys with Ivy League degrees crunching algorithms and figuring out if you spin your fastball up in the zone two percent more you're going to have this effect more.

Great. I understand it. I'm not naive to that. [But] there's a place in the game for guys who really know baseball.

"I think the Dodgers do a good job of that. As many guys as we have that are from Harvard or Yale or whatever, Ivy League guys, we also have Raúl Ibañez around. We have Chase Utley. We have Jamey Wright. We have a lot of guys around who played in the big leagues 15-plus years and that's invaluable.

"You have to have that around, almost to balance everybody out. Because a lot of guys up there—now some of them do it well—but a lot of them who didn't play don't really understand how hard the game is. They show you what to do and then they're like, 'Why is he not doing this? Why can't he do this?' They just kind of take the human element out, too. You need both. There's no doubt in my mind you need both."

Manfred thought he created closure to the Houston scandal by suspending for a season manager A.J. Hinch, general manager Jeff Luhnow and assistant GM Brandon Taubman (who was bounced for an ugly rant directed at female reporters). The penalties were harsher than any ever associated with stealing signs.

But Manfred acted only against Hinch and Luhnow for *a failure to act*. He did nothing about the actual actors in the schemes. Luhnow's hand-picked lieutenants—the technocrats—provided the runway to the trash-can banging scheme. They operated in-game schemes themselves under Codebreaker, the name they gave to their nefarious sign stealing first reported by the *Wall Street Journal*.

Opposing players could not reconcile the report with the subsequent disclosure of Codebreaker. To that complaint Manfred responded, "I think in their concerns about a lack of transparency is they don't quite understand how those two systems work together, which I think the report made clear. The Codebreaker system in and of itself could have been perfectly legal. It started as a non-in-game effort to decode signs. Lots and lots of teams do that. It doesn't violate our rules.

"What the report made absolutely clear was that at the same time they were developing Codebreaker the video monitor/trash can system emerged. They got a little nervous about that. Then they started using Codebreaker in an inappropriate way."

What the Astros did with technology should scare Manfred about where the game is headed.

"Stem cell management, cleats that allow you to jump five feet, and what else?" Boras said. "We need to have an independent medical board to be ready."

LUHNOW, THE MAN RUNNING the Astros baseball operations, did not love baseball enough to make it his life's work. "At no point was I planning to go into sports or baseball," Luhnow (Penn '89) once told *The Daily Pennsylvanian*. For 14 years he worked as an engineer, a McKinsey consultant and a tech entrepreneur. His only connection to baseball was taking part in a fantasy league.

Then in 2003 a former McKinsey colleague helped him land a job with the Cardinals. The Astros hired him in December 2011.

In June of 2013 Luhnow posted an opening in his baseball operations department. He didn't want an actual baseball person. He wanted someone from banking. Taubman (Cornell '07) answered. Taubman was a Wall Street derivative valuations expert who last played baseball on the junior varsity team at Syosset High School on Long Island, N.Y. He was making side money beating people at online fantasy baseball with a statistical model he once described as a "hacked-together, Excel-spreadsheet, SQL-server-sourced" optimizer.

It wasn't too big a leap to treat major league players as derivatives or fantasy picks. He took a pay cut to work for Luhnow as "economist, baseball operations." Luhnow promoted Taubman four times in the next five years, all the way to his right-hand man as assistant GM.

Three months after hiring Taubman, Luhnow hired Tom Koch-Weser (Illinois '04), who had been manager of advance information for the Seattle Mariners from 2009–13. Shortly after his hiring, Koch-Weser pulled aside Dave Trembley, a baseball lifer who was Houston's bench coach after serving the previous season as third-base coach.

Trembley, 68, told the *Post and Courier* of Charleston, S.C., that Koch-Weser told him, "Be careful giving signs from the bench. Last year in Seattle we played you guys 18 times and we had a camera on your bench coach and third-base coach and we had all your signs."

Such use of technology to steal signs was illegal in baseball since 2000 under protocols established under MLB executive Sandy Alderson.

Said Trembley, "A red light went on for me. It was like, 'Why is this guy here?' In my wildest dreams I could never have imagined that this is where it would end up. But the culture there was just different."

That same year, in February of 2014, Luhnow hired Matt Hogan (Wisconsin '09) from Stats LLC as an apprentice in advance information. Hogan rose quickly. In 2017 he was the coordinator of Major League Advance Information when, as he told investigators, Luhnow saw him and other personnel Codebreaking in the video room. Luhnow denied seeing such work.

In spring training 2016 Luhnow hired a fellow Penn graduate as a Spanish translator. Derek Vigoa (Penn '12) had worked four years in sponsorship and consulting businesses.

Six months later, Vigoa was in the clubhouse when Astros rookie third baseman Alex Bregman mentioned that other teams were better than Houston at picking up signs from second base, an accepted practice in baseball. Vigoa offered help. He created an Excel-based application in which an Astros employee would input the catcher's signs and the outcome of the pitch. An algorithm in the app decoded the signs.

On Sept. 22, 2016, Vigoa showed his work to Luhnow in a PowerPoint presentation. The name of the app was Codebreaker. Luhnow told investigators he considered it legal advance scouting.

Two months later, Luhnow promoted Vigoa to manager, team operations.

Early the next season, 2017, Koch-Weser sent two emails to Luhnow regarding "our dark arts." In the first one, on May 24, Koch-Weser seemed to acknowledge the ethical line they were crossing when he wrote, "I don't want to electronically correspond too much about 'the system' but Cora/Cintrón/Beltrán have been driving a culture initiated by Bregman/Vigoa last year and I think it's working…"

Luhnow wrote back, "How much of this stuff do you think [Hinch] is aware of?"

Taubman proudly referred to the codebreakers, analysts and quants as "The Nerd Cave." When the 2017 season began, they were hard at work decoding signs from the video replay room behind the dugout using a live feed. Two months into the season, DH Carlos Beltrán wanted an even better system. The trash can scheme was born. It did not emerge out of nowhere. It emerged from the behavior and culture of the front office.

In August, with the trash can system in full force, according to reports, director of pro scouting Kevin Goldstein sent an email to his scouts asking them to spy on potential postseason opponents with electronics. That same month the Astros laid off eight scouts as they transitioned to a team that relied more on data and video for information than human observation.

Two months later, the Astros trailed Boston, 3-2, in the top of the eighth inning of ALDS Game 4 when Bregman pulled a 2-1 slider from ace Chris Sale for a home run. Vigoa was in the clubhouse with players at the time watching on various screens. "As soon as he hit it, we all erupted," Vigoa told *The Pennsylvania Gazette*. Houston would go on to win, 5-4, to clinch the series.

The Astros won the World Series. Vigoa and Hogan received promotions. Vigoa was promoted again last November to director of team operations, just as the scandal was about to break. Koch-Weser, Goldstein, Vigoa and Hogan all remain with the club.

The next year, 2018, the Astros stationed someone named Kyle McLaughlin in camera wells near the dugouts of the Indians (their ALDS opponent) and Red Sox (their ALCS opponent) to surveille those teams with a cellphone camera. The Astros claimed to have done so as a means of "playing defense" against sign stealing. McLaughlin was not listed as an Astros employee, but did have connections to Crane.

McLaughlin (University of Florida Online '19) is from Palm City, Fla., where he was recruited to pitch for Farleigh Dickinson. After suffering a shoulder injury, he transferred to Central Florida. According to UF Online, McLaughlin then enrolled in online classes at Florida, which allowed him to work "in operations in Palm City and Texas." Palm City is home to The Floridian, an exclusive golf club owned by Crane. McLaughlin has been photographed with Crane and in front of an airplane bearing the logos of Crane's businesses.

The money quote from Manfred's report, which got lost in the noise over the low-tech absurdity of the trash can and the suspensions of Hinch and Luhnow, is this, with emphasis added:

"The baseball operations department's insular culture—**one that valued and rewarded results over other considerations**, combined with a staff of individuals who often lacked direction or sufficient oversight, led, at least in part...**to an environment that allowed the conduct described in this report to have occurred**."

AS MUCH AS WE WANT BASEBALL to be a refuge, it can be a mirror on society. Jackie Robinson took the field at Ebbets Field five years before the Supreme Court began to hear *Brown vs. Board of Education*. Cocaine and performance-enhancing drugs took root in clubhouses as they did so outside of them. Now the fight for the game's soul is not unlike our struggle to grasp how quickly technology is changing society, in which being "liked" by strangers can hold more social value than being liked (without quotes) by known persons.

Ask front office executives about the style of baseball they have wrought and they will talk proudly about its improved "efficiency." (The stolen base becomes the rotary phone.) But in truthful moments they also admit as an entertainment option the product is awful. It is the dilemma of the age: executives, who have seized power from managers, are motivated by ruthless efficiency but draw no motivation from aesthetics.

"Analytics have come into the game not because it's a championship-driven dynamic," Boras said. "It's a cost-savings dynamic and in my mind is about how we better use the less talented players."

Baseball set an all-time home run record last year. Runs per game increased by more than three-quarters of a run. It marked the eighth time since 1970 that runs per game jumped by 0.60 or more. But this was the first time that attendance went down with such a sharp increase in offense:

Highest Runs Per Game Increase Since 1970

Year	Runs Per Game Increase	Attendance Per Game Percent Change
1973	1.04	Up 6.8%
1993	0.96	Up 16.7%
1977	0.96	Up 12.3%
2019	0.76	Down 1.6%
1976	0.72	Up 4.9%
1994	0.64	Up 0.9%
1987	0.62	Up 9.4%
1982	0.60	Up 11.1%

Here's what that means: the game needs so much fixing that not even more offense alone can save it. The biggest crisis facing baseball is the slowing of the pace of action—one ball put in play every three minutes, 42 seconds. Players dawdle, but here again the growth of information is at work. Pitchers carry cards in their hat with numbered sign systems to use with the catcher, guarding against the technology-driven espionage in every clubhouse. Teams use multiple signs sometimes even with nobody on base.

"It takes a lot out of you," Vogt said. "It takes a lot more thinking. It takes the pitcher off his game a little bit and the catcher. You're thinking about what sign and what system to give them, not just the next pitch. And the pitcher is looking in trying to remember what sign system you're using in every situation. It definitely takes a lot more mental focus. It definitely changes the mindset and changes the emotion. It changes a lot."

Manfred has nipped and tucked at the pace problem with insignificant results. Worse, this year he crossed the Rubicon by messing with the strategy of the game. He is tying a manager's hands with an illogical risk:reward equation: pitchers must face at least three batters, up from one, even though the use of such specialty relievers has declined steadily and the net time saved is about 30 seconds per game.

"These one-offs are not doing anything to the game," said one executive. "I have told the commissioner's office I am in favor of any comprehensive proposal that gets the game down to like 2:45. I personally think the time of game thing is real, not just pace or action. Time is a big deal.

"So let's put a comprehensive plan together in which we can prove within some margin of error how much time we're taking off the game. It's going to include some things players aren't going to like. It's going to include pitch clocks. It's going to include batter's box rules. But you sell it as a way to get to 2:45. Going from 3:05 to 3:02 does nothing."

Astros players are in for a miserable season. They will expect the blowback to stop, but it will not. The choices made by the players, regardless of the front office culture around them, are so injurious to the integrity of the game that they must wear the questions, scrutiny and ridicule without complaint.

"To me it was unfathomable," Vogt said. "I couldn't even wrap my mind around the fact that that actually happened. I couldn't. It blew my mind. The fact that it was actually happening…it's just so far from my radar, so far from any thought I've had, I literally could not believe it."

Vogt began to think about a game on April 28, 2017, in Houston, when he was behind the plate as the Astros pounded three Oakland pitchers for nine runs and 14 hits.

"I remember specific pitches where I was like, 'Man, there's no way a human being can take that pitch,'" Vogt said. "Stuff like that. It's not the hitting—well, obviously, it is—but to me it's the 1-2 slider that gets taken that everybody in baseball swings at. That makes the catcher and the pitcher wonder if something is going on."

The 2017 Astros led the majors in runs. They hit nine points higher than any other team, including a major league high .294 with runners in scoring position. They hit eight points higher against breaking pitches than any team. They had the lowest swing and miss rate.

"Looking back on it, I feel bad," said one executive, "because we went through some hitting coaches, like a lot of teams did. We wondered why we weren't getting results the way Houston did."

In the coming weeks Manfred and Clark need to sit together at a news conference and give fans confidence this cannot happen again. The first step is confining technology to a tool to prepare for games, not a "dark art" to decide them in real time.

"Turn it off," Cubs manager David Ross said. "I understand why guys go back there. But I also know it's a powerful thing to have teammates all out there on the bench cheering you on, knowing that they are more invested in your at-bat in the moment than they are in their own at-bat from the last inning."

Said Kershaw, "I wish it was that black and white. Me personally, I don't need it a bit. I know what I'm trying to do and it's not going to make sense for me to use it there. I just need to go compete. Some guys just love to see their swing and see how they approach the ball, and that helps them in whatever way. I don't think you should take that away from them.

"That stuff is valuable, so to me it's not super black and white. What is black and white is no ability to relay signs in real time

to the hitter. We do away with that. Whatever it may be—put the
TVs on a delay, take away the centerfield Hawkeye camera for
that game and let them see it after the game…But once the game
starts it's off. Whatever it is. I don't know the answer, but to me
that's plenty. I'm great with that and it'll get back to the way it was."

Vogt and Kershaw are not talking about getting back to an
age of flannel uniforms. It was only 10 years ago that the average
nine-inning game took 15 fewer minutes than one from last year.
It was only five years ago that Kershaw and catcher A.J. Ellis had
the Dodgers' video room virtually to themselves, poring over
hitters to see who had trouble with a down-and-in slider, for
instance. Now the room is filled with non-uniformed wizards
scouring data and video for the smallest incremental edge.

As Clark said, the next several decades of baseball are on
the line in the next few weeks. Manfred and Clark must decide
what kind of game they want. Do they want R&D departments,
click-clacking on laptops and dissecting video, to be part of the
in-game competition, like bullpens and benches? Do they want
championships decided by who can build the next Codebreaker?
Do they want players hanging out in video rooms when in the
course of looking at their swing they can pick up signs? Do they
want a game that continues to lose fans by giving them less action
over a longer period of time?

These are complicated times. But baseball's guiding principle
through this crisis must be simple. It should be the most basic
demand we have of all sporting competition: that the outcome is
decided by the players in the arena, all in full view of us.

Tom Verducci has covered major league baseball for 40 seasons. He is a four-
time Emmy Award winner, two-time National Magazine Award finalist, two-
time *New York Times* bestselling author, the only dedicated baseball writer to
be named National Sportswriter of the Year three consecutive years, and in his
roles with FOX the only writer to call the World Series as a television analyst.
The Penn State graduate lives in Montgomery Township, New Jersey, with his
wife, Kirsten. They have two sons, Adam and Ben.

Inside the Rise of MLB's Ivy League Culture: Stunning Numbers and a Question of What's Next

JOON LEE

FROM ESPN • JUNE 30, 2020

At a time when industries across America are facing a racial reckoning following the killing of George Floyd by Minneapolis police and the rising support of the Black Lives Matter movement, Chicago Cubs president of baseball operations Theo Epstein spoke out recently about the homogeneity of today's Major League Baseball front offices. Including his own.

"I've hired a Black scouting director, [a] farm director in the past, but the majority of people that I've hired, if I'm being honest, have similar backgrounds as me and look a lot like me," Epstein said earlier this month. "That's something I need to ask myself why. I need to question my own assumptions, my own attitudes. I need to find a way to be better."

MLB's analytics revolution has brought sweeping changes to the game on the field, from the proliferation of launch-angle data, which has led to players swinging more for the fences, to the implementation of defensive shifts against batters, something that was an anomaly not much longer than a decade ago. And it has fundamentally altered how teams approach roster construction, with a heavier emphasis on young, cheaper stars.

But the rise of analytics also has resulted in another massive shift: an influx of white, male graduates of Ivy League schools and other prestigious universities into teams' front offices. In a data analysis conducted by ESPN, the percentage of Ivy League graduates holding an organization's top baseball operations decision-making position—which, depending on the club, could be its president, vice president or general manager—has risen from just 3% in 2001 to 43% today; while the percentage of graduates from *U.S. News & World Report*'s list of the top 25 colleges—both universities and liberal arts schools—holding the same positions has risen from 24% to 67%.

This rise coincides with a drop in former players running front offices over the same period, from 37% to 20%, while the percentage of minorities running front offices has risen, but from just 3% to 10%. Additionally, no woman holds the top baseball operations position for any of the 30 major league clubs.

To be clear, MLB front offices have always lacked diversity. It wasn't until 1994 that the Houston Astros' Bob Watson, a former player, officially became the first Black GM in the history of the league. (Atlanta Braves executive Bill Lucas essentially was the team's GM in the late-1970s, but team owner Ted Turner elected to keep the title for himself.) And there wasn't an Ivy League culture to blame for that exclusion. Indeed, the only graduate from an Ivy school running a front office at the time was Oakland Athletics GM Sandy Alderson, a Dartmouth alum, and more than half of the teams were run by former players. Baseball didn't see its first Hispanic GM for another eight years, when the Montreal Expos hired Omar Minaya.

Still, the 2002 hiring of Epstein by the Boston Red Sox helped spark the current Ivy League trend in MLB, which represents one of the most significant barriers to entry in baseball today. And that makes what Epstein said all the more instructive in defining and attempting to solve a major diversity problem in the sport as it stands in 2020.

How we got here
The success of Epstein—who helped snap historic World Series title droughts in both Boston and Chicago—and A's vice president of baseball operations Billy Beane, of "Moneyball" fame, created a template for winning through data-driven decision-making. For the first decade of hires following Beane and Epstein, the addition of similarly minded general managers marked progress in the diversity of thought in the sport. Epstein's hiring, and his 2004 World Series championship, validated the hiring of 28-year-old Cornell alum Jon Daniels by the Texas Rangers and 28-year-old Tulane alum Andrew Friedman by the Tampa Bay Rays in 2005.

But the trickle of young graduates from prestigious colleges filling baseball front offices soon became a flood. Today, many minorities and women working in the sport—from on-field personnel to baseball operations staffers—say the pendulum has swung the other way, with analytically driven executives, mostly white men, no longer representing a fresh approach to the game, but the predominant one.

"There are teams that were too much the other way, too many baseball guys," said one Hispanic American League baseball operations staffer, who, like others in this story, spoke on the condition of anonymity. "You can't have too many baseball guys. Now, we have figured out that doesn't work. They have biases. We're kind of doing the same thing, but now we're doing it with smart, rich, educated white guys."

Among the emblematic recent hirings was Jeff Luhnow, born in Mexico City to white American expats, by the Astros in 2011. His extreme strategy of tanking produced a string of losing seasons but also a treasure trove of high draft picks, which Luhnow turned into foundational roster pieces such as Alex Bregman and Carlos Correa. His tenure included a controversial, trash-can marred World Series championship team in 2017 that ultimately cost Luhnow his job.

Before his public fall, Luhnow had leveraged his degree from the Wharton School of the University of Pennsylvania, his MBA from the Kellogg School of Management at Northwestern University and his experience at the management consulting firm of McKinsey & Company to create the definitive modern baseball front office.

The years after Luhnow joined the Astros saw the 2015 hiring of then 30-year-old Harvard graduate David Stearns by the Milwaukee Brewers, the 2016 hiring of then 40-year-old Princeton graduate Mike Hazen by the Arizona Diamondbacks and, more recently, the 2019 hiring of then 36-year-old Yale graduate Chaim Bloom by the Red Sox. Bloom had gotten his start in baseball from the Rays, a team led by 44-year-old Harvard graduate Matthew Silverman. What baseball once called a smart hire in the front office has become similar candidates getting hired again and again, opening after opening.

"If I'm going to put my geek cap on, it's a statistical impossibility that every—that the best candidate for every position in baseball is a middle-aged Caucasian male," San Francisco Giants president of baseball operations Farhan Zaidi, a 43-year-old Muslim Canadian American with Pakistani roots and a degree from MIT, said to PBS in 2015.

Chicago White Sox vice president Ken Williams, who is Black and a Stanford graduate, told *USA Today* in December: "The natural assumption is that it's a racial problem and it's easy to jump to that. But there's much more to it. The Ivy League–educated, analytically based, PowerPoint-savvy individuals are being hired because they speak the same language as ownership groups. They're hiring people in the limited circle that are new to the industry because they can relate to them."

Those on the field see the same trend.

"There's big-time discrimination of age and salary, along with the intellectual thing," Astros manager Dusty Baker said in that same *USA Today* story. "It's not a question of whether you went to school, but where you went to school. Now it appears they're just hiring their friends."

Baker continued: "Nothing against the Ivy League, but how many minorities are friends and fraternity brothers of those who went to those schools? Most of us weren't at those schools, or if we played baseball, we weren't in that fraternity."

A 2017 story on IvyLeague.com detailed the paths of A's general manager David Forst, a Harvard graduate; Diamondbacks assistant general manager Peter Woodfork, a Harvard graduate; and Cleveland Indians general manager Mike Chernoff, a Princeton graduate, toward jobs in big league front offices.

"As more Ivy League graduates found their way into front offices, networks began to develop that helped younger alums find jobs," the story reads. "Chernoff worked under Princeton graduate [Mark] Shapiro in Cleveland. He followed the path of fellow Princeton alum Mike Hazen—now the general manager of the Arizona Diamondbacks—who interned with the Indians two years prior to Chernoff."

The Ivy League creates a networking bubble for many in baseball. Forst, Woodfork and Colorado Rockies general manager Jeff Bridich all played on the same Harvard baseball teams. Pittsburgh Pirates general manager Ben Cherington received his first opportunity with the Red Sox in 1999 when he was hired by Dan Duquette, a fellow graduate of Amherst College (one of the so-called "Little Ivies").

"The one thing that does not change between the old front-office and the new front-office makeup is that people will hire their friends or people who remind them of them," said one minority baseball staffer who has worked in the sport for more than a decade. "People will hire people like them."

It's not that minorities don't graduate from Ivy League schools: For example, according to a 2015 *Harvard Crimson* survey of students enrolled in the Class of 2019, 23.5% identified as Asian, 12.5% identified as Hispanic, 11.2% identified as Black,

6.5% identified as South Asian and 1.4% identified as American Indian. Harvard's graduation rate ticks in at 98%, among the highest at American colleges and universities.

But pulling from a hyper-specific group of Ivy League graduates means inheriting that group's diversity and classism problems, including the legacy admissions programs notorious in elite colleges that favor white and wealthy applicants. Yale University currently boasts four undergraduate alumni running baseball teams, tied with Harvard for the most represented school among top baseball executive undergraduate alma maters. In 2018, the acceptance rate at Yale was 6.9%, with the cost of attendance in 2020—which includes tuition and living expenses—estimated at $78,725.

All of the Yale graduates running teams, including Epstein, Bloom, Mike Elias of the Baltimore Orioles and James Click of the Astros, who replaced Luhnow, are white men. Among the Harvard graduates—Bridich, Stearns of the Brewers, Silverman and Michael Hill of the Miami Marlins—Hill, a Cuban American, is the lone minority. White Sox GM Rick Hahn also attended Harvard Law School after graduating from the University of Michigan. According to the Harvard Law School website, the cost of attendance prices at $100,625.

Since 2001, the average acceptance rates of the alma maters of top baseball operations executives have fallen from 50% to 26%. The drop in acceptance rates also has coincided with a rise in the average cost of attending these colleges in 2020, from $47,049 to $64,012. The growing homogeneity of front offices is directly tied to the exclusivity and expense of attending schools that all but qualify a graduating student for successfully pursuing a job in baseball.

Just 0.4% of all college students in the United States attend one of the eight private Ivy League institutions, while nearly 74% of all college students in America attend a public college, according to data from the U.S. Department of Education. In 2020, just five (17%) of the top baseball operations executives graduated from public colleges.

"Systematically, you're missing minorities who may have less of an opportunity to go to those places and be exposed to the things that those types of school exposes you to, that ultimately makes you a better candidate to get in," said one female National League baseball operations staffer.

And as an Asian American baseball staffer explained, "The more we entrench ourselves in analytics, we're entrenching ourselves in by nature a more privileged group of job candidates who have the ability and financial ability to get into a school to learn data manipulation and things like that."

The influx of analytics across the sport changed the entry-level jobs available. Whereas 20 years ago, many began their careers in baseball front offices as scouts or assistants, today, many first jobs require data analysis and fluency with programming languages such as Python and R.

"You get these teams looking for these very technical and very specific skills, whether it's R or Python," said one minority baseball operations staffer, a participant in MLB's Diversity Fellowship Program, which provides entry-level positions to minority college graduates. "When you look at the landscape of colleges and where you are going to find those skills, it leans towards Ivy Leagues and other prestigious colleges where people take computer science courses, mathematics courses, but aren't doing the scouting that once prevailed in baseball."

While Harvard admitted a majority-minority Class of 2023, a *New York Times* study from 2017 suggests that even with affirmative action, Black and Hispanic people are more underrepresented at top colleges than they were 35 years ago.

Why it matters

When the American League baseball field staffer with a Latin American background began his first job in baseball out of college for an organization run by an Ivy League graduate, he immediately felt he didn't fit in. Most of his colleagues were white men, he said, who shared similar education backgrounds and who all seemed to dress similarly. Without many colleagues on his team going through an equivalent cultural transition, he felt isolated.

"It was something I wrestled with inside pretty deeply," he said. "My first year, I was trying to be somebody that I wasn't because that's what I perceived they wanted. I wanted to be an Ivy League guy. I thought that was the way to go about things instead of trying to be myself. I was a young guy trying to make my name in baseball and have a career in the game of baseball, and I didn't want to be an outcast."

As one of the few minorities working for his team, the field staffer struggled with speaking up in meetings, afraid of going against the grain in a room full of people who tended to share similar baseball philosophies and private education backgrounds. The experience can be similar for former big leaguers. Once a defined and clear career trajectory to someday run a team, former players now find themselves in the minority in front offices. A lack of diversity—cultural, educational or otherwise—in the room can keep minorities silent when roster-building decisions are made.

"If you're the former player that's a special adviser, and then you're sitting at a roundtable with all these guys, you already probably feel a bit inferior from a cerebral standpoint," the field staffer said. "Granted, you played, but you also know I don't want to be the guy that says no, and then they're like, this guy doesn't agree with our stuff, he's not buying in, let's get him out of here. It's what you always face as the minority in the room."

The American League baseball staffer also sees how the lack of front-office diversity affects the development of minority players.

"There's so much that goes into making a big league player a big league player, and for Hispanic players, who are an important part of our game, being able to make them feel at home is so important," he said. "We're missing that diversity to mirror it off the field."

Every baseball operations staffer interviewed for this story expressed a similar opinion: that the homogeneity in front offices has led to a decrease in interpersonal skills, known colloquially as "feel" around the sport.

"When we view the game more analytically, the players become more of an asset, less of a human being. We're forgetting or leaving behind this interpersonal approach to the game that not just impacts on the field but impacts off of it," one female scout said. "With that comes a loss of feel, because the more that you're dealing with real people, the more that feel is important, the more that the appreciation for the human being playing the game is important."

Those we spoke to said the Wall Street culture, exemplified by the Astros, of valuing data and wins above all, has now spread across every front office. Wall Street and Ivy League schools have long been tied together, with 29% of Harvard graduates in 2011 taking finance jobs and a constant stream of recruiters interviewing students on those campuses.

"I feel like we're really fake. We're trying to run like a corporate company, when really baseball isn't that or traditionally hasn't been that," the American League field staffer said. "So it's really interesting just because the work dynamic is so different. We're trying to run it like a Fortune 500 company, and it just causes a very toxic, almost Wall Street–type environment. We're trying to look good on the PR side, being the most forward-thinking organization. Now I think that's more valuable than even winning a World Series. We want to be the most forward-thinking organization."

Diversity issues don't stop at team front offices. All eight men running MLB's executive office are white, with commissioner Rob Manfred and deputy commissioner Dan Halem both graduates of Cornell. The MLB Players Association, led by former big league first baseman Tony Clark, who is Black, represents a player base that is 28.5% born outside the United States and 7.7% Black.

"There's definitely a separation between being a player and a front-office guy or a coach and a front-office guy," said the American League field staffer, who often serves as an intermediary between the groups. "I think it's just a misunderstanding of people, maybe sometimes on our end, feeling like [the front offices] look down on [non–Ivy Leaguers], and then on the other side, us looking at them like they're a bunch of nerds."

What's next?
Debate continues over the effectiveness of the NFL's Rooney Rule, which requires teams to interview a minority for every head-coaching opening or senior operations position. The policy hasn't solved many of the diversity issues among the coaches. Research from professors at Georgetown, George Washington, Emory and Iowa State in 2016 found that white position coaches and assistants were twice as likely to be promoted to coordinators than their Black peers.

Baseball's equivalent, the Selig Rule—named after Manfred's predecessor as commissioner, Bud Selig—requires teams to interview a minority candidate for any managerial or front-office opening. But that hasn't prevented teams from operating around the mandate. In 2015, the Marlins even made general manager Dan Jennings their interim field manager despite no prior coaching experience. And while nearly 30% of major leaguers have Latino backgrounds, only four managers—Rick Renteria of the White Sox, Charlie Montoyo of the Toronto Blue Jays, Luis Rojas of the New York Mets and Dave Martinez of the Washington Nationals—share those roots.

Minorities and women within the sport we spoke to said the Selig Rule doesn't do enough to address the systemic problems preventing minorities from getting their first job in the industry, let alone rising in the ranks of power.

"There's a huge flaw in the system of forcing owners or GMs to interview minority candidates for high-level baseball jobs both on the field and off," said one Hispanic American League baseball operations staffer who graduated from an Ivy League school. "That's a mistake because it opens the door for the token interview. We're going to interview you, you're a Hispanic or African American or you're a woman who could be in this conversation, but we're not even taking this seriously and we just need to check a box and we're going to check the box with you. That's almost more disrespectful than not interviewing anybody at all."

Kim Ng, the senior vice president of baseball operations for MLB who has served as assistant general manager for the New York Yankees and Los Angeles Dodgers, has interviewed for nine top baseball operations positions without an offer. In 2018, Ng interviewed for the top Mets job, which went to former agent and Stanford graduate Brodie Van Wagenen—who had no previous experience working in a front office. Will Ng become the league's first female general manager?

"The idea that this is all sitting on my shoulders—it's a lot of pressure. It's hard," Ng told her alma mater's *University of Chicago Magazine* in 2018. "But I think someone's going to have to do it. At the end of the day, if this doesn't happen, I'm not going to see it as, 'My career was a failure.' That might be other peoples' take, but that's not mine."

Other women are rising through the game's ranks, including Eve Rosenbaum, a Harvard grad hired by the Orioles in January as director of baseball development. But for many minorities and women who entered the sport in the past decade, getting their first job meant convincing power brokers who largely hire candidates with backgrounds similar to their own. Once inside, a lack of role models to follow has left minorities and women with another hurdle as they navigate the politics of their workplace.

"We can be grassroots with this and really taking a more active stance towards this as opposed to a passive one, which is when it's time to look for interns," said the Hispanic American

League baseball operations staffer who graduated from an Ivy League school. "We're going to look for these guys or these men and women, we need to be doing this more proactively and cultivating these candidates in the same way we would be scouting an amateur player, when they're a sophomore, junior in high school or a non-draft-eligible college player. We need to view it the same way."

Two years ago, MLB implemented its Diversity Fellowship Program, designed to address this issue. The fellowship, which lasts 18 to 24 months, gives its recipients a window into the inner workings of baseball front offices via entry-level positions. The league's first class featured 22 college graduates, not just from Ivy League schools but also from historically Black colleges and universities such as Morehouse College and public schools such as Jackson State and Arizona State. The large majority of the first fellowship class continue working in the game today, according to LinkedIn profiles.

Still, those we spoke to who participated in the program said the fellowship is merely a starting point. More must be done.

"Baseball needs to do a better job of reaching out to minority communities," said the participant who now works in a front office as a baseball operations staffer. "When teams are doing their hiring, you notice they reach out to Ivy League schools, but they need to do a better job of reaching out at an even earlier point, whether that's high schools that are historically minority-driven or HBCUs. Going beyond the scope of the elite colleges where everyone is hiring from is a good starting point, but don't wait for people to reach out to you.

"If you take the premise that a baseball team is more than just a baseball team and more than just a business, but also socially responsible for the things happening in our society, then it needs to be a conversation that happens continuously, more than just diversity hiring. Right now, there's a nature of not being socially responsible for the benefit of baseball, and teams need to think about those things and how they affect the way minorities and women perceive their organization and the sport in the long run."

As Americans continue to take to the streets protesting the killing of George Floyd, minorities working within the sport hope to see the words of power brokers like Epstein turn into action to create systemic change.

"It shouldn't just be when it's convenient or at the forefront. It shouldn't just be Theo Epstein saying it's a problem when it's convenient for him to say it's a problem," said the diversity fellowship recipient. "That's the burning question right now: Are we going to conform to be one of them, or are they ever going to try to be more like one of us? Or will the pendulum swing back and will this fade as a distinct era in baseball operations?"

Joon Lee is a staff writer for ESPN. He previously worked for Bleacher Report with bylines in *The Washington Post*, The Ringer, and SB Nation. He was born in Seoul, South Korea, and grew up in Brookline, Massachusetts. He graduated from Cornell University in 2017.

Shades of Grey

ASHLEY STIMPSON

FROM Longreads • OCTOBER 2020

It's been nearly a decade since the numbers were tattooed in her ears, but they remain remarkably legible. In the right one, dots of green ink spell out 129B: Vesper was born in the twelfth month of the decade's ninth year and was the second in her litter. The National Greyhound Association (NGA) gave that litter a unique registration number (52507), which was stamped into her moss-soft left ear. If I type these figures into the online database for retired racing greyhounds, I can learn about her life before she was ours, before she was even Vesper.

Smokin' Josy was born to a breeder in Texas, trained in West Virginia, and raced in Florida. Over three years, she ran 70 races. She won four of them. In Naples on May 12, 2012, she "resisted late challenge inside," to clinch victory, according to her stat sheet. In Daytona Beach on April 17, 2013, she "stumbled, fell early." Five days later, after a fourth-place showing, she was retired.

There's a picture of her on this website. Taken on an unidentifiable track, her leash is held tight at the collar by a man who is cut off at the torso. His left Reebok is planted between her front legs. Vesper—Josy—looks directly at the camera, her brown eyes full of something I could translate as either desire or worry, anticipation or anxiety. Perhaps her expression is simply confusion at the unfamiliar contraption pointed in her direction. She is wearing a sunny yellow tank top emblazoned with a black number six.

She's recognizable—younger and leaner of course—but different. This picture reminds me that so much of my dog's identity is invented by who happens to be looking at her. When I see this picture, my chest swells for this cherished creature, a girl who is tall (and brave) enough to steal table scraps, who has no use for squeaky toys but sometimes spins her body in so many circles that she is still panting 10 minutes later. When the person who took this picture uploaded it to the site, he likely saw a working dog, a racing dog, an animal both fulfilling and fulfilled by its genetic destiny. The dog in the picture, like Shakespeare's rose, doesn't change but everything else does—the tone, the stakes, the moral obligation of the viewer.

This subjective ambiguity defined the battle over and ultimately led to the passage of Florida's Amendment 13, which effectively banned greyhound racing in the state after 2020. On one side of that argument were well-meaning citizens and well-financed animal rights stalwarts who alleged dogs were confined, abused, and discarded. On the other were breeders, trainers, and adoption organizations who claimed racing dogs live happy lives, that abused greyhounds wouldn't win races, that nearly 100% of retired dogs end up on couches.

In the run-up to the vote and in the weeks after, newspapers and magazines published articles about recent industry controversies, empty grandstands, and an anachronistic pastime. But few articles asked the questions that to me seemed most pertinent: If 97% of greyhounds bred annually in America were racing greyhounds, what would happen to the breed if the sport were to end? How is dog racing different from the many other forms of casual animal exploitation our society sanctions, like horse racing, a sport we not only condone but celebrate with minty cocktails and flowery hats? Most importantly, what could the racing ban tell us about our evolving-but-ambivalent relationship with dogs? With all domestic animals?

Our democracy demands that we vote on issues we almost never have the time nor inclination to truly understand. But the greyhound racing ban felt personal—because I have a greyhound, obviously—but also because my life (my diet, my clothing, my concrete city built on top of forest) depends on cruelty far more sinister than dog racing. I wanted to know something the ear tattoos couldn't tell me; I wanted to know if the dog in the picture needed my help.

VESPER'S LIFE BEGAN in liquid nitrogen. It began in pellets of semen the size of a lentil, collected by a breeder from a brindle sire named Lonesome Cry and implanted in a dam named Jossalyn. This is the way it begins for the majority of racing greyhounds—on purpose, in the hands of a professional like Dr. Kent Law.

Law didn't intend to become a foremost greyhound vet, but when he opened his practice in Abilene, Kansas, two miles north of the NGA's headquarters, things just turned out that way. Today half of his patients are house pets and farm animals, and the other half are greyhounds.

The day I visit his clinic, on the outskirts of town, Law is recovering from heart surgery. As we speak, he clutches a small, green pillow to his chest and submits to frequent coughing fits. Yet he maintains the air of measured authority that 35 years in the business has earned him.

It was the early '90s when he and his partner began freezing semen, at the behest of kennel owners looking for an easier, more efficient way to produce high-quality dogs. Freezing semen wasn't just convenient—dogs no longer had to endure stressful travel for forced and unpredictable mating sessions—it also allowed owners to choose from a wider variety of stud dogs, sometimes from around the world or beyond the grave.

Near the front room of the clinic, Law stores thousands of semen specimens, stacked in tanks of liquid nitrogen. Some of these specimens are shipped as far away as Australia. Some are used for implants right in this office. Law prefers surgically implanting the sample. He asks if I'd like to sit in on a procedure and I warily agree.

I push myself into the corner as a vet in bedazzled jeans casually slides her fingers into the side of an anesthetized dog. It is remarkable how little blood there is. Still, I am made so dizzy and so breathless by the procedure that I forget to jot down the dog's fanciful name, just that she is from Texas and the semen is from Minnesota. Soon, the vet finds what she is looking for—the gummy-pink uterine horn. After triple-checking they have the right semen sample, the vet and vet tech inject it directly into the organ. It then travels up the horn to the oviduct, where the developing egg is waiting.

While I am flattered to have a VIP seat for the surgery, I could have easily watched from a window: Law's office is resolutely open-concept. Large picture windows broadcast the goings-on of every examination room. This is by design. "I want owners to be a part of the process and they want to be a part of it too," he says. Law tells me some owners even like to be in the room when their dog's semen is manually collected. Some owners even like to do it themselves, off-site. (That means what you think it means.)

Law's methods are modern, but this kind of breed devotion goes way back.

The greyhound is a member of the sighthound family, notable for being among the first distinct dogs ever portrayed in art. Depictions of hounds with long torsos and spindly legs have been identified in Neolithic petroglyphs, paintings, and funeral vases in what is now Algeria, Turkey, and Iran. In the warm, wide-open spaces of the Middle East, these dogs developed a heightened sense of sight, to hunt over vast distances in the desert. Webbed toes provided traction in the sand, a deep chest meant greater stamina, and a jointed spine allowed for a steady, cat-like gait. Thanks to the arid climate, long hair and body fat were unnecessary. Uniquely adapted to their surroundings, greyhounds evolved into the singular, sinewy form that makes them so recognizable today. (Once when I was walking Vesper, a little girl we passed asked her mom, "why is that dog so weird-looking?" Her mother scolded her, but I wasn't offended. The first few months of living with a greyhound feel like sharing a space with a deer, an alligator, a great blue heron. As the French poet Alphonse de Lamartine said, "These are not dogs, they are four-legged birds.")

In Egypt, greyhounds were revered. Tax revenues were used to fund elaborate canine funerals, while the dog's family shaved their heads and fasted to mourn. The Egyptians also gave the hound a place in the firmament: Canis Major, or dog star, is part of the Sirius constellation, which now faithfully returns every year to watch over the hottest hours of summer, what we still call the dog days.

The Greeks loved greyhounds. Alexander the Great's dog Peritas died in battle, protecting his master from an elephant. After a state funeral for Peritas, Alexander named a city after him. Homer's Argos was likely a sighthound. When Artemis transformed Actaeon into a stag, he was ravaged by dozens of hunting hounds, whose names survive today (and, in fact, can be found on Wikipedia).

The Romans were largely responsible for Italian greyhounds, who were pampered, perfumed, and perched on cushions like living statuettes. When roving Roman soldiers came upon the Gauls racing their dogs, the greyhound's fate was sealed.

Law guesses that in the zenith of American dog racing, his practice was inseminating upward of 18 female greyhounds a day. What he's most proud of, what he wants to convey the most about this process, is that artificial insemination has produced better—and fewer—puppies and improved conception rates, meaning that while the female may spend a few uncomfortable hours licking her stitches, it's a one-and-done process, and soon she'll be back on the farm preparing for a new litter.

ON MY WAY TO HIS FARM, Michael Strickland calls to ask if we can push back our meeting. "My dogs ran their hearts out today," he says, "I need to spend some time with them."

I've come to Abilene during the NGA's Fall Meet, where breeders like Strickland show off their pups to kennel owners from around the country. An insistent prairie wind batters the banner that has been strung across 3rd Street: Abilene ❤ Greyhounds!

When I arrive at Strickland Sires (30 minutes later than originally scheduled) I am far from the only visitor. The meet has brought old friends and professional acquaintances to town. I am greeted by a tousled farm dog who insists on inspecting (the inside of) my rental car.

Strickland isn't shy about giving tours of his sprawling farm, where he raises about 120 dogs at a time. A sturdy man with shaggy brown hair who looks younger than his 46 years, Strickland is a third-generation greyhound breeder. His maternal grandfather was involved in greyhound racing in Arizona and his mother, a woman who "has a deep passion for dogs," introduced his father, David, to the stud business. The elder Strickland honed his animal husbandry skills at the U.S. Meat Animal Research Center in Nebraska and had been raising cattle and hogs until he married into the greyhound family, when he started breeding dogs, too. Some years he made more money on the dogs.

David Strickland was instrumental in the industry's shift to artificial insemination through frozen semen and for a time the business employed two veterinarians to perform surgical implantations. The Greyhound Hall of Fame (also in Abilene) recognizes him as a pioneer of the industry.

Strickland inherited his father's interest in breeding and raising animals and was heavily involved in Future Farmers of America as a teenager. He became fascinated by what he calls "genetic stuff" and went to Kansas State University in Manhattan for a while, until he realized that his agriculture business syllabus was basically a rundown of things he had been practicing on his father's farm for years. He returned to Abilene.

His parents, now Arizona snowbirds, still help out during the warmer months, but today Strickland runs the business largely on his own.

The tour of Strickland's property captures the first 18 months of a typical racing dog's life. We begin in the brooding barn, where a shiny black dam is nursing her rowdy litter. They will stay here, with her, for the first two months, or until she gets tired of their endless needling. Next, groups of four or fewer from the litter will be moved to a large run, where every night they will still pile up together to sleep in a small, insulated shed. At around six months, they move again, this time to a run that stretches almost twice as long as a football field. This is where they begin to demonstrate their speed and aptitude for racing, competing with each other up and down the fence line.

By the time we reach the finishing barn, the dogs are anywhere from 10 to 13 months old. They are no longer divided by litter and now wear muzzles to protect their thin skin from horseplay souvenirs. It is during this phase of their development that Michael trains them to run, using a trash bag and squawker that, tied to 1,400 feet of string and a motor, acts as a lure.

At the end of their time on the farm, the dogs reside in a kennel-like building that simulates what their lives will be like at the track. The greyhounds in this area are astoundingly athletic, with comically large thighs and butts.

As we move around the farm, Strickland is constantly leaning over to tussle ears and offer silly greetings. "Your half brothers and sisters raced today," he tells the teenagers as they jump up to greet him. "Yes! They did! They did good!"

When I ask if he gets to know each dog well, he says yes. "This is not a turnstile." He guesses that just one litter requires a $24,000 investment.

While most domestic dogs today are bred for cuteness, racing hound breeders don't consider appearance. Strickland looks for "confidence and sociability, independence and the ability to relax," and, of course, athletic prowess.

Dr. Jennifer Ng, a vet based in Columbia, South Carolina, who has a special interest in greyhound care and owns a racing greyhound herself, explained to me later that "breeding with athleticism as a priority keeps the breed healthy by selecting away from genetics that predispose to heritable orthopedic diseases, such as hip dysplasia, that are so common in other breeds." In other words, the reason why my pet-store boxer suffers from a slew of maladies while my greyhound has thrived into her senior years is because one was bred to have a lovable, smooshed-up face while the other got the benefit of forethought.

Ng worries that if novices begin to breed greyhounds, "there is a good chance they will lose many of the attributes that make the breed so unique," including their strong constitution. Additionally, the characteristics that make retired racers such ideal pets—their passive nature, their poise—are the "result of their early upbringing on the farm and the socialization and handling they receive at the track," she says.

On a phone call after my visit, Strickland speaks slowly and thoughtfully when I finally ask him about the racing ban in Florida. "I don't want to sound defensive," he says. "Regulation and oversight make sense to me. But if you applied the same standard to the average pet owner, nobody would have pets." Like most in the industry, Strickland feels that the statistics about racing injuries and deaths are manipulated, and pale in comparison to many dogs that are, for example, hit by cars every year due to human neglect.

Along with Ng, Strickland says he's "very worried" about the breed. The end of greyhound racing will "interrupt centuries of caretaking," and careful, controlled breeding. He maintains that every dog on his farm is treated like a superstar, if for no other reason than because it's impossible to tell which dog will actually be one.

"I'd be horrified if someone had my dog in their home and felt that they'd rescued it."

For much of the last millennium, someone like Strickland—that is, a middle-class person without a royal title or royal friends—would have been in a lot of trouble for breeding greyhounds. From 1200 to 1831, "nothing symbolized the divide between the Patricians and everyone else better than greyhounds," says Dr. Edmund Russell in his 2018 book *Greyhound Nation.* It was during this time that England's Forest Laws set aside broad swaths of land exclusively for the aristocracy and their hunting buddies. Greyhounds became dogs of the elite, and lived like them too, residing in spacious, elaborate kennels with shelter, fresh food, and water.

When Parliament finally opened greyhound ownership to all comers, the working class surged into hare coursing, in which greyhounds use sight, speed, and agility to pursue and oftentimes kill (read: eviscerate) a brown hare. The first Waterloo Cup was held in 1836 in Lancashire and would soon become a premier sporting event in Britain, attracting 80,000 spectators in its heyday. The democratization of greyhound ownership not only transformed the sporting scene, it forever changed the notion of the breed. "Once the minister only to the pastime of the kings or the nobly born, once the recognized companion of 'the gentlemen' only," a journalist wrote in 1897, "the greyhound is now the instrument of sport for the gambling multitude and the lodestar of the mob." The greyhound had gone street.

Coursing thrived in America, too, particularly the flat, open fields of the Great Plains. As the sport gained more followers, however, the audience became increasingly squeamish over the matter of the mangled hare (the Waterloo Cup itself ended in 2005 partly over complaints of animal cruelty). Greyhound racing may never have taken off in the States if it weren't for Owen Patrick Smith, a South Dakota engineer who quit his job to develop an artificial lure. At least 40 patents and thousands of dollars later, spectators were satisfied enough with the sport's newfound gentility for the show to go on. In 1919, Smith opened up his first (now-circular) track in Emeryville, California. Soon he was opening dozens of them around the country. For its sandy terrain and balmy weather, Florida became ground zero for greyhound racing, but only one of its tracks—St. Petersburg's Derby Lane—survived the Great Depression. Today it is the oldest continuously operating greyhound track in the country.

AS A YOUNG MAN IN IRELAND, Mick D'Arcy grew up dreaming about the neon lights and Art Deco allure of Derby Lane. "I used to get the magazines," says the County Tipperary native who walked his neighbor's greyhounds as a child. In them he saw photos of Derby Lane: "people with tuxedos…it looked good. I always had itchy feet for here."

Mick bought and raced a few dogs in England and Ireland before his wife Francis' job brought them to the U.S. After stints at tracks in Boston, West Virginia, and Kansas, the couple and their two children finally made it to St. Petersburg in 1994. Two decades later, Grey's Calibrator of D'Arcy's Kennels won the Derby Lane Million—the richest dog race in history.

There are a couple of pictures of Grey's Calibrator on the muted pink walls of the D'Arcys' modest home in the sunbaked suburbs of St. Pete. But there are dozens (and dozens) more of other dogs. Mick and Francis lead me through the framed photos—like the trophy room of a high school gym—first in the kitchen, then the living room and above the mantle, followed by the dining room and the office. Most of them feature dogs draped in satin, women held together by hairspray and pantyhose, and, of course, men wearing tuxedos. In fact, the only *people* that appear on the D'Arcy's walls at all are the ones standing behind the greyhounds.

Mick and Francis complete each other's sentences with sweet and lilting Irish accents. They say "'tis" and "'twas" and call New York City "high-posh." I couldn't track down Vesper's kennel owners, but I hope they were people like the D'Arcys—kind and thoughtful, deeply enamored of their dogs.

In their three-plus decades as kennel owners, the D'Arcys estimate that 4,000 to 5,000 dogs have passed through their hands and they can recall a startling number of them. They tell me about Canvas, who was part of a prisoner-rehabilitation program in which her handler taught her to sing and obey cue cards. Their first dog, Father Breen ("couldn't run at all"), their second dog, Cove Airport ("there's no airport in Cove"), and Isle of Skye ("with *Skye* spelled the right way"). There was Super Spring ("a superstar"), and "the blue one" their daughter dressed in pajamas to startle the mailman. There was Keegan, who remembered their daughter's belly rubs so fondly that, when he was reunited with her years later, immediately rolled onto his back to request one. There was Elwood (with one brindle leg and one fawn leg), who went away to Boston for a season and when he came back, remembered exactly where his former crate was; he was displeased to find it occupied. Oh, and Sidney, the old stud dog that was brought by his new owner to surprise Mick at the kennel's annual beach reunion: "there [were] pictures of us absolutely bawling," he says without shame.

There's no question that the D'Arcys adore the greyhounds they race. *My* question is whether or not they are the exception.

"There is a bad element, but they are way, way in the minority," says Mick. "Way, way."

But anyone paying attention to media coverage of the sport might have a hard time believing that. In 2017, about two dozen dogs tested positive for metabolites of cocaine at a track near Jacksonville. In 2010, eight greyhounds died of heat exhaustion in a transport trailer. In 2002, at least 2,000 dog carcasses were found in a makeshift Alabama cemetery, bullet holes laced through their skulls. According to authorities, the alleged executioner—a security guard at a Pensacola track—had been paid $10 a dog by several Florida trainers. It is something of an open secret that before the advent of adoption groups, greyhounds at the end of their racing days were taken en masse to be euthanized. The most common excuse? Greyhounds were treated as agricultural animals. (Who would want a 45-mph farm animal as a *pet*, the thinking went.)

He can't deny this grisly past or the more recent bad actors, but Mick laments that "they tarred us all with the same brush." Furthermore, he wonders why, if people were so concerned about the dogs, there were no provisions in the legislation to care for the thousands already in the racing pipeline. Ostensibly, Derby Lane could suspend operations at any time, and since the track owns the building his kennel is housed in, the dogs would have nowhere to go. In another irony, Amendment 13 outlawed betting on greyhound races that take place in Florida but it did not outlaw the simulcast of races run in other states, meaning money will still be wagered and won on dogs in Florida.

Mick's name is on a lawsuit that could require the state to compensate kennel owners for the loss in revenue that the racing ban will mean for many in the business, as well as the value of the dogs and lost wages for workers. "The livelihood has been taken away from us by an act of government."

In Florida, the ban has impacted mostly the people who spend their days in the kennels or in the grandstands. "Bitter," Mick says when I ask him to sum up how he feels about it all. "I'm very bitter."

The couple thinks the breed they love will also be corrupted by misguided affection. "I call Hollywood the plastic people," Francis says. "You look at the plastic people out there and they have these little dogs with no hair, and they have dogs in pocketbooks—"

Mick finishes her thought: "We'll be looking down at ya, saying what have you done to my greyhounds?"

WHEN I MEET KATHI LACASSE, she is wrangling a dozen greyhounds into the paddock at the Sanford Orlando Kennel Club and wearing a shirt that says, "The Universe is made up of protons, neutrons, electrons, and morons." Having recently injured her knee in a horse-riding accident, she is walking with a subtle limp. Her dogs are nearly uncontrollable with excitement.

Lacasse is no stranger to journalists (a picture of her sitting with a dog in its kennel was featured prominently in a *Washington Post* article) or controversy (in 2017, she was accused of jerking a dog into a gate; a year prior she was suspended by track management for being verbally abusive to maintenance staff), but unlike many of her colleagues, she continues to speak on the record. Lacasse's boyfriend, who owns a different kennel, has stopped doing interviews, she tells me, because "he's been burned too many times." Distrust of the press, I found, runs deep in the greyhound-racing industry.

If the D'Arcys are the CEOs of the sport, people like Lacasse and her boyfriend are the laborers, the people who get up early, stay late, and scoop a lot of poop in between.

Lacasse is the trainer of record for Bolton Racing near Orlando. On any given day she's responsible for about 100 greyhounds—and her own two whippets that come to work with her. She arrives at the kennel around 5 a.m. to let the dogs out, shake out their bedding, clean the crates. The dogs that are racing that day will get weighed, brushed, maybe an ear-cleaning. The dogs that race the following day get a manicure, a rub-down, a once-over for any issues. Afterward, Lacasse heads outside to fill in all the holes the greyhounds dug in the dirt ("kills my back," she says), the ones they like to roost in like pheasants. Then it's time to run. Some days are "schooling days," where the dogs go to the track to practice. Some days, it's the sprint path outside of the kennel.

Today, though, Lacasse has made time for me. We find a seat in the clubhouse, next to the windows that overlook the track. The crowd is surprisingly diverse. Retired white guys in Yankees caps. Baby-faced lovers pulling from the same pack of Pall Malls. Slick-haired, serious gamblers parked in front of simulcasts jotting down numbers and adjusting their earbuds. The facility is compact and aging. All the fixtures in the bathroom are still the do-it-yourself kind. Behind the sink there are two framed photos—one of hounds mid-race, eyes wild, sand flying; the other is of loaded nachos. Across the street—Dog Track Road—it's probably fourth or fifth period at Lyman High School, home of the Greyhounds. On the corner, the lunch rush is starting at the Post Time Lounge Cafe.

In her mid-50s, Lacasse has thick bangs and a bright, make-up free face. Her start in the industry came 38 years ago with a summer job at a track in New Hampshire that eventually led her to full-time work in Florida. She's good at what she does—so far this year, her nearly 100 dogs have 615 wins. The second-place kennel has 526.

In Florida, Lacasse has seen the industry transform over time. She readily admits that as recently as the '80s, dogs at the end of their career were disposed of by the truckload. "I look back now and wonder how I did it," she says. "Even now, if we have a dog that's critically injured or critically sick, it kills me. I don't know how I did it. It was a different mindset back then."

As the industry modernized yet again to become more humane, working closely with the many adoption groups that began to spring up in the '90s, efforts to end the sport intensified. Lacasse had seen the campaigns to ban racing come and go, but Amendment 13 was different, she felt it from the start. "Number one, our side didn't have the money that that side had. I mean, our money goes back into the dogs....they stole a lot of our pictures and they darken[ed] them and add[ed] weird music to them—like spooky music."

Christine Dorchak, president of GREY2K USA, an organization that calls itself the largest greyhound protection organization in the world, disputes this allegation. She said in an email that "industry images were used as-is."

Facing opponents flush with cash and celebrity endorsements, Lacasse says the industry's common-sense arguments were drowned out. This is a phrase she uses a lot during our time together: "common sense." But as I drive around Florida in the days after, past billboards advertising gator farms and monkey islands and Sea World, I can't help but wonder if common sense is ever a winning platform in a debate about animals.

Lacasse argues that greyhound racing is highly regulated, that the winning dog is urine-tested after every race. Her kennel can be inspected any time the state sees fit. In the last few years, the track has added a safety brake and a safety rail to prevent accidents. Furthermore, what benefits the dogs benefits the trainers. "Sick, scared, and unconditioned dogs are not going to make money and therefore neither are we," she says. It's just common sense.

That's why according to racing advocates like Lacasse, Amendment 13 was about much more than greyhound racing. Talk to anyone in the industry long enough, and they'll point you toward the casino owners, who were sick of the 1997 law that required them to offer (increasingly unprofitable) wagering on live races in order to operate (very profitable) card rooms. Talk to them longer, and they'll start telling you about voter fraud, voting machine glitches, conspiracy theories. It is Florida, after all.

Lacasse isn't sure what she'll do when racing ends for good in Orlando. She and her boyfriend are in the process of moving to Texas, but the uncertainty is taxing. To unwind, they go to auctions; he likes autographs, she hunts for collectable glass. Still, she confesses, "My stomach is not good. I take Advil PM to fall asleep every night."

As for the dogs, Lacasse doesn't have high hopes. "Everyone is like, 'Oh, we'll breed dogs for pets.' They're the way they are because of the way they're raised. Your average dog is taken away from everything it knows at eight weeks and made to conform to human standards. Whereas greyhounds spend the first year of their life with their littermates. They're in big runs. They're allowed to be dogs."

Near the end of our interview, the first race of the day begins. We turn to watch. "I have the four dog, she's not very fast," Lacasse says.

The four dog's name is Sleek Silver, in the kennel they call her Sweetie. Sweetie's on the verge of "pet-dom," Lacasse calls it—adoption.

"Oh my god, they're so beautiful," I whisper, oblivious to who is winning. "Yes," Lacasse laughs, "she's toast already."

IT IS IN THEIR "PET-DOM" that most people meet the greyhound. The average racing dog is retired around age four, picked up by adoption groups at the track, fostered, kid-tested, cat-tested, and rehomed. Adoptions groups were vocal in the debate over Amendment 13, but not on the side you might expect. More than 100 groups came together to form Greyhound Adopters 4 Racing, including Greyhound Crossroads, one of the largest adoption agencies on the East Coast.

Kim Owens started Greyhound Crossroads in the mid '90s, a few years after meeting a greyhound named King at a South Carolina flea market—"the skinniest and most stunning dog I'd ever seen," she remembers. King's racing trainer (as well as a memorable hug from King) convinced Owens and her husband to adopt a dog from the next batch to come up from Florida. In the end, they took three: Stubby, Sunshine, and Angel, all littermates.

It's a gusty summer day in Greenville, South Carolina, when I meet Owens. The heavy air portends a thunderstorm. We convene on rocking chairs in the enclosed porch of Joanne Johnson, who facilitates most of Greyhound Crossroads' adoptions, and Neil Roepke, an active member of the group who Owens has invited to talk about the political side of things. We are surrounded by four greyhounds in varying states of repose: Topper, Stutz, Sugar, and Peanut.

For Owens, who works full-time as a computer technician for a school district, it's very important that people understand Greyhound Crossroads is not a rescue organization. "In the last 15 years, we have not taken in one dog that was abused during its life as a racer," she says. "When people adopt a greyhound from us, they aren't doing us a favor. It's not like they are saving a dog, because the dogs are not in any kind of danger." Owens is so used to being challenged on this point that she often pulls up YouTube videos as evidence, "this is the marshmallow video," she says when I ask her about life at the track, "it's a really good way to show the relationship between the dogs and the trainers."

While Owens is changing minds with (truly) precious videos, what Roepke is peddling is good old-fashioned outrage. An unlikely racing proponent, Roepke never wanted a greyhound. When his wife suggested they adopt a retired racer, he told her he didn't need "somebody else's headache." Even Johnson remembers his skepticism. "I really didn't know if that adoption was going to work because he came in with such an attitude, like this was a poor, abused dog…and that she was going to have all these problems. And I was like 'this is the best dog!'"

Sara (racing name Sarandon) did turn out to be the "best dog ever," according to Roepke. "Crazy and just loads of fun." His profound affection for the greyhound compelled him to call her breeder, "to thank him for raising a great dog." The breeder, a farmer in Iowa, was in the middle of a hardware store when Roepke called but eager to reminisce about Sara, who he remembered, and about greyhound racing in general. The conversation lasted an hour and a half.

"I was pissed off that I had been deceived so bad," Roepke says. He got more involved with Greyhound Crossroads. He also sent a 47-page complaint to the IRS about the tax-exempt status of GREY2K USA.

It's not only GREY2K spreading lies about greyhound racing, according to the group. It's also the ASPCA and the Humane Society of the United States (HSUS). When I wonder whether slandering a beloved institution like the HSUS is a great PR tactic, they explain that the national arm of the HSUS is simply a lobbying group (the local chapters are the ones doing the admirable, boots-on-the-ground work, the ones who deserve our money and support). Johnson argues that these "organizations know the least" about greyhounds but are continually sought out by reporters as an authority on the matter.

It's how, according to the folks assembled in front of me and the many others I've talked with, so much bad information circulated prior to the vote in Florida. Those arguments—that dogs are kept too long in cages, that many are killed or injured—were supported with arguable statistics, altered photos, and outdated grievances that were addressed years ago, they say.

Accuse the greyhound racing industry of cruelty in 1980? Sure—they would have given you that. But in 2019? Owens has spent the last three decades working to rehome greyhounds and categorically rejects those claims. "It is my job to protect these dogs. Why would I lie?" she says.

In response to these allegations, GREY2K's Christine Dorchek reiterated that all material used in the 2018 campaign in Florida "was recent, relevant, and sourced to state and track records, and the images used in our television ads were those posted by the kennel operators and greyhound breeders on social media." Kate MacFall, HSUS Florida State Director, echoed Dorchek's statement and suggested that voters were most disturbed not by statistics, but by the thought of dogs in cages. "That bothers people," she said.

Owens says Greyhound Crossroads will help resettle the last of the dogs coming out of Florida before it likely winds down operations. "The dog that has literally taken up half of my life will no longer be there. No matter how much we talk about it, it's not the same thing as going home and realizing that the crate is empty, and the dog bed is going to be empty."

"If this breed were in the wild, it would be on the watch list as an endangered species," Roepke says. "It would be a borderline protected species."

If Owens is nearing the acceptance phase of her grief, Roepke is still bargaining. "Do I get to decide that you can no longer have a cheeseburger?" he poses. "Hell, that's the ultimate cruelty. Do I get to make that decision? Who makes that decision?"

Maybe the problem isn't about *who* is making the decision, but that the decision is always posed as a binary choice. The conversation about greyhound racing in Florida is considered only black and white, abandoning the gray space of nuance, the contradictions and complexity that arise when we explore what animal welfare looks like from multiple perspectives—including the animals; we love our dogs more than ever, but shouldn't loving them mean something other than dressing them up and slathering our Instagram feed with their photos? Shouldn't our love also mean breeding them more thoughtfully (under, yes, stricter regulation), allowing them, whenever possible, to experience the natural milestones of their own development, and rescuing their curious minds from the cruel monotony of the couch? If ending racing was a step in the right direction, its momentum is thwarted by our premature self-congratulations.

I don't mourn for greyhound racing and its long-delayed reckoning. I do sympathize with working-class people who genuinely love their dogs and who feel overlooked and overpowered by the currents of political change. And selfishly I feel sad that I'll probably never have another dog like Vesper; I so love the bony ridge of her spine, the way her teeth chatter when she gets excited, the skin that clings to the cartilage between her eyes, softened by so many hands like an ancient piece of pottery. I don't know if she was happier in the starting block at the track or tucked into her monogrammed bed here with me, but I'm open to the possibility that it was the former.

AFTER MONTHS OF REPORTING, I waffle about attending the National Greyhound Association's annual Hall of Fame induction ceremony. When I call ahead to get details about the event, I am mostly looking to be let off the hook. I can hear the woman on the other end flipping through pages to tell me about this year's canine inductee. "It's a dog named Lonesome Cry?" she says like a question. "I know who that is," I tell her. It's Vesper's sire.

Nearly everyone I interviewed was dissatisfied by the NGA's response to Florida's constitutional battle, but no one wanted to speak on the record about it. The gist, they told me, was that NGA leadership is composed of older men—dog guys, handshake guys; farmers, not Facebook-ers—who had no idea what they were up against, no idea how to win a war of public opinion in 2019. Maybe they've failed to notice the tectonic shift in our attitudes about dogs, maybe they don't follow the hashtag #doggo. For their part, the NGA maintains that it is simply a registry, not a political entity.

The Hall of Fame is a surprisingly well-executed endeavor, manned by a small group of volunteers and two retired racers, Gary and Ginger. The night of the induction, about 150 people gather in a large conference room in the back of the building, shuffling around finger foods and tight coils of stackable chairs. I had expected festive, but the vibe feels strangely subdued. I find Kathi Lacasse in the crowd, who looks pretty in a lace-yoked shirt, but just as weary as the last time I'd seen her.

"Did you hear the news?" she asks. I hadn't. "Southland is closing. They announced it today."

Southland is the 64-year-old greyhound track in West Memphis, Arkansas. One of the five that would have been left after Florida's go dark. With little fanfare, the casino, owned by Delaware North, and the Arkansas Greyhound Kennel Association had struck a deal to phase out racing by 2022. No one saw it coming.

When NGA Executive Director and Secretary-Treasurer Jim Gartland steps behind the podium, the room settles to an anxious hush. "This ain't gonna kill us," Gartland begins, swallowing tears. "That's for dang sure." For a moment he pauses with a fist on his lip, then introduces the board of directors. "Their hearts are broken, too," he says.

I wonder if he is crying because in two or three or five autumns from now, he can imagine this room dim and voiceless. I wonder if he's crying because it's hard to lose money and harder to lose a fight. If I summon all my generosity, I can imagine the tears are simpler—the empty crate, the empty dog bed.

I don't stay to interview anyone after the ceremony; there's an emotional fatigue in the space that doesn't feel right to exploit. Regardless, I need to pack. My flight doesn't leave until the next morning, but I want to be ready. I want to go home. I want to see my dog.

Ashley Stimpson is a freelance journalist based in Columbia, Maryland. Her work has appeared in *The Guardian*, *National Geographic*, Atlas Obscura, *Johns Hopkins Magazine*, *Blue Ridge Outdoors*, and elsewhere. She shares her home with a retired racing greyhound named Sable.

A Nameless Hiker and the Case the Internet Can't Crack

NICHOLAS THOMPSON

FROM *WIRED* • NOVEMBER 2, 2020

In April 2017, a man started hiking in a state park just north of New York City. He wanted to get away, maybe from something and maybe from everything. He didn't bring a phone; he didn't bring a credit card. He didn't even really bring a name. Or at least he didn't tell anyone he met what it was.

He did bring a giant backpack, which his fellow hikers considered far too heavy for his journey. And he brought a notebook, in which he would scribble notes about *Screeps*, an online programming game. The Appalachian Trail runs through the area, and he started walking south, moving slowly but steadily down through Pennsylvania and Maryland. He told people he met along the way that he had worked in the tech industry and he wanted to detox from digital life. Hikers sometimes acquire trail names, pseudonyms they use while deep in the woods. He was "Denim" at first, because he had started his trek in jeans. Later, it became "Mostly Harmless," which is how he described himself one night at a campfire. Maybe, too, it was a reference to Douglas Adams' *The Hitchhiker's Guide to the Galaxy*. Early in the series, a character discovers that Earth is defined by a single word in the guide: *harmless*. Another character puts in 15 years of research and then adds the adverb. Earth is now "mostly harmless."

By summer, the hiker was in Virginia, where he walked about a hundred miles with a 66-year-old woman who went by the trail name Obsidian. She taught him how to make a fire, and he told her he was eager to see a bear. On December 1, Mostly Harmless had made it to northern Georgia, where he stopped in a store called Mountain Crossings. A veteran hiker named Matt Mason was working that day, and the two men started talking. Mostly Harmless said that he wanted to figure out a path down to the Florida Keys. Mason told him about a route and a map he could download to his phone. "I don't have a phone," Mostly Harmless replied. Describing the moment, Mason remembers thinking, "Oh, this guy's awesome." Everyone who goes into the woods is trying to get away from something. But few people have the commitment to cut their digital lifelines as they put on their boots.

Mason printed the 60 pages of the map and sold it to Mostly Harmless for $5 cash, which the hiker pulled from a wad of bills that Mason remembers being an inch thick. Mason loves hikers who are a little bit different, a little bit strange. He asked Mostly Harmless if he could take a picture. Mostly Harmless hesitated but then agreed. He then left the shop and went on his way. Two weeks later, Mason heard from a friend in Alabama who had seen Mostly Harmless hiking through a snowstorm. "He was out there with a smile on his face, walking south," Mason recalls.

By the last week of January, he was in northern Florida, walking on the side of Highway 90, when a woman named Kelly Fairbanks pulled over to say hello. Fairbanks is what is known as a "trail angel," someone who helps out through-hikers who pass near her, giving them food and access to a shower if they want. She was out looking for a different hiker when she saw Mostly Harmless. She pulled over, and they started to chat. He said that he had started in New York and was heading down to Key West. She asked if he was using the Florida Trail App, and he responded that he didn't have a phone.

Fairbanks took notice of his gear—which was a mix of high-end and generic, including his black-and-copper trekking poles. And she was struck by his rugged, lonely look. "He had very kind eyes. I saw the huge beard first and thought, 'It's an older guy.' But his eyes were so young, and he didn't have crow's feet. I realized he was a lot younger." She was concerned though, the way she used to be concerned about her two younger brothers. The trail could be confusing, and it wouldn't be long before everything started getting intolerably hot and muggy. "I remembered him because I was worried," she added.

Six months later and 600 miles south, on July 23, 2018, two hikers headed out into the Big Cypress National Preserve. The humidity was oppressive, but they trudged forward, crossing swamps, tending aching feet, and dodging the alligators and snakes. About 10 miles into their journey, they stopped to rest at a place called Nobles Camp. There they saw a yellow tent and a pair of boots outside. Something smelled bad, and something seemed off. They called out, then peered through the tent's windscreen. An emaciated, lifeless body was looking up at them. They called 911.

"Uh, we just found a dead body."

IT'S USUALLY EASY TO PUT A NAME TO A CORPSE. There's an ID or a credit card. There's been a missing persons report in the area. There's a DNA match. But the investigators in Collier County couldn't find a thing. Mostly Harmless' fingerprints didn't show up in any law enforcement database. He hadn't served in the military, and his fingerprints didn't match those of anyone else on file. His DNA didn't match any in the Department of Justice's missing person database or in CODIS, the national DNA database run by the FBI. A picture of his face didn't turn up anything in a facial recognition database. The body had no distinguishing tattoos.

Nor could investigators understand how or why he died. There were no indications of foul play, and he had more than

$3,500 cash in the tent. He had food nearby, but he was hollowed out, weighing just 83 pounds on a 5'8" frame. Investigators put his age in the vague range between 35 and 50, and they couldn't point to any abnormalities. The only substances he tested positive for were ibuprofen and an antihistamine. His cause of death, according to the autopsy report, was "undetermined." He had, in some sense, just wasted away. But why hadn't he tried to find help? Almost immediately, people compared Mostly Harmless to Chris McCandless, whose story was the subject of *Into the Wild*. McCandless, though, had been stranded in the Alaska bush, trapped by a raging river as he ran out of food. He died on a school bus, starving, desperate for help, 22 miles of wilderness separating him from a road. Mostly Harmless was just 5 miles from a major highway. He left no note, and there was no evidence that he had spent his last days calling out for help.

The investigators were stumped. To find out what had happened, they needed to learn who he was. So the Florida Department of Law Enforcement drew up an image of Mostly Harmless, and the Collier County investigators shared it with the public. In the sketch, his mouth is open wide, and his eyes too. He has a gray and black beard, with a bare patch of skin right below the mouth. His teeth, as noted in the autopsy, are perfect, suggesting he had good dental care as a child. He looks startled but also oddly pleased, as if he's just seen a clown jump out from behind a curtain. The image started to circulate online along with other pictures from his campsite, including his tent and his hiking poles.

Kelly Fairbanks works at the Army and Air Force exchange store on a Florida military base. She normally monitors the CCTV cameras for shoplifters, but if there's no one in the store she might sneak a look at Facebook. It was a quiet moment, and suddenly the picture popped into her feed. There he was: eyes wide open and looking up. She recognized the eyes and the beard. "I started freaking out," she says. It was the kind man she'd seen on Highway 90. The sheriff's office had also posted a photo of the hiker's poles, and Fairbanks knew she had an image of the same man holding the same gear.

She clicked right over to the Collier County Sheriff's Facebook page and sent in two photographs she had taken of Mostly Harmless. She got a message back immediately asking for her phone number. Soon a detective was on the line asking, "What can you tell me?"

She told him everything she knew. And she shared the original post, and her photo, all over Facebook. Soon there were dozens of people jumping in. They had seen the hiker too. They had journeyed with him for a few hours or a few days. They had sat at a campfire with him. There was a GoPro video in which he appeared. People remembered him talking about a sister in either Sarasota or Saratoga. They thought he had said he was from near Baton Rouge. One person remembered that he ate a lot of sticky buns; another said that he loved ketchup. But no one knew his name. When the body of Chris McCandless was found in the wilds of Alaska in the summer of 1992 without any identification, it took authorities only two weeks to figure out his identity. A friend in South Dakota, who'd known McCandless as "Alex," heard a discussion of the story on AM radio and called the authorities. Clues followed quickly, and McCandless' family was soon found.

Now it's 2020, and we have the internet. Facebook knows you're pregnant almost before you do. Amazon knows your light bulb is going to go out right before it does. Put details on Twitter about a stolen laptop and people will track down the thief in a Manhattan bar. The internet can decode family mysteries, identify long-forgotten songs, solve murders, and, as this magazine showed a decade ago, track down almost anyone who tries to shed their digital skin. This case seemed easy.

An avid Facebook group committed to figuring out his identity soon formed. Reddit threads popped up to analyze the notes he had taken for *Screeps*. Amateur detectives tracked down leads and tried to match photographs in missing persons databases.

A massive timeline was constructed on Websleuths.com. Was it possible, one *Dr. Oz* viewer asked, that Mostly Harmless was a boy featured on the show who went missing in 1982? Was it possible that Mostly Harmless was a suspect in Arkansas who had murdered his girlfriend in 2017? None of the photos matched.

The story pulled people in. Everyone, at some point, has wanted to put their phone in a garbage can and head off with a fake name and a wad of cash. Here was someone who had done it and who seemed to have so much going for him: He was kind, charming, educated. He knew how to code. And yet he had died alone in a yellow tent. Maybe he had been chased by demons and had sought an ending like this. Or maybe he had just been outmatched by the wilderness and the Florida heat.

It just wasn't a normal story in any way. And, as Fairbanks said, "he was a good-looking dude," which, she notes, might explain why so many of the searchers are women. In mid-October, one woman in the Facebook group posted a slideshow comparing his photos to those of Brad Pitt. "Actually I think MH looks better. ☺," one commenter wrote.

The dude, though, seemed to have followed, to near perfection, the hiker credo of "Leave no trace." None of the clues panned out. Nothing actually got people close to solving the mystery. An industrious writer named Jason Nark spent more than a year obsessively tracking down leads and then wrote an elegy to the hiker that began, "Sometimes I imagine him falling through space, drifting like dust from dead stars in the vast nowhere above us."

Natasha Teasley manages a canoe and kayak company in North Carolina. As business slowed when the coronavirus hit, she started to spend more time online, and she started to fill the gap in her life with the hunt for Mostly Harmless. She sent flyers to the Chambers of Commerce in every city where people thought he might have come from, including Sarasota, Florida, and Saratoga Springs, New York. She tracked down details about every car that was towed out of Harriman State Park, where he likely started his journey. She scoured missing persons databases. I asked her what motivated her to spend so much time looking for a man she'd never met. She responded achingly, "He's got to be missed. Someone must miss this guy."

WHEN WE THINK OF DNA TESTS, we normally think of their miraculous ability to give us a yes or a no. The unique thread of base pairs that make us who we are exists in every cell. So we take the genetic information found at a crime scene, or in the saliva on a coffee cup, or on the hand of a deceased hiker. Then we look closely at roughly 20 chunks, or what geneticists call markers, and we search in a database of collected samples to see whether the markers match. Imagine if a book, 1 million pages long but without a cover, washed up on the shore. And then imagine you could scan one page and search all the books in a giant database to see if that exact page appeared. That's conventional DNA testing.

But DNA also can tell the story of human history. By running a different kind of test, you get beyond yes or no and into a million variations of maybe. The genetic markers in your body are closer to those of your first cousin than your third. And they're closer to those of your third cousin than your sixth. There's a little bit of each generation in each of us, from our parents to our great grandparents to the early apes of the forests of Africa. So now imagine that book, and imagine that instead of comparing one page, you could compare everything in the book with everything in all other books, to find similar words, syntax, and themes. You would need complicated math and pattern tracing, but, eventually, you might figure out the author. And so, early in the summer of 2020, the organizers of the Facebook group searching for Mostly Harmless' identity sent news about the case to a Houston company called Othram. It had been started two years earlier and pitches itself as a one-stop shop for solving cold cases.

Othram's founder, David Mittelman, is a geneticist who had worked on the original human genome project, and he was drawn to this odd case. The company asks the public for suggestions for mysteries to solve, and that's one of the best parts of the job. "I like doing the cases from the tip line," Mittelman told me. "Lab work for the sake of lab work is kind of boring." If he could crack the hiker's identity, he'd get attention for his technology. But there was something else, too, drawing him in, a riddle he wanted to answer. The hiker seemed to have found an internet family but had no connection to his real one.

Othram called up the Collier County Sheriff's Office and offered to help. DNA analysis is expensive, though, and the company estimated that the whole project—from evidence to answers—would cost $5,000. The sheriff's office couldn't spend that much money on a case that involved no crime. But it would love Othram's help if there were another way to pay for the work. And so three of the great trends of modern technology—crowdfunding, amateur sleuthing, and cutting-edge genomics—combined. Within eight days, the Facebook group had raised the money to run the analysis. Soon a small piece of bone from the hiker was on its way west from Collier County to the Othram labs.

The first step for Othram's team was to extract DNA from the bone fragment and to then analyze it to make sure they had enough to proceed. They did, and so they soon put small samples of DNA onto glass slides, which they inserted into a sequencer, a machine that costs roughly a million dollars and looks like a giant washing machine made by Apple.

Unfortunately, it's a washing machine that has a long run cycle. And it doesn't always work. Sometimes the pages of the book you find are ripped or blurry. Sometimes the process is iterative and you have to tape fragments back together. So, as the sequencer spun, the Facebook hunters fretted that, once again, nothing would come of a promising lead. But by mid-August, Othram had a clean read on the DNA: They knew exactly what combination of As, Cs, Gs, and Ts had combined to create the mysterious hiker. A company spokesperson appeared live on the

Facebook group's page to detail the progress; posters responded with gratitude and euphoria.

Science sometimes gets harder with every step, though, and having the sequence was just the beginning. In order to identify Mostly Harmless, the team at Othram would have to compare his genetic information with other people's. And they would start with a service called GEDMatch, a database of DNA samples that people have submitted, voluntarily, to answer their own hopes and questions—they want to find a lost half-sister or a clue about their grandpa. That collection of DNA has become a cornucopia for law enforcement. Each new sample submitted provides one more book for the library that can be searched and scoured. It was through this technique that investigators in Contra Costa County, California, found the Golden State Killer in the spring of 2018, connecting a DNA sample of the killer to GEDMatch samples of relatives. Just this past week, Othram helped law enforcement identify the murderer of a 5-year-old in Missoula, Montana, a case that had gone unsolved for 46 years.

It's been over a month since Othram started looking through the GEDmatch database. It won't say anything about what it has found, and the Collier County Sheriff's Office is keeping quiet as well. But one source outside of the company who is familiar with its progress says that, while Othram doesn't know Mostly Harmless' name, it has found enough matching patterns to identify the region of the country from which his ancestors hail.

That isn't sufficient though. Knowing for sure, for example, that his relatives came from Baton Rouge doesn't mean Mostly Harmless came from Baton Rouge. His parents could have been born there and moved to Montreal. He could have been born in Louisiana and dropped on a doorstep in Maine. But, right now, the data scientists at Othram are combing through all the DNA samples in GEDMatch, looking for patterns and trying to circle closer to his identity. They're most likely building out a family tree. Let's say they found someone in GEDMatch whose DNA seems like a fourth cousin of Mostly Harmless, and then perhaps someone who seems like a third cousin. How do those two people connect? Through this sort of slow, painstaking analysis, they can get closer to an answer. Soon they might find his extended family, and then perhaps his parents' names. And then law enforcement will be able to solve a case that has stumped them for more than two years.

They might get there, and they might not. A source familiar with the work suggests that the earliest we'll get an answer is December. Unless between now and then, perhaps, someone reading this article or browsing a Facebook group recognizes his face. Or puts together clues that have eluded everyone else. Finally, he won't be "Mostly Harmless"; he'll have a real name.

And then, with that mystery solved, a new one will open up. Why did Mostly Harmless walk into the woods? And why, when things started to go wrong, didn't he walk out?

Update: Six weeks after this story was published, the hiker was identified: he was a former computer engineer from Baton Rouge named Vance Rodriguez who had indeed been working in New York City before heading out on the Appalachian Trail. He had lived a troubled, complicated life and was estranged from his family. You can read about his story in an article published by the author on WIRED.com.

Nicholas Thompson is the CEO of *The Atlantic* and the former editor in chief of *WIRED*.

The Master Thief

ZEKE FAUX

FROM *Bloomberg Businessweek* • JULY 1, 2020

It was the play that turned "Manning" into a bad word in Boston. There was a minute left in Super Bowl XLII. The New England Patriots—Tom Brady's undefeated New England Patriots— needed one defensive stop to beat the New York Giants. On third down, multiple Patriot defenders pushed through the line and grabbed quarterback Eli Manning's jersey. But Manning slipped away and chucked a wobbly pass downfield, where a mediocre receiver, David Tyree, leapt, pinned the ball against his helmet, and somehow hung on to it as he crashed to the turf. Manning, the interception-prone doofus with the look of a confused middle schooler, would go on to beat Brady in the sport's biggest game.

Sean Murphy seethed as he watched from his weed dealer's couch. It was February 2008. Skinny, with deep-set brown eyes, Murphy was a typical Patriots fan. He pronounced "cars" as "cahs," got his coffee at Dunkin' Donuts, and had a mullet and a horseshoe mustache, at least when his girlfriend didn't make him clean up. He moved furniture for a living in Lynn, Mass., a down-and-out suburb on the North Shore, and on Sundays, when he could get tickets, he made the 40-mile drive south to Foxborough to root for the Pats.

But there was another side to Murph, as his friends called him. On Saturday nights he put on an all-black ninja suit and went out looking for things to steal. He was a cat burglar—the best in a town where burglary was still regarded as an art form.

A FEW WEEKS AFTER THE GAME, Murphy was at the Boston Public Library, browsing the internet and planning his next break-in, when he came across an article about the Giants' Super Bowl rings.

Michael Strahan, the team's star defensive end, had told Tiffany & Co. that he wanted a "10-table stunner"—one that could be seen from 10 tables away in a restaurant. Tiffany had complied, designing a bling-encrusted monstrosity: a thick white-gold band with the team logo and three Super Bowl trophies rendered in diamonds on top. Each ring, engraved on the side with the score, "NYG 17 NE 14," was to have 1.72 carats. The Giants were producing 150, enough for the players, the front office, and the owners' families. More noteworthy to Murphy, the rings, according to the article, were going to be manufactured by E.A. Dion Inc., a family-owned jeweler in Attleboro, two towns south of Foxborough.

After dark on June 8, Murphy and a friend slinked behind the company's office and workshop. The industrial park surrounding the white, one-story building was deserted, and it was so quiet they could hear cars pass on the highway a half-mile away. They wore their usual—black jumpsuits, black gloves, black booties over their shoes, and black masks with slits cut for their eyes— and carried crowbars, power saws, drills, and a cellphone jammer, a large metal box with four antennas.

They climbed onto the roof. Murphy found an outlet, plugged in the jammer, and turned it on. His accomplice walked the perimeter, trying to make calls with a burner cellphone as he went. No signal. Perfect.

Murphy leaned over the edge and cut a black wire coming from a telephone pole. Then he plugged in a drill and a power saw and started going at the roof itself. The grinding of metal on metal echoed through the industrial park. Once he completed a square hole, he jumped down onto a cage on the shop floor.

Inside the building, Murphy and his buddy found gold rings, gold necklaces, gold plates, boxes of gold beads, and drawers full of melted-down gold. Unable to crack the safe, they lifted it on a jack and pushed it through the loading dock onto their 24-foot box truck. Murphy was sweeping gold dust off the workstations when his accomplice came out of an office, his hands glittering with diamonds. There was a Super Bowl ring engraved "Strahan" and a few others that read "Manning." By the time Murphy had finished loading up the box truck, he had more than $2 million of gold and jewelry and more than two dozen Super Bowl rings.

F--- 'em, he thought. They don't deserve them.

IN LYNN, A TOWN OF 90,000 filled with vinyl-sided houses and abandoned factories, burglary was a trade, passed down from criminal to criminal. "Lynn, Lynn, the city of sin / You'll never come out the way you went in," a popular rhyme went. In the 1970s and '80s, when Murphy was growing up, local thieves specialized in prying open the doors to pharmacies at night and stealing pain pills to resell. "I didn't think we were doing anything wrong—we're from Lynn," a burglar joked after a drugstore break-in, according to a police officer.

Murphy was introduced to burglary in the summer after eighth grade. One night his brother and some friends came home riding freshly stolen Yamaha dirt bikes. They told him if he wanted one, he'd have to sneak into the store and grab it for himself. He did. That Christmas, on a sleepover at his aunt's house, a cousin helped him crack his first pharmacy.

Murphy's father, Teddy, worked at the General Electric Co. jet engine plant that's still the town's biggest employer. But in the '70s, when his son was in school, Teddy spent most of his free time at the Lynn Tap & Grill, where he sometimes brought his kid to bet on Pats games. This was before Bill Belichick, before Tom Brady—back when the Pats usually lost. Teddy never asked his son about his new source of cash, not even when he bought a midnight-blue Camaro. In high school, Murphy spent his loot on epic keggers and smoked as much weed as he wanted, which was a lot.

He first went to prison at age 17, after spinning out a stolen Corvette in a police chase and then, when the cops showed up at his parents' house, fleeing on foot. It wasn't as bad as he'd imagined. "Everybody's scared about jail," Murphy says during one of our many conversations over the past year. "I got there, and my whole neighborhood was there."

Murphy got out after a few months and spent much of the '80s and '90s hanging with his buddies, cruising Lynn in his Camaro blasting Mötley Crüe, and burglarizing stores. He wanted to be the best the town had ever seen. He abstained from alcohol, mostly, and he didn't use any of the painkillers he stole. But he loved lighting up a joint, sitting back in a chair, and thinking through his next caper.

Heist by heist, Murphy honed his technique. He practiced how to disable alarms, how to tie a climbing rope to rappel down from a roof, how to cut steel with a plasma torch, and how to crack a safe with an electromagnetic drill press. He was fanatical about not leaving evidence, concealing his fingerprints with gloves, his footprints with rubber booties. He once even sprinkled a crime scene with cigarette butts collected from a homeless shelter to confuse any attempt at DNA analysis.

During a prison stint, he wrote an instruction manual titled *Master Thief: How to Be a Professional Burglar*, which he planned to sell to wannabes. Among his rules: Break in at nightfall on a Saturday, leave as the sun rises on Sunday. Cut the phone line, smash the alarm, and take the security tapes. Take half the score and let everyone else split the rest. And no weapons, because they lead to a longer prison sentence, and most places aren't guarded at night anyway.

"I'm not one of those cowboy-type guys," Murphy says. "The idea is, sneak in, do what you gotta do, and get out of there with nobody seeing you."

Each time he got busted, Murphy saw it as a fluke, chalking up his failure to an unreliable accomplice or bad luck, even as he compiled a rap sheet of convictions on more than 80 counts. Somehow, prison time only increased his determination to be a criminal genius. During one seven-year stretch in the '90s, he taught himself law so he could argue his arrests were improper. He also read widely on electronics; he was particularly impressed by a *Popular Science* article that explained how some alarm systems had cellular connections to police that could be defeated using an industrial-strength signal jammer. "An alarm is only as good as its ability to call for help," he says.

Armed with a jammer, Murphy felt like he had superpowers. He could break into safes at leisure, free from fear that the authorities were coming. He coined a verb: to murph, meaning to cut communications lines and block wireless transmitters. He was so proud of his trick that he wrote to the president of Costco saying his "elite team of experts" had robbed its stores in "high-tech heists" and offering his services to stop other criminals. "You can now hire my security consulting firm to utilize our expertise," Murphy wrote, signing his full name and address. Costco referred the letter to the FBI as a possible extortion attempt, but the feds didn't pursue it.

BY THE EARLY 2000S the Patriots were the best team in football, and Murphy was the undisputed top burglar in Lynn—the one other burglars turned to for loaner tools or legal advice. He started a furniture-moving company, Northshore Movers, which really did move people's furniture, but also gave him a convenient excuse to keep a warehouse full of tools and trucks. Other than that, not much had changed. He was approaching middle age, but he still lived in the house where he'd grown up. He still watched the Pats with the same guys, drove the same muscle cars, listened to the same hair-metal music, and smoked weed every day. He also still threw keggers for high school kids.

At one of them in 2003, he met Rikkile (pronounced "Ricky-Lee") Brown, then a junior at Lynn English High School. She'd come to the party with some girls from her social studies class, who'd told her about an older guy who gave them cash to buy DV8 jeans that other kids couldn't afford. A few years later, after meeting again by chance at a courthouse, they started dating.

Brown was 19, an aspiring radio news anchor with wavy brown hair. She also was addicted to prescription painkillers. Murphy, by then 42, kept a roll of cash and would give her some whenever she asked. "My life was always hard," Brown says. "He made things very easy."

Four or five other women Brown's age had similar arrangements with Murphy. They settled into a bizarre imitation of domesticity: dinners out, group trips to the movies or a Kid Rock concert, vacations in the Bahamas and Hawaii. The women would alternate who spent the night with Murphy. They helped him run the moving company, and sometimes they'd sell stolen cosmetics for him at a flea market in neighboring Revere. When he was flush from a score, he bought all of them breast implants. "When you're a young girl and you're having whatever you want thrown at you, that's tempting," says another former girlfriend of Murphy's, who was 20 when they met. "You grow up and you realize the creepiness. It was a very weird, twisted situation."

Brown eventually moved in with Murphy. She says he called her the "Queen of the Castle" and talked about going straight and settling down with her—just as soon as he pulled off one last big job. But there was always one more. And though he told her he didn't love the other girls, he kept looking for more of them. In August 2007, one came home from rehab with a 21-year-old friend. Her name was "J," and she soon became Murphy's favorite. (*Bloomberg Businessweek* is withholding J's name to protect her privacy.) She moved in, and Murphy soon suspected her of stealing his electronics, to pawn them for drug money. Brown was baffled by Murphy's patience with the new girl, especially because he told her J was just a friend. "It didn't make sense to me," Brown says. "Kick this bitch slut out!" Instead, he told Brown to move out, though they kept seeing each other.

As the 2007 Patriots crushed team after team, Murphy's luck went cold, and he started to run low on cash. He was double-crossed by an accomplice who stole a large part of a 1.8 million-pill score. A few other burglaries were foiled when he or his tools were spotted ahead of time. After reading about the Super Bowl rings in the library, Murphy had high hopes. He told J that after this, they wouldn't be poor anymore.

But then, a week before the robbery, he saw the Giants on TV: They were receiving their rings. "You can buy a lot of stuff, you can't buy one of these," Strahan said at an after-party at the Hawaiian Tropic Zone in Times Square. "You can't take it away."

Murphy decided to go through with the plan anyway, figuring that E.A. Dion, which he'd read had revenue of at least $10 million a year, would have other jewelry worth stealing. But as he discovered the night of the burglary, many of the Super Bowl rings hadn't been distributed yet. Now they were his.

When Murphy got home, he spread the haul on his bed, where his girlfriends could admire it. Brown was on his good side that day, so he gave her one of the rings. J got the booby prize: a different ring intended for RadioShack employees with the store's logo on it.

Murphy was thrilled when the burglary made the news. "A GIANT HEIST" was the *New York Post* headline. "Giant Jewel Heist Baffles FBI," wrote the *Boston Herald*. Kate Mara, the *House of Cards* actor whose family co-owns the Giants, told *New York* magazine that her ring was among those missing. Some writers joked that the Patriots' Belichick was the prime suspect. But the notoriety also meant that Murphy couldn't sell the rings. He stashed his share in a safe deposit box and sold, traded, or gave away most of the rest of the E.A. Dion loot within a few months.

In October, Brown finally lost it over Murphy's relationship with J. One day, she scratched the word "SLUT" onto the hood of one of his cars. A scuffle ensued. Brown said at the time that Murphy hit her, though she now says they shoved each other. In any event, he was charged with domestic assault and battery, but he was allowed to remain free. He figured he'd make up with Brown before the case reached trial.

Lieutenant Al Zani had been after Murphy since about 1990, when he was an overachieving Massachusetts State Police officer assigned to Lynn. Raised in Danvers, a nicer suburb a few miles north, he was built like a fire hydrant, liked to box with other cops for fun, and believed he could personally make a dent in Lynn's crime problem. He and two local detectives made a list of more than 135 professional burglars and associates in the city and set out to bust them all. He dubbed them "the Lynn Breakers." Murphy topped the list.

Over the years, Zani earned a reputation in Lynn's underworld as someone to avoid. He wasn't the smartest officer, but he was the most dogged. Once, the story went, Zani jumped down from a hiding spot in a tree to make an arrest. Other times he posed as a drug addict or delivery driver.

In 2008, Zani was assigned to the FBI's Boston bank robbery task force. It wasn't as exciting as it sounded. Bulletproof barriers, dye packs, timer locks, and high-resolution security cameras had scared off all but the most desperate criminals. Most bank robberies were being committed by "note passers," drug addicts who hand a piece of paper to a teller asking for money and walk out with a couple thousand dollars. Zani would wait for them to slip up. They usually did. When he found one at a homeless shelter near the scene of a crime, the man still had a note in his pocket that read "Count $3,000 no dye pack I have a gun."

The E.A. Dion burglary had initially been investigated by local police. But after a couple months with few leads, the task force was called in to help. Zani says he knew right away that Murphy was the only burglar in the area who could pull off such a sophisticated break-in. He also knew Murphy was so cocky that he'd almost certainly hold on to the Super Bowl rings. "He's a smart kid," Zani says. "But he's not smart enough."

Zani and his partner, FBI agent Jason Costello, started driving by Murphy's house and his moving company's warehouse, but they didn't see much. Zani called an old accomplice of Murphy's, who wouldn't talk. Then he found the domestic violence report. It listed Rikkile Brown as a victim and J as a witness. Costello paid a visit to Brown's apartment. She wasn't home, but he noticed her doormat, which read, "Come Back With a Warrant."

Zani had more luck with J. She had an outstanding warrant for burglary, so he arranged to have her arrested. On Jan. 15, 2009, he and Costello approached her at the courthouse. They told her they wanted to talk about her boyfriend, Sean Murphy. They expected her to be unhelpful, but it turned out her relationship with Murphy had soured. When she later asked if Murphy would know it had been her who'd informed on him, Zani sheepishly admitted that he would. "Great," J replied. "I want him to know it was me who did him."

She said Murphy had bragged about his burglary skills and showed off his ninja suit and cellphone jammer. She also said Murphy had talked about doing something big that summer. Then she gave Zani what he needed: She complained that Murphy had given Brown a Super Bowl ring.

The next day, Zani went to the task force offices in downtown Boston to plan Murphy's arrest. Unfortunately for Zani, no officers were stationed outside Murphy's home that morning as he set off in a moving truck for Columbus, Ohio. And so no one was watching when he arrived at a squat, white-and-blue warehouse surrounded by a barbed wire fence in a corner of an industrial park. It was a Brink's armored car depot. And if Murphy was right about how much money was inside, he was about to attempt the biggest cash heist in U.S. history.

ASKED WHY HE ROBBED BANKS, the famed bank robber Willie Sutton supposedly said, "Because that's where the money is." Credit cards, ATMs, and e-commerce mean that's no longer true. A bank branch might hold as little as $50,000 to cover a week's withdrawals. But a Brink's depot is a different story, with enough cash in its vault to fill a dozen or more armored cars, each of which could supply several branches. Murphy had seen 40 trucks parked at the Columbus depot on a scouting trip, which he figured meant at least $20 million. That would have cleared the U.S. record: $18.9 million taken from a Dunbar Armored depot in Los Angeles in 1997. And, crucially for Murphy, all the workers who came in the morning left at closing time, suggesting it was unguarded overnight.

It was a Saturday, as usual, when Murphy cut through the fence behind the depot. He'd brought two accomplices: Rob Doucette, the weed dealer he'd watched the Super Bowl with, and Joe Morgan, a 26-year-old part-time car salesman who'd become Murphy's right-hand man. Murphy climbed onto the roof, set up the jammer, and cut the phone lines. "The building's been murphed," he told Doucette. Then he sawed through the roof, dropped to the floor, and epoxied the front door shut so no one could surprise them. Morgan pulled their truck up to a shipping dock, and they unloaded an oxygen tank, an oxy-acetylene torch, and a 10-foot-long steel pipe packed with smaller rods.

These were the components of a thermal lance, a heavy-duty tool normally used to demolish bridges or decommission battleships. The mechanism is simple: Pump pure oxygen to the end of the long pipe, then use the smaller welder's torch to light it. With enough oxygen, the fire can burn as hot as 8,000F—almost the same temperature as the surface of the sun. The lance consumes itself, melting down to a nub within a few minutes of cutting.

Murphy put on a welder's mask and a leather jacket. With Morgan supporting the back end of the lance, he brought the welder's torch to the tip and set off an explosion of sparks. The warehouse filled with smoke as Murphy touched the lance to the vault door, melting through it instantly. Molten steel dripped like lava, and the pipe burned toward Murphy's hands as he traced a small hole. A square of steel hit the floor.

Murphy looked through the smoking hole. He'd cut too deep. The money was burning. He sent Morgan for a hose.

Murphy didn't know it, but Brink's had stuffed its vault in anticipation of a busy week. There was $54 million waiting to be delivered to banks, $12 million on its way to the Federal Reserve and $27 million for ATM refills—a total of $93 million. Some of the bags of money were just inches from the door.

The burning cash smelled horrible. Doucette started vomiting. Murphy rigged a fan he'd brought so it would draw smoke out through the ceiling. Once the hole had cooled down, Murphy strapped on a painting respirator and squeezed through, burning his nose on an edge. It was so tight his buddies had to push him in by his feet.

Murphy had grabbed only one cash brick when he started to feel lightheaded from the smoke. He realized that if he passed out, he'd probably be left to die. He wiggled back out into the warehouse, and the three took turns reaching through the hole and pulling out as much as they could. The bills that weren't burnt were soggy from Morgan's hose. They borrowed a forklift and loaded their truck with 5 tons of coins—$396,290 worth. At 8:45 a.m., with the fumes still suffocating, Murphy left. When the Brink's guards arrived a half-hour later, smoldering bills were fluttering in the air.

AFTER A STOP AT A HOTEL and a 12-hour drive back to Doucette's house in Lynn, they dumped out the money and started counting. Murphy and his crew had stolen more than $1 million in cash. But the bills smelled terrible, and many were damaged. Doucette sprayed Febreze on them to try to cut the smell, but that didn't do much. They tried putting some of the bills through a laundry machine, which only crumpled them into balls.

They still hadn't dried and smoothed out all the money four days later when, just before sunrise, 19 police officers and FBI agents surrounded Murphy's house, shined a spotlight into his bedroom, and stormed in to arrest him. Murphy was wearing only boxer briefs when they cuffed his hands behind his back. Another group followed Brown to a methadone clinic, pulled her over, and brought her in for interrogation. A third team searched Northshore Movers.

Costello tried to butter up Murphy. "For my money, you're one of the top guys out there," the agent told him. Murphy just smirked. The cops had no idea he'd just robbed Brink's, and he was hoping they wouldn't find out. Brown threw up during her interrogation, but she didn't crack either.

At Murphy's house, police found two safe deposit keys and traced them to a bank in nearby Saugus, where Zani found 27 Super Bowl rings. They also found paperwork from a cash-for-gold liquidator where Murphy had been selling the stock from E.A. Dion. The liquidator told them that another man, David Nassor, had been selling gold for Murphy. After Costello arrested Nassor, he told the FBI agent that he'd gone to Ohio to scout a Brink's depot and that he believed Murphy had broken into it with Doucette and Morgan.

Costello decided to visit Doucette and bluff him. The agent told Doucette he knew all about the Brink's burglary. "I'm not here to arrest you today, but we will be coming back for you," Costello said. Within a day, Doucette agreed to cooperate, the agent says.

Murphy was held in prison, unable to raise the $3 million bail. After about a year, he was ready to make a deal. Given temporary immunity to negotiate a plea agreement, he confessed to everything. He gave tips about other burglars and even sat for a videotaped interview about his techniques for the FBI to show new agents. But the tips were too stale to be useful, Costello says, and the videotape was never used in training. (Murphy says this was intentional; he avoided giving the FBI anything it could use to charge anyone else.) The best deal prosecutors offered Murphy was about 10 years in prison for the Brink's burglary if he pleaded guilty, then a trial—and likely more prison time—for E.A. Dion.

Murphy wasn't about to accept that. His first lawyer quit after realizing Murphy wanted to try his luck in front of a jury. When his replacement told him to take the deal, Murphy decided to represent himself.

On Oct. 17, 2011, Murphy stood at a lectern in an Ohio courtroom dressed in a shirt and slacks from Men's Wearhouse for the occasion, with a remote-controlled shock band around his calf to make sure he didn't run away. He'd spent the night in his cell writing an opening statement. It was a tricky situation. Under plea bargaining rules, his confession couldn't be used against him, unless he contradicted himself in court. That meant he couldn't directly deny committing the crime. Doucette and Nassor had pleaded guilty and agreed to testify against him. ("We got caught because he gave a f---ing 20-year-old girl a Super Bowl ring," Nassor says. "F--- him.") And the prosecution had a copy of *Master Thief*, which had incriminating tips such as "be extremely careful when piercing the last layer of steel on the vault door."

Murphy decided to argue that he was, more or less, a burglary professor who was being set up by his pupils. "Have many of you seen the new movie, *The Town*?" he asked the jury, referring to one of his favorite films. He told them that his hometown of Lynn was full of professional burglars, like Boston's Charlestown neighborhood in the Ben Affleck movie. The prosecutor, Salvador Dominguez, just had the wrong guy, he argued.

"Sal's playing a game that we all played when we were little kids, every single one of yous played it when you were a little kid—it is called tag," Murphy said, sounding like Clarence Darrow as interpreted by Mark Wahlberg. "And unfortunately, I am it. But, ladies and gentlemen of the jury, by the time this trial is over, you are going to realize that I have tagged two other people, and I am not it."

While questioning witnesses, Murphy referred to himself in the third person and seemed to get sidetracked by his favorite subjects. Over the course of a five-hour cross-examination, he went over Doucette's muscle car collection, car by car, and asked him if the weed he sold was clumpy.

> MURPHY: Why don't you just admit to the jury that you took Murphy's professional burglary course?

> DOUCETTE: I've only hung out with you, and we smoked weed. And you told me, because you like to run your mouth, about how everything is.

> MURPHY: So you expect the jury to believe that you traveled halfway across the country, used cell jammers, deactivated alarm systems, cut open vaults, stole over a million dollars, and this was your first burglary?

> DOUCETTE: You are very convincing and good at what you do, and you only needed a follower. So, yes.

The jury found Murphy guilty on all charges, and the judge sentenced him to 20 years in federal prison for the Brink's job, reduced to 13 years on appeal. Doucette was sentenced to 27 months for his role, Nassor got three years, and Morgan 55 months. Brown was put on probation for receiving stolen property.

I WROTE TO MURPHY LAST YEAR. I'd read a little about his case and was curious if he was a Patriots fan like me and if he'd been out to avenge Brady's loss. Over dozens of phone calls, he told me his story. He'd been dragging the E.A. Dion case out for a decade in state court, outlasting two prosecutors, and in November, I went to see him represent himself at a hearing.

Murphy shuffled into court in Fall River, Mass., his ankles and wrists chained together. Now 55, he seemed small, wearing a way-too-large striped dress shirt and slacks, with reading glasses on top of his thinning gray hair. He carried his legal papers in a clear plastic bag. Happy to have an audience, he turned and gave me a thumbs-up.

Toward the end of the hearing, Murphy huddled with the prosecutor and the judge in a corner of the courtroom. He told me later that he'd cut a deal that should see him released next year, but the prosecutor on the Brink's case says he still has years left on that sentence.

Murphy has been in prison since 2009, long enough to watch the Patriots win three more Super Bowls, lose another to the Giants, and see Manning retire and Brady leave for the Tampa Bay Buccaneers. He's been inside so long that he's never used an iPhone or Instagram. He still doesn't mind prison. These days, he works as a block runner, collecting other inmates' meal trays and taking out their garbage. To raise money to pay his property taxes, he sues the prison, whether for opening his mail or charging him to make copies, and reads newspapers to look for tainted products so that he can sue, claiming food poisoning.

Amazingly, this sometimes works. Murphy says he's won about $10,000 from prisons in four settlements and $750 in a dispute over a bad batch of salami. "You fill your day up with a routine, and time just goes by," he says.

Murphy is proud that "murphed" has been adopted into Lynn burglar slang and that treasure hunters search for gold in his old house. But he says he's retired from crime. The only score he's plotting now is how he's going to get someone, preferably Ben Affleck, to turn *Master Thief* into a movie. It would be like *The Town*, only even more thrilling, he says. "I'm just as good, if not better, than them guys," he says.

Murphy says he's still got some of the Super Bowl rings, including the one with Strahan's name on it. (The Giants say the stolen rings were for team staff, and Strahan's never went missing.) Once he's out, maybe he'll slip it on his finger. He says he'd like to open a marijuana business now that it's legal, or maybe become a security consultant, for real this time.

"There's a lot of ways to make legitimate money out there," he says. "I'm just going to keep my hand out of the illegal cookie jar now."

———————

Zeke Faux writes for *Businessweek* magazine and *Bloomberg News.* Originally from Somerville, Massachusetts, his exposés of financial fraud have won the Gerald Loeb award and American Bar Association's Silver Gavel award.

The Bout

CARY CLACK

FROM Truly*Adventurous • FEBRUARY 19, 2020

The mingled smell of stale popcorn, beer and tobacco clung to the octagon-shaped interior. The 4,500-seat barn-like Sportatorium, south of downtown Dallas, was a beloved venue for wrestling shows and country music programs and, tonight, a one-of-a-kind boxing match.

For the last few years this was the site of the weekly *Big D Jamboree*, a Saturday night country music radio show broadcast across the country by KRLD over the CBS network. Established and rising stars from the Grand Ole Opry like Hank Williams, Sonny James and Johnny Cash would take the stage that sat at the center of the arena.

The Sportatorium had seen audiences even bigger than the nearly 2,400 gathered here on February 24, 1955, but maybe never one so rapt.

And the Sportatorium had never seated an audience so evenly distributed between Black and white spectators, although, this being Dallas, in 1955, Blacks and whites didn't sit together. They were segregated by alternating sections steeply rising towards the crisscrossing rafters. Tonight's crowd had sat through four preliminary matches and now, peering through the haze of cigarette and cigar smoke curling into the glow of the lights, looked upon a sight never witnessed in a Texas boxing ring.

The two men below mirrored the crowd. In one corner was a white boxer, in the other a Black one. The first was the young boxer with four professional fights, the other the veteran pugilist with a losing record in seventeen professional fights.

During introductions, Reagan "Buddy" Turman, the young high-flying white boxer, drew the louder applause. He was a familiar face who'd fought two weeks earlier in the Sportatorium. But the applause for I. H. "Sporty" Harvey, veteran, journeyman boxer, was generous, recognizing his long and incredible fight to enter that ring. It was an outpouring.

Late in the third round, Turman slammed an anvil disguised as a left hook into the right side of Harvey's face, dropping him to the canvas and sending the crowd to its feet, some with cheers, others with hearts dropping as hard as Harvey had.

The referee's voice cut through the roar and groans.

"One! Two!"

This was the end that had been predicted, even preordained. Turman was more skilled and powerful than Harvey.

"Three! Four!"

In a story running that day in newspapers across the country, a UPI sportswriter, previewing this fight, noted Harvey's battles to make the fight happen. *But tonight, at least, he may wish he had never launched his campaign. For the 20-year-old Turman is expected to make short work of the veteran Harvey.*

"Five!"

Searching for clarity and his legs, Harvey struggled to get off the canvas. *Short work of the veteran* indeed. Watching, holding their breath, and trying to will him to his feet were entire sections of Black people not ready to give up a dream.

"Six!"

Harvey wasn't the first Black Texas boxer to imagine himself having a chance to fight for the title of champion. But he was the only one who imagined it so strongly to the point of forcing that image into existence.

"Seven!"

Ding!

The bell ending the round could give him another chance if he could get up. Few thought he had fight left in him. Their mistake.

TWO YEARS BEFORE, during the 1953 session of the Texas Legislature, a young, white civil rights attorney and state representative from San Antonio named Maury Maverick Jr. introduced a bill he knew wouldn't pass.

A 32-year-old who'd served in the Marines during World War II, Maverick, in his second term in the legislature, was already one of the leading liberals in that chamber and in the state. It was a position he came by through intellect, convictions and heritage. Crusty and gruff even as a young man, the sad eyes on his oval-shaped face were offset by the wry remark that always seemed ready to spring from a mouth pulled back just shy of a smile.

During the 1960 presidential campaign, Maverick Jr. was giving John F. Kennedy a tour of the Alamo when Kennedy, late for another appointment, asked him to lead him out the back door.

"There is no back door," said Maverick. "That's why there were so many heroes."

"Maverick" had come to apply to anyone independent and willing to think in unconventional ways because of Maverick's great-grandfather, Samuel Augustus Maverick. A signer of the Texas Declaration of Independence and a wealthy landowner, he didn't brand his Longhorns, a strange choice at the time. When one of his animals strayed from the herd it was called a "maverick" by cowboys.

Maury Maverick would always remember being a teenager and hiding with his parents and sister with family friends after their home was surrounded by an angry mob wanting to lynch his father. Maverick's father, a two-term New Deal U.S. Congressman and San Antonio Mayor, had allowed a Communist Party rally to be held in the city's Municipal Auditorium in 1939. That memory seemed to animate his father's advice: "When you've got a famous name, you've got to use it to speak up for people who can't speak up for themselves."

Maverick's proposed bill of 1953 would repeal the ban on interracial boxing and wrestling matches, declaring, "it is discrimination and unfair to deny a boxer or wrestler the right to make a living by reason of his race, color or creed."

The two-decades old ban also wasn't popular with the boxing and wrestling communities. After Maverick's bill was filed, the *Austin-American Statesman*'s Buster Haas wrote, "We have talked to every leading boxer in the state, in addition to all fight mangers, and have heard no dissenting vote against allowing Negro and white fighters to box...In fact, most boxers and managers, in addition to promoters who predict an upswing in boxing popularity if the bill passes, say that 'mixed' bouts are the only salvation for boxing in Texas."

The pre-history of Maverick's bill went back to February 25, 1901 in Galveston's Harmony Hall, when a white veteran fighter from California named Joe Choynski slammed a right hand into the face of a young Black Galveston fighter in the third round. Knocked cold, the young fighter fell into the arms of Choynski before hitting the floor. The young fighter was Jack Johnson, who in seven years would become boxing's first Black heavyweight champion of the world and one of the sport's most gifted fighters in its history.

Texas Rangers arrested Choynski and Johnson for fighting not because theirs was an interracial prize fight but because it was a prize fight with money on the line, which was illegal in Texas. The two men were jailed for three weeks and sparred every day in prison, often before an audience, with Johnson playing student to Choynski's teacher. Upon their release, they left Galveston.

In 1933, the Texas Legislature banned boxing matches between white fighters and Black fighters. Historian Dr. Francine Romero explores the motives for the ban in "There Are Only White Champions," an essay on segregated boxing in Texas. "The significant legislation that appeared in 1933 in this regard was not the segregation of the sport, but approval of the resumption of legally sanctioned boxing in the state after a thirty-eight-year absence…it is this reauthorization that prompted legislative debate and public scrutiny, not the limit on mixed matches quietly attached to it."

The institution of segregated matches was a natural consequence of the era's raw and unapologetic racism and segregation. No matter how talented or bursting with promise, a Black fighter could never be champion of any boxing division in the state of Texas. He could, like Johnson, become champion of the world by taking a detour out of Texas but the road to being recognized as the best in his state would always be blocked.

The same legislation banning mixed-race matches repealed the ban on all forms of boxing in the state, which through licenses and permit fees alone would deprive the state coffers of $30,000 annually, a value equivalent to over half-a-million dollars today.

That was twenty years before Maury Maverick's attempt to change or challenge the ban. A realist, he had an idea of how it would play out.

"My bill was sent to the State Affairs Committee which meant from the start that the Speaker wanted it killed," Maverick recalled years later.

He got a hearing but was stung by the "good old boy humor" that led up to the bill being killed. He knew that the bill would probably die, he just didn't expect it to die as quickly as it did. Recounting the experience in a letter, Maverick wrote, "It made me feel sore." He needed to find another way to win.

That summer, Maverick was in his law office on the seventh floor of the Maverick Building in downtown San Antonio when a muscular, well-dressed Black man walked in who would change everything.

"I'm Sporty Harvey," said the man, introducing himself. "I could be champ of Texas in the heavyweight division but they won't let me box."

He caught Maverick off guard.

"I was bewildered at first," he'd recall. "I didn't quite know what to make of him."

"I want to file a lawsuit with you," Harvey explained. "I want to talk to you about dignity for my people."

HARVEY WAS BORN ON JULY 21, 1925 in Hallettsville, TX about a hundred miles east of San Antonio. He was the firstborn of Charlie and Rosella's six children and was named I.H. That's his name in the Lavaca County birth registry and would be his name on his headstone. What the initials stood for, if anything, has been lost to history, even to his family.

"(I) never knew," his son, Lymont Harvey, says when asked why. "His mother just gave him that name. I guess it was the thing to do."

As a child, Harvey chopped wood and picked cotton. His formal education stopped after sixth grade. In 1937, he moved with his family to San Antonio.

Somewhere between Hallettsville and San Antonio, he began to box. His nickname, "Sporty," unlike those of Joe Louis' "Brown Bomber" or Jack Dempsey's "Manassa Mauler" came not from any fighting technique but from his well-groomed style and sartorial taste outside the ring. "I.H. 'Sporty' Harvey was invariably a colorful lad," wrote Mark Batterson, an *Austin-American Statesman* sports columnist, in 1953. "He affected bright, bright ring garments which established a trademark for him."

If the nearly four decade ban on prizefighting had tamped down enthusiasm for the sport in Texas, national popularity grew with major fights broadcast live over radio, seen in movie reels and covered in newspapers. The heavyweight championship of the world was the most coveted and recognized title in sports and whoever was the champ was one of the most famous men in the country.

Joe Louis won the title shortly before Harvey's 12th birthday. Louis' reign lasted a dozen years, extending into the first two years of Harvey's professional career. The second Black man to win the heavyweight title, after Harvey's fellow Texan Jack Johnson, Louis was the dominant fighter of Harvey's youth and a man who carried the hopes of Blacks each time he entered the ring.

If Louis could do that for Black people across the country, why couldn't Sporty Harvey do it for Black people throughout the state of Texas?

For one thing, Harvey was the ultimate underdog. Starting off as a light-heavyweight, he was knocked out in Pittsburgh, in 1947, in his first professional fight. It didn't get better. Harvey was knocked out in his first four professional fights and lost his first eight, six by KO and two by TKO. His first win came in San Antonio's Municipal Auditorium against a fighter making his pro debut who quit between rounds.

We will never know Harvey's actual record as a professional fighter and he probably didn't know. BoxRec, Boxing's Official Record Keeper, lists his record as 10–23–2. They also list him as J.D. Harvey, an alias Sporty appears to have used to score more fights.

That record doesn't include some of his fights in San Antonio East Side out-of-the-way venues like The Ritz, a former movie theater, or at Fort Sam Houston, a military base. Nor does it include his fights in Mexico where he'd challenge Mexican and white boxers. Whatever the number of fights, they probably added up to a losing record.

He was an everyman, not a superman. But by all accounts he was a popular and entertaining fighter who, years before Muhammad Ali, did windmill windups before throwing a punch.

Mark Batterson observed: "I.H. 'Sporty' Harvey used to come to Austin to engage in his profession. Just what this profession was sometimes wasn't clear. On at least two occasions, he definitely appeared to be a boxer. On another he seemed to be an entertainer, an imitator, sort of, who was giving his comic impressions of a boxer…A more memorable trademark in this case, however, was the way he jutted out before and aft when he scampered into battle. At times this style made him look more like a Studebaker than a boxer."

There were more talented Black fighters in Texas than Harvey but because of the ban against matches between Blacks and whites they were no closer than he was to winning a championship or maximizing earning potential.

Neither talent nor the guts to take physical punishment from another man in the ring would be enough to change the law. Such change demanded a different type of courage, the courage to challenge an entire state's legal system and way of life and risk all the forms of punishment the state could inflict.

ON THAT JULY DAY IN 1953, Maury Maverick listened to his unexpected visitor tell his story in a drawl not so different from his own.

Harvey had read about Maverick's attempt to change the laws prohibiting Black boxers from fighting white boxers, which is what brought him into the office. He quickly convinced the lawyer he should represent him in his cause. Harvey couldn't afford an attorney. Maverick wouldn't have charged him anyway.

Change was in the air. Just a few weeks earlier, a bus boycott by Blacks in Baton Rouge, Louisiana had won concessions from that city. The slavery era and Jim Crow dictums of Blacks "knowing their place" was challenged with greater frequency and variety as "their place" became any place where they'd be afforded the same rights and opportunities as whites; those places included schools, public accommodations, voting booths and, just maybe, boxing rings.

Maverick hatched a plan. He asked his new client to write a letter to M.B. Morgan, the state's Labor Commissioner whose office governed professional boxing, asking for permission to fight a white boxer. When the office predictably denied the request within a week, Maverick prepared to sue.

In deploying the legal system, often used against Blacks, to assert his right to professionally fight white men in his home state, Harvey tread uncharted and dangerous territory, inviting the threats and assaults that attended Black men and women refusing to stay in their place. Physical harm always loomed but more common, even likely, was the economic retaliation of losing jobs and being denied credit in stores.

Harvey's family supported his quixotic lawsuit, but not without reservations. "We were kind of afraid for a while but we were with him all the way," his sister, Lottie, told a reporter years later.

Potential harm to the family appears to have spurred Harvey to move his family out of state. "From what I remember my mom telling me," Lymont Harvey says, "I think he moved us to California before the fight because of fear for the family."

To help fund the case, Maverick reached out to the state NAACP that, at its state convention in San Antonio, voted to underwrite $500 of court costs. He also assembled a diverse dream team of legal talent hailing from San Antonio in Bexar County. They included Harry Bellinger, a scion of one of San Antonio's most powerful Black families; two future judges and a future district attorney; and, most notably, Carlos Cadena, a legal scholar and future chief justice of the Fourth Court of Appeals.

On August 13, Maverick filed a lawsuit in the 126th District Court in Austin challenging the legality of banning professional boxing matches between white and Black boxers, calling it, "wholly unjust, arbitrary and capricious." The suit claimed that the law denied Harvey rights guaranteed by the Fourteenth Amendment to the Constitution as well as the Federal Civil Rights Act.

Maverick's decision to file the suit in state court instead of federal court met opposition from civil rights advocates, like the NAACP, and even by his own colleague, Cadena. All believed, with history as their guide, that minority plaintiffs had greater success at the federal level than in state courts, especially Southern state courts.

But Maverick's devotion to justice and Constitutional principles paralleled his love of his state. He wanted to show that Texas could do the right thing.

"We have a great Bill of Rights in the Texas Constitution of 1876 and no one has ever paid any attention to it," he wrote in some notes. "I do believe in State's Rights, but to have those you have to have State's Duties. Blacks, browns, poor whites in state courts always got the short end of the stick, historically, and that's why everybody went to the federal courts. But, hell, I love Texas. Why not have good Texas courts?"

AS HARVEY NAVIGATED the maze of the legal system, a world of opportunity was open for white boxers with similar ambitions, with fellow-Texan Reagan "Buddy" Turman a prime example. Born in the East Texas hamlet of Noonday in 1933, the same year of the birth of segregated boxing in Texas, Turman was a 6'1" young heavyweight with great promise.

He began chopping wood on the family farm when he was six, and not long after his family gathered around the radio to listen to the fights of one of their favorite boxers, Black phenom Joe Louis.

After a stint in the Navy, Turman came home, worked the oil fields and began his amateur boxing career. While building a record of 20–5–1, he developed what would be his most dangerous punch: the left hook.

Turman became Texas' amateur light-heavyweight champion. He had one goal, just like Sporty Harvey, and he wouldn't let anyone stand in his way to reach it: world heavyweight champion.

ON JANUARY 26, 1954, Maverick, Harvey and team walked into Judge Jack Roberts' 126th District Court seeking an order directing M.B. Morgan, the State Boxing Commissioner, to allow Harvey to fight any professional fighter, no matter his ethnicity. They also sought a ruling on the constitutionality of the segregated boxing law.

Testifying for the state, Morgan, 63, argued that banning the professional boxing contests between Blacks and whites prevented hostility and race riots and that the law should stand as a bulwark against those threats.

Morgan claimed "the people of Texas, from the conversation I have had with folks, are of the opinion that the customs and habits and traditions of the citizens of Texas are satisfied with our present law and think it would be best to keep the law on our books."

Contradicting Morgan's position, Maverick's witnesses included longtime Texas sportswriters who had attended countless mixed-race sporting events, including amateur boxing matches, without observing racial tension, much less violence, rising from the competition.

Then came the star of the proceeding. Wearing a dark, double-breasted suit and thick black-rimmed eyeglasses, Harvey said he would never have the chance in Texas to win a championship because of his race.

"The guys I want to fight I can't fight because I'm a Negro," Harvey testified, even though he worked out with white boxers and that had never caused any problems because of his race. He was treated well by the boxing community in San Antonio but had to drive a truck and handle freight to support his family. Harvey's household included his wife Hazel Lee, whom he met when she was at nursing school, and a growing brood eventually including four children.

Harvey couldn't get enough fights to make a living as a boxer because of the limitations placed on him.

"It helps to have an economic deprivation which, of course, we had here," wrote Maverick. "If Sporty could box he would make more money, thus, because he was Black he was being denied an equal opportunity to make a living." Maverick could attack an unconstitutional law by arguing that it denied Harvey grocery money to take care of his family.

Not much food landed on the table from his meager boxing earnings, unless it was food he caught with his hands. Once, he and some other fighters from San Antonio drove to Beeville for a four-fight card in a tent. The eight fighters were supposed to get a share of the gate. But the gate total was $11 to be divided between the fighters and a promoter. Having fought for $1.22 purses, Harvey and Tony Castillo, a San Antonio bantamweight, left the tent disgusted and hungry. They saw two turkeys wandering around. In their most vigorous workout of the day, Harvey and Castillo chased the turkeys around the tent until they each caught one to take home.

None of this would change until Harvey and other Black fighters could fight those who held championships and drew bigger gates and paydays: white fighters. Harvey now sat in court because he couldn't just wait around for that day to arrive.

There were two instances when Maverick feared Harvey's testimony would hurt his cause.

Wanting to show the absurdity that Harvey couldn't fight a white man in Laredo, Texas but could go across the border five miles in Nuevo Laredo, Mexico to fight the same white man—which Harvey had done—Maverick asked him, "Sporty, isn't it true that you boxed a white man in Nuevo Laredo, Mexico?"

The courtroom was silent and Maverick grew more uncomfortable with Harvey's silence. They'd rehearsed this but now Harvey appeared confused.

"Naw," he finally answered. "I didn't fight no white man—"

Maverick, not believing his ears, thought they'd get thrown out of court but Harvey continued, "—I boxed a Spaniard."

Laughter spilled out over the courtroom.

Under cross-examination, the assistant attorney general of Texas took notice of Harvey's thick eyeglasses and Maverick panicked again, worried that the glasses would allow the state to say that they were turning Sporty down because of his bad vision and not his race.

"Mr. Harvey," asked the assistant attorney general. "Because of those glasses, you can't see well, can you?"

Harvey answered, "I have perfect vision. I wear these eyeglasses for sport. That's why they call me Sporty."

He smiled and the courtroom laughed again.

"Sporty could play the fool," Maverick would say. "But the next minute break your heart."

The state used Harvey's subpar record as a fighter against him. Asked what his record was, Harvey said he was only "guessing" but that he'd won 18 out of 21 professional fights. The state countered, saying he had only seven wins in 17 fights and that his lack of talent was the barrier to his fighting for a championship.

Harvey was the only Black man in a courtroom filled with white men who were lawyers, judges, politicians, and journalists; men practicing their crafts and making a living in the professions they chose and wanted. All were gathered because the lone Black man in their presence was fighting for the right to do what they did, a right they took for granted: the opportunity to practice his craft and make a living in the profession of his choice.

Yet here he sat listening to these officials of the state in which he was born and raised talk publicly about how bad they thought he was at his craft; so bad, they claimed, that he should be denied the opportunity to see how far he could go. He was mocked for lacking skills and techniques by the very people denying him the opportunities to hone his skills and techniques.

Just two weeks earlier, two members of Harvey's legal team, Carlos Cadena and Gus Garcia, had argued a case that would make them the first Latino attorneys to win before the United States Supreme Court. The landmark *Hernandez v. Texas* ended the exclusion of Mexican Americans from jury pools based on the Fourteenth Amendment's protections for all nationalities, not just white and Black. Cadena now argued that Harvey's talent wasn't the issue, that in fact he was being denied the opportunity solely because of his race.

During the day's testimony, Judge Roberts consistently ruled with Harvey and against the state on objections about evidence. Signs pointed toward a victory. But on February 3 came heart-breaking news. Roberts ruled against Harvey and upheld the law, citing Harvey's losing record. His decision may have been swayed by electoral concerns.

A state district judge such as Roberts depended on the ballot for his position, in contrast to a federal judge appointed for life. Years later, when Roberts was a federal judge, he ran into Maverick and told him, "If I had been a federal judge when you brought the Harvey case before me, I would have held with that nigger boxer."

WHILE HARVEY WAS FACING a major setback, Buddy Turman, nicknamed "The Golden Boy from Noonday," got a boost in his quest for boxing glory. This came in the form of a man named Bobby Joe Manziel. The boxing promoter and wealthy oilman was impressed with what he saw in the anvil-of-a-hook on the Tyler product. Small and lithe, Manziel wore a signature fedora. Underneath was an angular face with thick eyebrows, mischievous eyes and tight smile, features that would be shared by his great-grandson, future Heisman Trophy winner, Johnny Manziel.

"You come with me and you'll become the heavyweight champion of the world," Manziel told Turman the first time they met (according to Joe Garner Turman, brother and biographer of Buddy). "You can train on my farm, and I'll set up a ring and everything else you need. I'll get you the best trainer available. Listen, I know a lot of people in the boxing world. I can get you the fights you need to move you toward becoming a top contender."

Brash, aggressive, and calculating, Manziel looked for the angles which would most quickly elevate him to the top of every endeavor. Manziel had originally moved to East Texas to wildcat oil wells. It was a $400 loan from boxing legend Jack Dempsey that allowed him to strike oil on the grounds of a Black Baptist church that showered both men in riches. Settling in Tyler, Manziel would own hotels, banks, other real estate, newspapers, fighting roosters and pilot his own plane after taking off from a runway on his farm. He was also a promoter who lost his license after accusations of fixing a professional wrestling match.

Turman signed a contract with Manziel on a chilly fall day. To bring Turman to the next level, Manziel hired a Black trainer named Robert "Cornbread" Smith, who fought in the 1930s and who'd worked the corners of world champions like Fritzie Zivic and Lew Jenkins. He now trained young fighters in a gym he owned above a liquor store in South Dallas.

Turman ended his last amateur fight with a first round knockout, and picked up right where he left off in his professional debut, on September 27, 1954, when he knocked Bobby Babcock off his feet three times en route to a unanimous decision. The referee for the fight was Manziel ally Jack Dempsey.

What Manziel couldn't bestow on Turman was patience. Just like the young boxer, Manziel was driven to reach the top rung fast.

In Turman's second fight against Max Baird, repeated left hooks knocked out the overmatched Baird in the second round and sent him to a hospital for observation. Then, in just his third professional fight, Manziel pitted Turman against Birmingham battler Oscar Pharo for the Southern Heavyweight Championship. Raising the ante, Manziel said that after Turman beat Pharo, he'd try to arrange a fight against the formidable Rocky Marciano. Turman lost to Pharo on points, and suddenly his way forward became unclear.

THOUGH LOSING IN JUDGE ROBERTS' COURT had been a crushing blow to Harvey's case, Maverick and his team felt that Roberts, consciously or not, set up Harvey for appeal. But Maverick had yet to receive the $500 promised by the state NAACP to cover state costs. He hurried out a letter to Thurgood Marshall, executive director of the NAACP Legal Defense Fund and future Supreme Court Justice, and within 72 hours had received the funds to help keep the case moving.

Harvey's appeal reached the Third Court of Civil Appeals on October 13, 1954. In the interim, on May 17, 1954, the U. S. Supreme Court's decision in *Brown v. Board of Education* ruled that racial segregation in public schools violated the Equal Protection Clause of the Fourteenth Amendment.

Against this backdrop of upheaval, Maverick asked the appeals court to consider sociological as well as legal reasons for overturning the ban on interracial prizefights.

"We have this nation holding itself up as a democracy to the colored peoples of the world," said Maverick, a gifted orator. "And yet we have this law here where a Negro man can't even have a professional fight with a white man."

On October 27, the Third Court of Appeals ruled in Harvey's favor by reversing the state district court's decision and sending it back to retrial. The court did not invalidate the 1933 law, supposedly because doing so also would have nullified the necessary parts of the law, such as requiring strict physical examinations for fighters and the licensing of fighters and managers.

The court dismissed the state's argument that mixed-race matches would lead to race riots, saying that, "Even if riotous conditions did result from mixed boxing exhibitions we doubt if this statute would be sustained by the Federal Supreme Court in view of language which we find in some of its opinions." The first of those opinions it cited was *Brown v. Board of Education*.

The thrust of the court's decision called for regulations so that mixed-race bouts would no longer be prohibited. On January 19, 1955, the Texas Supreme Court sustained the judgment of the appeals court, making it official: Sporty Harvey had just beaten the state of Texas.

After the decision, a jubilant Harvey said, "I'm going to really get started good in boxing now that I'm going to get my big chance."

JUST MINUTES INTO A BUDDY TURMAN FIGHT at the Dallas Sportatorium on February 10, 1955, Turman's vicious left hook staggered Bobby Babcock and left him covering up and clinching until the bell ended the round.

This fight suddenly had new stakes. It was announced that the winner would go on to challenge Sporty Harvey—now known far and wide as a trailblazer in the courts—in two weeks. In the last few months since Turman had stumbled against the hulking Oscar Pharo, he had put on ten pounds and cut a more dangerous figure than ever. This fight with Babcock could be a stepping-stone to Turman's redemption and his biggest spotlight yet.

Just 55 seconds into the second round, another Turman left hook drove Babcock into the ropes as a follow-up right to his jaw knocked him out. Ringside, Turman was swarmed by a crowd of more than 200. Babcock lay on the mat with only his doctor and trainer, and a few concerned friends. It would be fifteen minutes before Babcock got to his feet.

During Harvey's battle with the state, Turman, who'd idolized Joe Louis, sparred with Black fighters and had his Black trainer in his corner, voiced his support for Harvey's case and offered to fight him if it would help. He told his guru Manziel, "Since I'm a white Texan, I'll volunteer to fight Sporty. This will force the issue with the Texas State Legislature."

But Manziel, the savvy promoter and businessman, wanted Buddy to fight Harvey for a more practical reason. "He knew the fight would generate a lot of publicity for Buddy, and he would make boxing history in Texas," recalls Joe Garner Turman. "This would move Buddy along in the boxing world."

Sporty Harvey had scored a chance to follow his dream, and now had drawn Buddy Turman, a human threshing machine.

Turman was fast, with astonishing power in both hands, and a bob and weave later admired by Rocky Marciano, the heavyweight champion of the world. Many experts saw in Turman the potential to become the future champion. Dempsey said Turman was "the best young prospect I've seen in the last twenty years."

He had movie star looks and newspapers called him Handsome Buddy Turman or Handsome Heavyweight Buddy Turman, as if that were his given name. (In stories and headlines, Harvey's name was often preceded or followed by "Negro" as in "Negro Sporty Harvey..." or "...Harvey, a San Antonio Negro boxer...")

The irony was that Harvey took on the state of Texas for the right to fight white boxers so that he might have a chance to contend for titles. Now the manager of a white boxer wanted to fight Harvey to expedite his star fighter's title chances. Harvey looked to be a sacrificial lamb to a white fighter, a killer in the ring whose opponents had to peel themselves off the canvas.

THE WEEK OF THE FIGHT, Sporty, true to his nickname and reputation, arrived in Dallas wearing a light tan coat, brown pants, a pink shirt, purple tie, robin's egg blue hat and brown suede shoes.

In less than two weeks after the Harvey-Turman fight, Elvis Presley would perform there for the first time. But on the night of February 24, 1955 Sporty Harvey was the headliner for the first time in his career. Walking from his dressing room to the ring and the biggest spotlight of his life, a sweeping glance of the arena would have informed him that half of the audience, if not more, were Black.

Extra security was on hand, just in case the defense made at trial by M.D. Morgan and the state of Texas for segregated boxing came true in the form of a riot.

Years later, Turman would tell the *Dallas Morning News*, "Oh, sure, people were saying this or that might happen at the fight but it didn't seem like any big deal to me. I'd sparred a lot with Black fighters. I was just thinking about trying to win. That whole thing about not allowing Blacks and whites to fight seemed stupid. But it was that way all over the South."

The chasm in talent between Turman and Harvey was seen by some as so wide as to render the fight absurd. *San Antonio Express* sports editor Dick Peebles, who'd testified on Harvey's behalf in court, wrote that the idea that Harvey could make a good fight of it was like thinking "a horse that draws a milk wagon is going to win the Kentucky Derby." He thought that Harvey's presence was merely a sign of the promoters "trying to capitalize on the novelty of a white fighting a Negro."

Attached to Turman's future as a fighter were adjectives like "promising" and "up and coming" which had never been used to describe Harvey. Fighting is what Turman did for a living. Fighting is what Harvey did when he could.

Turman, with the backing of a multi-millionaire manager who believed he'd win the world title, had trained daily by running four miles, chopping wood and sparring 12 rounds. All the more intimidating, the immortal Jack Dempsey was said to own a "piece" of Turman's burgeoning career and future.

Harvey, when not driving or handling freight, trained by running or going to a gym, of which the most iconic was the San Fernando Street Gym, on the western edge of San Antonio. There, he'd work the heavy and speed bags and spar under the eye of well-regarded but relatively obscure trainer, Jimmy Scarmozi. Harvey continued his workout regimen the day before the big fight.

Harvey had boxed only three times during his court fight with the state and had lost twice. At 29 years of age, Harvey weighed in at a "ponderous" 196 pounds, heavier than he'd ever been. Turman salivated for an easy match. According to a story the day before the fight on WBAP-TV of Fort Worth, Turman "says he is in good condition and can take the Negro without trouble."

At the opening bell, Harvey moved towards a 21-year-old, 177-pound dynamo who in two of his last three fights had sent one man to the hospital and left another unable to get up for a quarter of an hour.

The first two rounds were uneventful as Harvey and Turman felt each other out but in the third, Turman's advantage became clear as he snapped jabs, bobbing and weaving while trying to set Harvey up for a knockout punch. With less than ten seconds remaining in the round, he decked Harvey with the notorious sledgehammer of a left hook. The hit on Harvey was called "thunderous" by one beat reporter.

A former opponent had said of Turman's power, "When he hits you, you get so weak you can't stand up."

At the count of eight, a weakened Harvey, struggling to get up, was saved by the bell ending the round. One minute later, when the bell rang for the fourth, Harvey was rising to his feet, ready to brawl. "[Harvey] appeared confident in the face of all odds at all times," reporter Mark Batterson had marveled, "and you finally had to get around to admiring him very much for this quality." Harvey ended up against the ropes, "eyes glazed and knees sagging," as the bell gave him yet another chance.

Knowing that Turman was best while fighting long range where he could jab and plant his feet for his power punches—especially that murderous left hook—Harvey stayed close, smothering him and pounding blows to the body.

This confused the younger fighter who was inexperienced in handling the pressure of infighting.

In the fifth round—already a dramatically longer match than many had predicted—Harvey continued carrying the fight to Turman, forcing him against the ropes, smothering him and belting him with hard body shots; fighting not as someone who didn't want to lose but who believed he could win. Desperation circled Turman. Twice in the fifth round, Turman was nabbed for hitting after the ref called a break. In the sixth, Harvey dominated, sending Turman "coasting and retreating" away from him, as described by Turman's hometown paper. Each man had to catch his breath in the seventh.

But a Turman combo in the eighth signaled the end. Turman dug a left into Harvey's gut before driving a right cross to the head, sending Harvey crashing hard to the mat.

"One! Two!"

IN MAKING THIS A FIGHT for eight rounds, Harvey had surprised almost everybody at ringside.

"Three! Four! Five!"

He'd given the customers their money's worth, a chance to see history and a good fight.

"Six! Seven! Eight!"

Eight. This was the eighth round and two remained. If a man is going to headline his first ten-round fight, he should finish it.

That's when the Sportatorium shook. Because Sporty stood up.

Buddy Turman went on the assault, intent on ending the fight in a knockout. He left his opponents crumpled up in a corner, and this showboat wasn't going to go the distance with him. Hell no,

Turman wasn't going to let that happen. He ripped a left hook into Harvey's face that banged him to the canvas for the third time.

Then the roof might as well have come off the place: Harvey stood up again.

As the round ended, Harvey pressured Turman, hammering punches and trying to pummel his way to an upset win. Maybe the world was just using him, like others had said, but he'd show the world.

Harvey kept charging into the ninth, shocking Turman with powerful combos to the head, leaving the favored fighter drained. In the tenth round, Turman flicked jabs and crosses, wanting to unload another left hook as he "tried for the kill." But it didn't happen.

The final bell rang, and Harvey was standing, face-to-face, toe-to-toe with his opponent.

ON A 1978 VISIT TO SAN ANTONIO 22 years later, Sporty Harvey, now 52 with a face lined with more wrinkles but his still-unmistakable smile flashing, sat down with reporter Dan Cook. He recalled segregated life in San Antonio during the 1950s, perhaps throwing in some hyperbole.

"Sitting in the back of the bus was just a pride thing and Black people got used to so it wasn't any big deal. It wasn't, that is, unless the back of the room was crowded. The real problem, in those days, was finding downtown public toilets and getting something to eat out of a restaurant's rear back door. After I got everything changed, me and Maury Maverick Jr., I caught a city bus and plopped right in the first seat."

When Harvey returned to San Antonio over the years to visit his mother and friends, you'd never know what he'd be driving. One time it was a camper. Another year it was a baby blue Cadillac.

Harvey told Cook he was going to see Maury Maverick while in town. "He might need me to help bust down some more color lines."

As for the fears, looking back to 1955, about what his ground-breaking boxing match between a Black man and white man would stir up? The race riots these pugilists would ignite for practicing their craft? Police had reported only one disturbance in the stands. A fight between two white men.

Harvey could look back at his big fight with pride and some lingering bitterness. After the last bell rang, Turman won a unanimous decision by wide margins on the scorecards of the referee and two judges. But the amazing fact was that Sporty Harvey was still on his feet. What had knocked him down again and again was not as powerful as what lifted him up. And what lifted him up, leaving him standing, was a strength scorecards could never gauge.

The older Harvey believed his technical loss in the ring was payback for taking on and beating the state in court. "They got back at me and gave the decision to Buddy."

"The only thing I know is that I did my best," he had told his wife Hazel after the fight. "I thought I put up a good fight."

HARVEY AND TURMAN WOULD MEET in the ring again. In a June 1955 rematch in Tyler, Turman knocked Harvey down two more times before winning on another unanimous decision. After his two fights with Turman, Harvey would fight ten more times, losing eight of them. Harvey never fought for the Texas state title. The closest he'd come to the world heavyweight championship was sparring with Sonny Liston and Joe Frazier. He settled into a career working for the Jones Tire Company in Los Angeles.

As for Buddy Turman, he would later reflect on the fight. "I was delighted to have an opportunity to demonstrate my attitude toward integration. I felt, and still do, that sports is a field where each man is proven by his feats and not by his social or ethnic background."

Late summer of 1955, in his tenth fight, Turman outpointed "Red" Worley for the Texas heavyweight title. Turman also would never fight for the world heavyweight title but in November of 1960 and March of 1961 he fought light-heavyweight champion, Archie Moore, losing both fights on unanimous decisions. Their first fight, in Dallas, was close enough that Turman thought he'd won. He wasn't the only one. In his dressing room, afterwards, Turman was visited by a young heavyweight who'd recently won his first professional fight.

"You beat that old man," said 18-year-old Cassius Clay to Turman.

Turman primarily would be remembered in Texas boxing circles as Sporty Harvey's partner in history. No footage or photographs of their groundbreaking bout have surfaced.

IN THE SUMMER OF 1997, Maury Maverick called me to ask a favor. I was a columnist and reporter for the *San Antonio Express-News*, thanks to Maverick bringing me to the attention of some editors. At that paper, I would become the first African American on the editorial board of any San Antonio daily, as well as the first metro columnist.

"Kiddo," he said, his nickname for anyone younger than him. "Do you think you could drive me to Sporty Harvey's funeral on Thursday?"

Harvey had died in Los Angeles from heart disease on June 5, 1997 at the age of 71. His wife, Hazel, had promised his mother that when he died she'd bring him home to San Antonio.

After a long career as a civil rights attorney, including a 3–0 record arguing before the U.S. Supreme Court, Maverick, now 76, was penning a regular Sunday column for the *Express-News*.

Maverick was one of the few white people in the predominantly Black church we entered. Hard of hearing, throughout the service, he'd turn to me and ask, "Huh? What did he say?" or "What did she say?"

Inside the funeral program, a picture of Harvey in boxing gear sat above the Samuel Ellsworth Kiser poem, "The Fighter" which ends with the lines:

My victories are small and few,

It matters not how hard I strive,

Each day the fight begins anew,

But fighting keeps my hopes alive.

Not long after the trailblazing fight of 1955, Charley Eskew in the *Austin-American Statesman* had already begun to mark Harvey's legacy not as a boxer, but as a fighter. He made the case that despite his middling record overall, Harvey would be voted into a hypothetical Texas sports hall of fame "for making his greatest stand outside the ring and, as a result, bringing life again to Texas boxing."

"He took it upon himself," says Dr. Francine Romero. "There are so many people who no one hears about who challenge big things. Because of them, we can say, 'hey, it's starting to crumble a little bit. You can see it happening.'"

Harvey v. Morgan was cited when a similar law forbidding mixed-race boxing matches in Louisiana was overturned by a federal court in 1958. "You don't know how many people it affected," writes Romero of *Harvey*. Sporty Harvey's breakthroughs joined a slew of events still brewing—such as the campaigns of 1960s Birmingham and Selma—that helped dismantle segregation and establish political and economic justice through smaller, specific, and achievable remedies.

Harvey and his family were proud of what he'd done. The children wrote school reports about how their father had "knocked out" Jim Crow.

"I think he did a great thing at that time of his life and with what was going on in this world," says Lymont Harvey of his father. "I'm very proud of him and glad he stood up and spoke his mind and that people listened and agreed and he won. By the time the [Turman] fight started, he'd won and opened the doors for other people."

 279

After the funeral's minister eulogized Harvey for his courage in challenging a racist law, he asked if anyone wanted to come up and say a few words. Without hesitating, Maverick rose from the seat, excusing himself as he eased past others in the pew to get to the aisle. As he approached the pulpit, some in the church recognized him and smiled or pointed toward him.

"I'm Maury Maverick Jr. and I had the honor of representing Sporty in his lawsuit against the state of Texas," he said as people nodded in appreciation.

He recounted the summer day they met, when Harvey strolled into his office with a smile and a mission. As Maverick spoke, his rumbling drawl picked up pace and volume as it rolled over a growing chorus of "Amen!" "Tell it!" and "Preach!"

"I had two college degrees," Maverick thundered. "But that Black man…" he pointed to Harvey's gray casket, "with a sixth grade education taught me more than I taught him!"

When he finished, there was applause, more Amens! and shouts of Yes! Yes! As the lawyer walked past the casket, many in the congregation were doing what Sporty Harvey did against the state of Texas and Buddy Turman.

They stood up.

Cary Clack is a native of San Antonio and was a columnist for the *San Antonio Express-News* from 1994 to 2011, where he is now a columnist and editorial writer. Inducted into the Texas Institute of Letters in 2017, he is the author of a collection of his columns, *Clowns and Rats Scare Me*, and is currently editing what will be the first anthology of Black Texas writers for a new book series as part of the Wittliff Collections, to be published by Texas A &M University Press.

The Bubble of a Dream

PETER BROMKA

FROM MEDIUM • NOVEMBER 23, 2020

A dream doesn't make a sound when it dies. With no reason to exclaim, the aspiration simply slips away with a sickening silence.

January 19, 2020
Exhausted and stunned, I stumble forward reluctantly.

Dehydrated and sore from having just battled 26.2 miles of windswept streets, I pause in panic, fearful of moving forward because once I leave this chute it's over. Accepting a finisher's medal will mean this dream is done.

Salt covered and in a daze, I stare out in search of support, but all I find are the faces of fans pressed up against the fence of the 2020 Houston Marathon straining to find their loved ones. They have no idea how much my world has just altered.

Having failed to qualify for the USA Olympic Marathon Trials by a handful of seconds, for the third time, I fight back tears with slow breaths that decompress me into the air outside the bubble of purpose and passion I've lived within the past two years.

Two years earlier…
My mind raced to make sense of how life had just changed while my tired body rested in the seat of a plane rising gently up over a setting Northern California sun.

To this day I was a steadily improving amateur marathoner moving up year-by-year amid the masses. I'd sought and gained meaning from breaking one threshold after another. An enjoyable hobby that had brought me from Boston to Chicago to New York. But I'd begun to fear that my ascent was approaching its peak.

I'd broken 3, then 2:50, 2:40, and even 2:30. But as my ability increased I began to question the value of shaving another few seconds off my personal best. I'd enjoyed moving up the ranks of nonprofessionals, but questioned the value in dedicating so much time to a hobby.

Running 2:29 felt like an arrival; a distinction understood by fellow runners. A subsequent 2:28 was a feather in my cap, but did this mean I'd reached the end of the road? Since what difference would running 2:27 make? How much could a 2:26 or even 2:25 alter my reality? I'd wondered.

But we had just run 2:23.

My teammates and I had tossed caution to the wind that morning in Sacramento—and it'd worked.

"*BROMKA WHAT ARE YOU DOING?!*" A friend had shrieked in alarm at halfway. But we'd finished what we started, only slowing slightly by the end. This leap forward moved my teammates and me from the no man's land of amateur marathoning onto the brink of sub-elite distinction: *The 2020 USA Olympic Marathon Trials.*

"*Are you gonna try for it?*" my wife Julia questioned before I'd even had time to conceive of what "it" would demand. The prospect of earning entry to the dream competition two years away made my mind race and stomach churn. Running the required time of 2:19:00 felt nearly unfathomable.

Almost. But that glimmer of a chance held my eye.

Earning the opportunity to run in a race where the top-3 qualify for the Tokyo Olympics felt like a goal worthy of engrossing my heart and sapping my body. The problem was I had no idea what it would take to even have a chance to try. Sure, in theory, it would simply be more of the same. More training, more focus, more intent. But that sounded too simple.

Failure was probable.

Injury was likely.

The only guarantee was weariness. The act of even trying consistently for something this difficult for that long would demand more, for longer, than I've ever attempted.

Raised a runner, I've known the sport since my earliest memory. My father brought me along to road races as an infant and mentioned history's greatest athletes as typical dinner time conversation. As a teen, I wanted to be fast, just like all children exploring their newfound strength, but I was mostly marginal.

By college, I was all consumed. Each day was spent in the spellbound state of a student-athlete: the imbalanced excitement of amateurism. Trying to cram more of everything you love than can fit into each day. Foolishly believing that if you just "want it" more you'll be better. Sadly, that mostly led to injury and heartbreak. Led to forcing in a sport that demands patience.

Such is youth.

All of that felt like a lifetime ago because it was. Over a decade gone by, a career, a wife, and now a son added to life's juggle, I was concerned about becoming all consumed by an outlandish ambition.

Dreaming this grandly felt almost childish. But reimagining myself this late in my athletic life was mesmerizing. Improving these past years was one thing, but qualifying among the nation's best, while approaching forty, offered a chance for a crisp title of distinction: "Olympic Trials Qualifier." That's the type of thing you could be remembered by forever. But what would such a dream even demand?

I poured everything I understood of the endeavor into an essay titled, "Burn the Boat," an homage to an idea I'd read about that the only way to achieve something heroic is to eliminate all other options. Part road map ahead, part love letter to the sport, part ode to the doubters—I explained to the world, as well as myself, the ridiculousness of the dream in detail. Cutting another 11 seconds per mile from my pace was unlikely at best, harmful at worst. I needed to own the improbability of success to prevent others' doubts from dissuading me once I begin.

With my intent posted for the world, and before I understood the significance of our commitment, my teammates and I were forging a path toward an attempt to qualify a year later at the 2018 California International Marathon.

Stepping into this dream out of curiosity, over the following two years it would impact nearly each of my days, affect almost all my relationships, and leave an indelible impression on my identity.

Spring 2018

Anxious, I began the final training run of my week at a shuffle. By the time I beeped my watch to finish, I'd stare at the 12-miler with pride for what it completed: my first 100-mile week.

And I wasn't broken!

Of course, the body doesn't understand exact mileage. An injury can occur anytime, not simply while passing an arbitrary empirical threshold. Having run for over twenty years, I'd never accumulated triple-digits in a week.

But I'd need to.

Though our qualifying attempt was still eight months away, I was already in debt. My fastest teammates had either enormous talent or years of accumulated mileage. I had only modest amounts of either. Unable to rewrite my genetics, I needed to increase my training load as fast as possible without injury. It's the easiest mantra for a runner to say, such an elusive line to actually walk.

The essence of this dream was calculated risk.

A late Sunday in April, walking out of historic Hayward Field having just finished in 3rd place in the Eugene half-marathon, I was filled with subdued satisfaction. It was a good day, the plan was working, but we would need more.

The lesson I was learning was simple: running more makes running easier. That morning I'd felt more comfortable at a faster pace than ever before. An ego boost, but only a small step towards the goal.

A 2:19 Trials Qualifying marathon is two 69:30 half-marathons back-to-back. Ideally, you'd be able to pass through the first one well within yourself. At ease and breathing calmly. Having just run barely a minute better than that pace, 68:23, I was proud, but it only granted me marginal self-belief.

Pulling my phone from my bag revealed a text from my dad, *"Today was a great start toward December. Now just believe and do the work and savor every time you run."* A compliment wrapped in context. The day mattered mostly as momentum for the future.

Our endeavor in the fall was far from certain. We had half a year to get comfortable at 5:18 per mile pace. Though it might be possible, it was unlikely to ever be comfortable.

We had work to do.

Fall 2018

"Marathon training is kind of a trust fall," Patrick philosophized.

A methodical man of understated Southern manners, Patrick doesn't overstate or theorize indulgently like I do.

My closest training partner, I wouldn't be where I was without him. When we met years ago I was a marathoner, but I wasn't pushing hard. Participating, but not truly testing. I'd do easy long runs and a workout here or there. That isn't Patrick.

The man is a metronome.

He ran fairly well as an amateur in 2010.

Then slightly better in 2011.

And even better in 2012.

His progress continued each subsequent year.

Averaging over 4,000 miles annually for the past decade, he gets in a 10-11 mile run each day. Everyday. Regardless of life's bumps or curves.

I took his metaphor for our training as an omen, even he understood that this attempt for the Trials would be a leap. He'd been dusting me in workouts, but calculations for race day left him uncertain. We'd repeatedly turned up the dials on our training, but lacked the data to know how all of this effort and fatigue would translate into the final miles of a marathon.

Ten miles at qualifying pace after a ten-mile warmup gave us confidence, but how much?

Twenty miles at our previous race pace completed while chatting, felt great, but what did it mean?

I knew that no one workout signals the sum of a training block, but if I couldn't breathe calmly at qualifying pace it would be impossible to enter the race with belief. It's easy to explain failure in hindsight, to reason it away in the aftermath. What's difficult is anticipating being broken by a dream and still continuing on.

One Month till CIM 2018

The pressure of this endeavor was threatening to break me before the race even began.

"*What if I fail?*" I wondered.

As other marathons took place across the country and dozens of talented runners I knew failed to qualify it framed the difficulty of this dream. If these men, athletes who've beaten me on every occasion, couldn't even crack 2:20, what hope did I have to even finish the race at such an absurd pace?

Was I wasting my time reaching for this idolized echelon?

I didn't know. But I did feel strong.

I was able to shift gears with abandon and stretch out my stride further than ever before. This fitness felt incredible, but if I couldn't run below 2:19, was it all meaningless?

Such thoughts were compounding the existing fatigue from months of high mileage, sending me towards sadness.

Maybe I should simply play it safe, I considered.

Surely I could shatter my personal best. I could surge into the finish with satisfaction. The guys attempting to qualify would be off in the distance, but that would be okay, right?

Sadly not.

"*That's not what got you here,*" I remembered. I'd announced my goal to everyone I knew because if the dream was beyond me, maybe I could cross over to it on a bridge of belief built on the hopes and dreams of others. This attempt felt wholly outside of my experience. But that was the point.

I must endeavor to qualify because of what the threshold signifies—that I was among a group who are able. If I aspired to be with them I could not hide in the safe harbor of myself.

Like when you step right up to the edge of a cliff above the ocean and force yourself to peer down, I had to own the intent of this endeavor or it would end in regret.

Resigned to fear, which seemed certain, I swore off caution, which I could not afford.

The 1st attempt—The California International Marathon

Stepping to the line I was filled with a good fear. Though not quite at Patrick's fitness level I would follow him until I faltered. There were simply too many unknowns to go on this journey alone.

As the sun began to rise, a year removed from the race that changed how we thought of ourselves as runners, we were about to step up and hurl a half-court shot, together. If last year we reached the logical limit of ourselves as aging amateurs, this past year had been an exploration of how far we could make it if we truly dared to dream.

We were about to find out.

"*Crack!*" the starter pistol fired, and we were off in a stampede. Having raced a dozen marathons previously, the intensity of this attempt was unlike anything I'd ever experienced. A pack of so many men extended right to the edge of their ability, aligned in the same pursuit. Many of us would fail, that truth was understood. The point was we were there to try.

5:16
5:17
5:07
5:14
5:14
5:12
5:18
5:15

Splits are flying by faster than I'd ever experienced before. Having raced this course twice, I was experiencing it in an entirely new way. Like playing your favorite record at double speed, each rise and roll sent my breath gasping.

"*We're doing this!*" I celebrated internally, even as I understood that the true measure of a marathon wouldn't begin for an hour. Sure you can tuck away seconds under pace early on, but it's crushingly easy to hand back minutes in the end.

Rising up a slight incline into a slanting sun, my heart rate began to feel like an engine revving off its block. "Too hot" I cautioned. Panicked, I attempted to understand why the pack around me was surging now.

"Our splits are fine, no need to accelerate!" I whined inside, but this horde of humanity wasn't dictated by my desires.

5:11—a totally respectable mile, only to get dropped by the pack.

I was pissed.

Alone.

And over an hour from the finish.

"Shit. Shit," my wife muttered as Patrick traveled past her without a sign of me alongside.

Here I came up the road ten seconds later. How do you encourage an athlete as he begins to slip?

"*YOU GOT IT! COME ON PETER YOU GOT IT BABE!*" she screamed, I could tell she was hollering hoping to make it true. I couldn't spare the energy to acknowledge her encouragement, but I was still traveling at a rapid rate.

The final nine miles of a marathon are chapters of descending discomfort. The obstacles to running fast begin to compound as the body's temperature rises, the muscles dehydrate, and sugar levels fall off a cliff.

Not a single step of these miles would be easy, but I still had a chance.

5:20

"*Shit, there it is, over pace.*" It's the split I'd been dreading for a year. What will I do once I'm finally confronted with the threshold of failure? I'd wondered for 52 weeks.

The only thing there was to do: anchor and re-anchor my mind forward a block at a time to compel my body to continue.

This is where marathoners give up. Where defeat is so understandable it's almost assumed. In the final few miles, a marathoner's stride becomes taut. While before their body bounced and hung in the air, it now hits and jolts against the ground. My heart rate peaked as my stride began to shorten.

With close to a thousand steps per mile, the sensation of slowing from the qualifying pace of 5:18 per mile to a pace that is too slow, 5:25 per mile, was nearly imperceptible. The difference was only inches. It's each stride lasting simply a moment less. The cruelty of distance running: the difference was slight, but the distinction was significant.

Seeking to distract my mind from such mathematics, I focused on the truth that a friend had imparted:

"*Run fast because you can,*" she'd urged.

At the final stage of a race, there is no strategy. There is only effort. What's required is the audacity to check and recheck the empty bank account of your ability, to scour for any final deposits until the finish.

Nearing the final bend I understood that I was slowing. The past year of effort might not get me to the Trials this day, but I was sprinting down the streets of Sacramento faster and with more inspiration than ever before.

There's a cruel finality to a marathon run right at your edge, that after over two hours of running your mind can barely accept the challenge of the final few minutes.

It simply feels too difficult to grasp.

All the while your legs continue to churn, repeating on the flywheel you started before sunrise.

Turning the final bend to the finish my knees drove and back arched to reveal the clock having just rolled past 2:19. The qualifier was gone, but I was about to break 2:20. A time that only shortly ago would have felt unimaginable.

Embracing Patrick, he'd done it. He was a 2:17 marathoner and a qualifier for the 2020 Olympic Trials a year later in Atlanta.

Embracing Julia we simply sobbed. From sadness, from happiness, from pride, a bittersweet cocktail of them all intertwined. Arms wrapped around her, head hung forward, my tears dropped straight to the cement. Too exhausted, invigorated and inspired inside to worry about how I looked on the outside.

This dream brought me further this day than ever before. This dream took more from me the past year than I'd previously known I could give. Though not yet at their external standard, I was now a runner fully reinvented from my former self.

After taking moments to breathe I checked my phone. Scrolling across hundreds of texts, from congratulations to condolence, I stopped on one from a runner friend: "I'm missing out! *Let's go get that 2:18:59 together!!*"

A smile creased across my face as I realized the truth that had become obvious to everyone: this dream was just beginning…

Spring 2019

Approaching the 123rd Boston Marathon I felt unexpectedly light and excited. While ordinarily racing in Boston demands pressure and sacrifice, this time I was doing so with my focus set elsewhere, on another attempt at the Trials qualifier that coming December. So now I was somehow able to run America's oldest marathon without the usual burden of expectation.

Like an orbital slingshot, when they direct a rocket around a planet in order for it to pick up speed, I was aiming at this Boston excited to race, but mostly focused on using it to gain fitness en route to another flat course attempt in Sacramento.

"Heck of a workout this morning! Take confidence from this!" a friend texted after a morning in which I'd run four times four miles at close to my half marathon best pace. We were two months out from Boston and the splits I was running barely made sense, but they were not what I was focused on. I was simply attempting to keep up with my teammates. They were pulling me to personal best efforts weekly while I was just hoping to contribute to our collective goal of winning the 2019 team title in Boston.

The team competition is scored by the lowest total time from a team's top three finishers. As a group of amateurs, we'd supported each other in this exhausting hobby for years on end and figured we might as well try and earn a trophy together in the process.

By the time it was over I ended up finishing 1st for the team, 33rd in the race, and we won the team title together. Improving my Boston best by over five minutes somehow felt like a sideshow, a bonus, a supplement to the main affair.

I had seven months to prepare for my final attempt at the OTQ.

Summer 2019

"It takes an amazing amount of confidence in your condition, and belief in yourself, to rest."

Ryan Hall, America's fastest marathoner, said this in the latter half of his career after he'd broken himself repeatedly. His wisdom was gained through years spent not exhibiting such self-confidence.

For the half-year preceding my second attempt I aimed to emulate his intent, not his actions. I was in a circling pattern, an arc of training intended to ascend without overextending. A balance of strain and ease. It was a tricky tiptoe to walk when your mind simply wants to dive in.

Though my body was in a holding pattern, my identity continued to be absorbed by the pursuit of the dream.

"*How's training?!*" was friends' most common question. They understood that each of my days was marked in relation to a future date. And I began to notice that the goal served as both a sword and a shield in my daily life. It offered excitement to attack each day and braced my ego when I felt vulnerable.

Early one summer morning as I walked off the sky bridge onto a 737 aircraft to fly in coach across the country I was confronted with self-doubt as I encountered the 1st Class cabin.

Though subtle, I sensed their superiority.

Though unstated, I assumed their success.

If they have all of this, the wealth required to fly in such luxury, what do I have? I wondered.

My OTQ chase.

The pursuit of this goal, with its resulting strength and focus, had come to define my self-worth. I was proud of my pursuit. My identity consumed not just by being a runner, but by being someone committed to finding more speed each day.

Maybe he's an executive? I'm a marathoner.

Maybe he drives a Tesla? I've run 2:19.

Though I understood such judgment was petty and insignificant, I couldn't stop myself. I was consumed by a dream that I stumbled upon at a moment I'd been seeking meaning.

As a working professional, running was not my job. The main hours of my days were dedicated to earning a living, providing for a family. But after a decade as a business consultant, I'd begun to question the true meaning of my work. White-collar, professional service is a prudent pursuit that often lacks emotion and consequence.

As an amateur marathoner, I'd stumbled upon depths of personal meaning, vivid physical experience, and a rich international community, which had eluded me in the professional world. Sure, this pursuit was all for fun. But, decades removed from my earliest athletic endeavors, I'd begun to question if these games we play are in fact the essence of who we are.

With less than a year to go before the Trials, I wasn't the only amateur athlete attuned to this dream. A swelling crowd of men and women across the country had declared their intent to chase the OTQ. Already the largest field of qualifiers ever, the 2020 Olympic Marathon Trials was shaping up to be momentous. Though only the top-3 from each race earn Olympic entry, hundreds now saw the pursuit of qualifying as a life-affirming pursuit. But for me, it already felt like an old foe.

I would begin this fall as a dad approaching middle age who was faster and better prepared than ever before. If this was a form of mid-life crisis, it felt incredible.

The only thing to do then was begin.

Fall 2019
The 12 weeks between Labor Day and December's California International Marathon frame the fall as if the season was designed for runners to excel. If last year's attempt was a half-court shot that could have banked in on a fluke, this year's race was a 3-pointer. Like I was coming off a screen and sliding deliberately to a trusted spot behind the arc, I was waiting to receive an outlet pass that I knew I could hit, but was far from certain.

35 days before CIM
101 miles in 6 days. Two workouts faster than ever before.

Still, I was sad.

It was probably just fatigue. I was depressing my body with daily training. And by caring so much about something I couldn't control. It hadn't gotten any easier over the past year. If anything it was getting worse as the deadline approached.

21 days before CIM

"*What does that mean?*" I wondered. We'd just ran 16 miles at qualifying pace and it hardly felt hard.

"*I wish we could just do it right here, on our practice route,*" I told a teammate. But of course, that's not how the marathon works. Race day involves so many more variables than a practice run.

I attempted to appreciate the simple beauty of being this able. The journey of forming my body into something that can sustain at a previously unimaginable pace. The plan was working.

But it's those final miles that make the Marathon.

One day till CIM

"*I'll go 14-16, then roll-off,*" Patrick confirmed. He was there to pace several of us, and though his presence would be a comfort, he'd be gone by the time the real work started.

My father was there as well.

The pieces and people were in place for a great day. It was time to execute.

"*You'll need to finish it,*" I repeated to myself softly. There's a chasm between ability and belief, a divide that's not always clear how to cross. Sometimes it's something you step over without hardly noticing, "*Oh look, I did that!*" you delight in hindsight. Other times the span to overcome feels never-ending as if tiptoeing out into space blindfolded, continuing on faith alone.

At 38 years old I felt stronger than ever before, but reaching the finish line under 2:19 would take an extra leap.

The 2nd attempt—The California International Marathon 2019

The starter pistol cracked and we were off.

The most startling sensation was the size of the pack surrounding us. My teammates and I were engulfed in a mass of humanity—over a hundred men were rising and rolling the California hills in unison. A mass of Trials hopefuls much larger than previous years. Some settled, many stressed, it was early still and the breathing around me was already audible. I admired these men for dreaming, for arriving on the day prepared to try, but we had too far to go to be straining just yet.

"*Climb the ladder*," I reminded myself. Fearing I might obsess about the final miles and make a mistake before I arrived there, I settled on this mantra to keep my mind on the moment at hand. After all, you can't climb to the top of a ladder without stepping up the bottom rungs first. My mind screamed for the chance to take on the final miles where I had failed last year, but it'd have to wait for now.

Halfway—we were 23 seconds under qualifying pace.

The middle miles can gnaw at your psyche, twisting you into unusual versions of yourself.

"*Let's do this motherfucker!*" I snarled to a guy next to me after Patrick had rolled off. My mind was cycling through a carousel of emotions: excitement, fear, sadness, and anger. But no amount of trash-talking the marathon will have any effect. You simply do what you can to get yourself through.

Approaching the final 10k, moving faster, and feeling better than ever before, my mind was consumed by its arrival into the moment that it had fixated upon for months.

But my body was beginning to ache.

Muscle soreness is expected, what concerned me was the feeling I was being baked inside. It was the humidity, uncharacteristic for this wine region, that was softening my resolve. Not a sharp pain, but a woozy sensation of intoxicating systemic fatigue.

Expecting to suffer, I'd buttressed my mind in preparation. Two years in the making, I'd finally arrived at the moment I'd written about so long ago.

The moment I'd warned myself and others might be too much.

I had the chance that others envied.

"*They all wish they were here*," I reminded myself.

"*We're all rooting for you. You're a mini-celebrity over here.*" A friend had messaged me from New York the week before. I'd been overcome with emotion. These men, many I don't even know, cared about my success.

Why?

Maybe they've read my writing? Maybe they've followed my progress? Why were they so invested in my success?

I was one of the few left from my generation still fighting for more speed. Still believing their fastest days are ahead. If I could, maybe they could have, or even still can. Their care for me means I could not indulge in self-sorrow. This moment was my opportunity.

But all the well wishes in the world wouldn't close these final miles for me.

The final 5k I was surging, passing people, but something didn't feel quite right. Glancing at my watch, the status was grim. Like attempting to reconcile a stack of bills with a budget that just won't balance, I was slipping back seconds to the standard with too few to spare.

"*WAKE UP! You need to fucking face it!*" I implored myself. I felt better than ever before, but my past wasn't the measure of the Olympic Trials standard. The time wouldn't be moved by my effort. I was fighting through the fatigue by delusionally believing that I was still on track.

"*You've run so many good splits. You're gonna do it!*" I encouraged myself. If only positivity made it true.

And then I heard it, "*YOU'VE GOTTA GO!*" My teammates, standing at the marker for a quarter-mile remaining, screamed with utter urgency. Finally, the truth.

My knee popped up...my hand raised high, and I simply began to sprint.

At their essence, moments like these are all the same, the sensation identical to high school two decades ago when I dashed for the schoolyard finish line.

Rounding the final turn toward the California State House my head tilted up to the nauseating reality that I had only a dozen or so seconds to make it over a hundred meters.

Every step was a full body squat. Every arm swing ached like a bicep curl.

I might fall.

I may fail.

I just had to make it to the line.

Dad

Minutes passed without a word.

There's nothing he needed to say, and I couldn't summon a sentence. We'd been there before. My most memorable sports heartbreaks flashed through my mind.

The Cross Country races in college where I'd underperformed.

The District track meet in high school where I didn't hit the time.

Even my nearly undefeated elementary school soccer season that ended in defeat.

We'd experienced the heartbreak of sports together before, but it'd been a long time.

That's maybe what was most remarkable, how little the simple feeling of competitive disappointment had changed as I aged. Though a son approaching forty hardly needed his father for emotional support on Race Day, this day was different.

Because this goal was different. It had opened me up so widely, demanded so much intent and aspiration, that it stripped away the layers of emotional protection and perspective a grown man carries around with him each day.

All of a sudden I was back on that soccer field, standing in the cold November drizzle, sobbing as I struggle to make sense of the last-minute loss. I could still see the fir trees that lined that field as I recalled that first athletic heartbreak. To want something so much and realize it's not possible.

A father and son may be able to reminisce generally about the younger's successes and victories, but they can recall every detail and element of the losses and failures. In high school, it was .24 seconds that kept me from the State Meet. I cried about that split second for weeks and let it define me for a year.

This day it's two.

2:19:02

Angrily hurling my soggy singlet against a fence did nothing. A scream had no effect. Before I knew it I was back on the ground with my eyes closed, unable to take in any more of the moment.

The best race of my life. The fastest I'd ever run, the best I'd ever felt, was a failure?

Last year's 2:19:40 was clear: I tried and wasn't able. Capable but not that close.

Ironically, in some ways, I felt unburdened. Having carried the weight of insecurity about whether I'd be capable for over a year, I nearly had. Such a close miss meant that all that work, all that worry, every ounce of effort, had added up to something worthwhile. It meant that the plan I obsessed over and enacted for two years was in fact correct.

"*I am capable of being a Qualifier!*" I celebrated to myself between the tears.

And yet I wasn't.

I hadn't gotten it done.

Like the man who won the lottery but lost the ticket, I was successful, yet no different than before. Just as irrelevant to the OTQ.

Having my father there was welcome but unnecessary. After this many years, his care was understood, his guidance engrained. Quite simply, this entire chapter of my athletic life is a gift, because it was something he nearly missed.

Nearly a decade ago, when his heart stopped, I was no longer competing. I'd figured my days of endeavoring athletically were behind me. But as his arteries began to heal I had re-entered the competitive running scene, for no real reason except I had realized how soon the option to pursue speed would pass me by.

The gift he gave me as a kid had kept us close these past years. A father and son can't call each other constantly simply because there will be a day when they are unable, but they can use sport as an excuse to connect. Texting to celebrate a successful workout, discussing the final details before an attempt, or taking time together to consider what's next.

I will never know how much I'd care about running if he hadn't given it to me at birth.

The simplest sport used to build the most foundational relationship.

A day later

"*You'll know,*" my dad advised, softly.

Seconds passed with nothing to say. I may forever regret how the day before finished, but time was already moving forward.

My pride in how my teammates and I typically execute on race day threatened to swell into hubris. The question at hand was whether I should head to Houston for a final, unplanned attempt at the qualifier in just 41 days. The USA Olympic Marathon Trials qualifying window would close on January 19th.

I was incredulous.

This wasn't what I'd prepared for. I'd seen too many talented runners chase standards with decreasing returns to get caught up in such behavior. That was never supposed to be me. We prepare with intention and execute with composure. We don't hurry. We don't do vanity races or ego intervals. We pick our shot and hit it.

Except I hadn't.

So now I was forced to scramble. To seek advice for the future even as I was still processing the past.

Two days after

"*You failed. Sorry man, but that's the truth. You were over,*" a friend reflected on the harsh reality.

It hurt to hear but helped to process without sugarcoat or caveat.

"*Yeah, man. It's true. Thank you.*" I replied with the lump from Sunday still stuck in my throat.

"*I mean, I appreciate the support from everyone for sure. But you're either in or out.*"

I hadn't qualified. I wasn't a qualifier.

The overwhelming impulse is to support those who struggle. But the goal was to qualify, and any number of seconds over was too many. It hurt, but the truth was refreshing to face with a friend.

Two days removed from missing the standard for the second time I was reeling and tumbling like a tissue in the wind. Updrafts of excitement for racing at such a pace, followed by the sharp sinking realization that in terms of The Trials it meant nothing. Twenty-six and two-tenths miles completed, I'd fallen less than ten feet short.

"*You really thinking of trying again?!*" he questioned skeptically.

"*Considering it for sure,*" I replied hesitantly, hoping that saying it aloud would convince me.

Feeling so many things at once, the most consuming sensation was numbness. And the messages kept pouring in…

"*We've never met but I just had to say…*"

"*We don't know each other but I wanted you to know…*"

"*I admire…*"

"*You inspire…*"

A lifetime's worth of care and consolation. More love than any one runner deserves.

But I hadn't intended for any of this!

Qualifying was supposed to prove that wild dreams were worth chasing. That limits are simply cages we create for ourselves.

But no. I'd fucked it up. Entering the final mile I had 5 minutes and 28 seconds left to qualify. But I'd taken 5:30.

Frustrated at myself for failing, I continued to swipe open my phone to thank strangers for congratulations and condolences I appreciated, but couldn't fully accept. Like a birthday gift you get as a kid that's not the toy you asked for, I said thank you but wasn't fully grateful. A bratty perspective you just can't shake free from.

I hadn't gotten it done.

And yet the messages still kept appearing.

Somehow, to my surprise, the act of not qualifying appeared to be more inspiring than if I was 2 seconds better.

"*I don't know how you're handling this, I'm afraid I'd be shattered,*" a woman confessed to me.

Speechless, I continued to try and make sense of it myself.

Three days after

"*I still don't know if I understand it,*" I messaged a friend.

"*I don't mean to be naive, I appreciate the support, but why is coming up short more inspiring than if I'd qualified? What about all the guys who beat me and are going to Atlanta? Wouldn't it be better if I was like them, if I was faster?*" I questioned.

"*I think it's cause it was always going to be a razor-thin margin,*" he replied.

"*It was going to take everything you had and wasn't a guarantee. And you were still willing to give everything to it. That's what's inspiring to people.*"

Another deep breath and difficult swallow, I thanked him.

Clearly missing by so little reinforced to others what'd been painfully apparent to me: this dream was way out of my control. The truth that the marathon can't be tamed was so obvious that it had strung a thread of urgency and meaning through each day of the previous two years inside this dream. I had understood that if I wanted to achieve this outcome I needed to do more, try harder, and focus more intently than ever before.

And even after all that, I'd failed.

Again.

Shaking my head slowly, I continued clenching my fist in frustration, as tears welled in the edges of my eyes, days removed from the finish line moment I couldn't seem to get past.

Four days later

"*I have something I need to tell you,*" I offered Julia sheepishly.

"*What's that?*" she asked, bracing herself slightly.

"*I'm thinking of going to Houston.*"

"*Oh, yeah...I mean, I kind of assumed. I thought you were gonna say something bad.*" She sighed in relief.

Apparently, the task at hand was obvious to others.

"*I guess I'm just nervous. More than ever before,*" I confessed.

It felt silly to care so much, to get so worked up, about something of little consequence. After all, in a world of increasing complexity, that's heating up rapidly, tearing itself apart politically, and losing its way economically, what does qualifying for a footrace matter?

What had become most clear in attempting to qualify was that the point of all this was to maximize. To feel something. To turn the volume on life all the way up and stare straight at the scariest, most exciting challenge you could find without looking away.

But many of my peers from my running past had stopped. Most hadn't continued to select higher goals that scared and inspired their heart. I'd watched too many friends drift back to earth because they let the sails of their ambition fall slack. I understood that this window of my body's ability wouldn't remain open indefinitely.

No, the promise of faster tomorrows evaporates eventually without your approval. Having seen it close on others slowly at first, and then all at once, it was now painfully clear to me what the dream at hand demanded.

I had to run.

One day before the Houston Marathon

There was no way to know how the next day would go. The weeks after CIM I had felt sapped, dejected, and sad. Emotionally somersaulting each day between disbelief at my near miss and hope for a final chance.

With just 12 hours remaining before the final attempt at this wild dream something dawned on me: I felt incredible.

Having forced my body to begin moving through the motions of training before my mind could make sense of it I'd managed to complete several workouts that actually gave me hope.

"*You know, you did run your personal best, feeling your best, just a few weeks ago,*" I reminded myself cautiously.

"*What if, instead of thinking of yourself as an empty vessel, a spent rocket, you're actually a recovered racer with more ability than ever before?*"

"*What if tomorrow could actually go great?!*" I shocked myself with the most obvious question.

I was ready to race again.

The 3rd attempt—The 2020 Houston Marathon

A morning of déjà vu preparations. And we were off.

Today was crisp and fast.

"*Is this the 2:19 pack?*" a man inquired as he caught us from behind.

"*2:18 pack,*" I deadpanned.

"*Every second counts.*"

The men surrounding me were prepared. It was deadline day and we were on a mission.

And I was running free. Having familiarized myself with failure, my stride and spirit felt light, as if unburdened by the cloud of disappointment that had followed me the past month. Sprinting at pace through streets lined with well-wishers, I was where I belonged, thankful, and able for one last attempt.

The only issue was I was a bit stuck.

Off the back of a faster pack, and ahead of another, I was isolated without clear cover from the wind. Which would become an issue. Miles passed with ease and the spirit of the day began to carry me through. To feel this good, again, so soon, was a distance runner's dream.

But then we turned toward the gusts.

Still striding with strength, the blowback was subtle at first, then stronger, then stronger still. Glancing at my watch, the pace was precarious; not yet a disaster, but not quite fast enough to qualify.

A mile split: too slow.

Another: even slower.

Panicked, I was too far from the finish to go any faster.

"*Shit.*" A cloud of dread was forming over me even as the crisp sun rose.

I was fucked.

Slightly past half-way, the pace was too slow and I had too far to go alone. Being blown about by the increasing wind, I still felt incredibly able, I just wasn't moving quite fast enough.

Frantic, my mind scanned through options of what to do next.

"*Do I drop out?*" I puzzled. I only came here for one reason, what's the point in even finishing any slower?

"*Don't be absurd,*" I scolded. But the thought of covering the next dozen miles slower than qualifying pace was too much for my mind to process.

"*What an imposter!*" I screamed at myself inside. "*All those people, all those well wishes, and you're pissing it away again! You idiot.*" Wallowing, I continued to run without a plan.

But then I heard it.

The stampede was coming.

The steady pack of OTQ paced hopefuls was about to roll me up. I knew how this goes. I'd watched it many times as a fan. The struggling runner tries to hang on, gives it a shot, fights briefly, before the pack eventually, relentlessly, rolls on without him.

"*You've got one fucking chance to reattach and then it's over.*" Like a surfer about to drop in on the last big wave of his dream set, I breathed deeply and slipped in with the others.

Still processing waves of anger, disappointment, and sorrow for my race gone wrong, I was managing to hang on.

Fighting into the wind, we weren't running quite fast enough, but it didn't matter anymore. Having tried and failed to dictate the pace myself, I was now resigned to just hang on. My fate, the outcome of this dream, was in their hands. I saw the broken edge of a Texas sidewalk. Then the thick crimson stripe on the singlet of the man in front of me. Anything to distract my mind. There was no time left to think. Just run.

"Do these men believe more than me?" I wondered. Are they more talented, better prepared, or just mentally more willing to buy into the yet unfulfilled dream of being a Qualifier? Filled with doubt, I knew I was overthinking it, yet I couldn't stop.

"Shut up and run!" I screamed inside. But this was me. For good, bad, and complicated, I was 23 miles deep into my third OTQ attempt, and I was...still on pace! I had nearly given up. Then fought an hour's worth of mental battles. And yet remarkably, I still had a chance. But then came the wind again.

As the course turned, we were exposed once more, and surging once, twice, a third time confirmed that I could no longer keep up with the pack. I would have to fight these final gusts on my own.

Having spent two years fighting to cross the threshold of this marathon dream, the window closed in sixteen minutes.

No longer looking at my watch, I pushed harder.

Having burned through the inspirational power of all the well wishes I brought to Texas, I was down to one final figure, the person who always expects excellence of effort: my Dad.

Weeks before when I doubted whether I should come to Houston I had sensed his hesitation. I saw in his eye the perspective of an elder who understands the significance of a title. He would always love me regardless, but in these minutes, I had the chance to define myself for a lifetime.

I'd always run harder for him.

Kicking, surging, I was absolutely flying. Though likely slower than the Olympic Trials Committee demands, I was closing a marathon faster than I'd ever thought possible.

Rounding into the finishing straight, the scorching of my marathon legs was overcome by an ache inside my chest as I watched the lights dim and the curtain close on this amazing dream.

2:19:23

Waking up

Opening my eyes to a day outside the dream of the 2020 Olympic Trials felt like an organ had been ripped out of my chest.

Its absence was eerie.

A sound of silence lingered as the pressure of my purpose escaped and I decompressed into the feeling of daily life without direction.

I felt lonely and exposed.

The force that had propelled my running and absorbed my life for two years, was now gone. No matter where I was the past 25 months it had always been on my mind. Whether running a mile, hosting a meeting, or drinking a beer, I was aware of how that action fit in the scheme of my preparation towards the goal.

It had offered clarity, momentum, and meaning to each day.

"*I'm sorry,*" I texted Patrick.

Fully aware that remorse was unnecessary. That regret was implied. That hurling yourself against the castle walls of the qualifier three times only to come tumbling back down meant you tried entirely. But if you unraveled the dream completely, if you rolled it out fully, from a marathon goal, to a hope for running distinction, to a desire to be physically able, what you get to eventually is the simple vision of racing the best marathon of your life side-by-side with your friend.

We had an unspoken promise that we'd be there for one another at the Trials. Having given so much to me, my driving force during each attempt had been to be there for him on our sport's greatest stage.

But it wasn't a promise I was able to keep.

Although the ability to fly at such a speed is intoxicating, at some point I'd discovered that the quest to become a Qualifier stopped being only about running. Somewhere between rising for thousands of miles over years, and sharing the meaning of those moments with others along the way, I had propped open the door on our collective desire to dream that most often sits closed.

I had wanted to be good enough. For myself and everyone that had invested their emotions in me. Because amid life's ambiguous layers of meaning, I had spent these years longing for the crisp, clear, irrefutable stamp that I'd done something.

"*My heart beat for you today. I guess the world still needs heartbreak,*" a friend wrote to me. His message illuminating the meaning that had emerged from this endeavor. Our dream had rested on my shoulders. Stood on my legs. Only my two feet could achieve the outcome that had captivated our imagination.

It had never stopped being about being better. No silver lining, secondary meaning, or soft landing could ease the pain of this failure. Because the purpose was to feel, even when it hurts.

Maybe especially when it hurts.

The Olympic Trials

As the start of the race I wasn't running approached, my body began rattling with phantom nerves. Unsure of what was happening, I realized my mind was ringing an alarm that I had set long ago and forgotten to switch off.

The moment I'd dreamt of every day for years was about to occur, but I was standing inside sipping a cup of coffee. I couldn't converse casually because I hadn't prepared to be there as a fan.

As packs of our country's best runners circled the city I felt an intense need to experience the race alone. To connect directly with the racers I so wished I could call peers.

Finding a spot on a bridge one-kilometer from the finish I screamed until my lungs were coarse, and then I screamed some more. I implored the men and women to embrace this moment, to not look away at the horrible beauty of the thousand meters remaining.

It appeared terribly painful for them all, regardless of their place. The top few sprinted by in fear of getting caught for their podium position. The next few surged past gripped by the horror of seeing their Olympic spot slip away. Some were charging, accomplishing heroic runs in their nation's best marathon. But for many, I sensed in their eyes the ache of witnessing their long-time dream printed into reality. Watching as the goal that had motivated them for years faded from the glimmer of imagination to the muted tones of reality. Their salt-stained faces passed by in shock.

This was the dream. This was the moment we all longed for, taking place over a hilly, cold, windswept course. In all of its glory, agony, and prestige.

This was ugly.

It was wonderful and painful to watch. This course, under these conditions, had left the best marathoners in America exposed. Which was always the point: to find a test that would striate even our elite.

Such is the beauty of the marathon—making the most of themselves, together, there was nowhere for them to hide, not a moment to hold back.

Not racing there was a failure for me, sure, but in some ways, the entire event was about failure. The commitment of this whole endeavor was simple: to push until you lose control.

To reach that line.

Mine was right on the precipice of qualifying. For others, it was earning the "Qualifier" distinction only to be dropped off the back of the pack. And the pros, the very best who didn't earn a podium spot, they had their faces pushed right up against the glass outside Olympic distinction. Cruelly forced to watch their competitors showered with accolades.

But embracing failure is the essence of our sport.

The foundation of this dream was simple: the ability to run fast at length. But as it expanded I was surrounded by a community aiming to endure until we were unable. Dreaming this grandly meant becoming so acquainted with our limits, so accustomed to living past our perceived abilities, that we took our mortality down off its safe perch on the mantelpiece of our mind and tossed it about, playing daily games with our humanity.

It meant feeling so invested in a pursuit that despite all other responsibilities and obligations we rose each day aware of what it would require and closed our eyes each night dreaming of how success would feel.

And in the end, once we each reached our inevitable edge, we were guaranteed two things: the heartache that we couldn't go further, and the satisfaction that we spent each day along the way having never felt so alive.

Peter Bromka is an amateur runner and writer in Portland, Oregon. Growing up in Oregon, his father both gave him the love of running and flooded him with stories about the legends and lessons of the sports world. However, he didn't really begin writing his own stories until in his 30s when he realized that he finally had something to say.

Out There: On Not Finishing

DEVIN KELLY

FROM Longreads • SEPTEMBER 2020

I started to come apart sometime after midnight. I was cold, shiver-sweating, and shuffling alone on my 35th two-mile lap around a farm 40 miles west of Savannah, Georgia. I'll back up in a second, and offer some context. But, for now, let's remember the loneliness, and the absurdity. Let's remember the darkness and how the stars looked like light shining through a thousand pinpricks in the vast blueblack tapestry of the night sky. And let's remember how, when I shifted my head-lamped gaze from the few feet right in front of me to the big sky above, hoping to have a moment with the stars and witness something beautiful, the headlamp erased them, and I became a single low beam of light caught in the act of disappearing. Let's remember how that felt: to expect something so great and be faced with its opposite.

Beginning on October 20, 2018, ultrarunner Courtney Dauwalter took on Johan Steene at Big's Backyard Ultra, a wildly conceived race where runners must complete a four-mile loop every hour on the hour. Runners can complete the loop as quickly or slowly as they desire, but they must be on the start line when the gun goes off each hour. Dauwalter and Steene battled over three days, running 279 miles each until Dauwalter, after 67 hours, shook Steene's hand and let him finish his last loop alone. Steene later wrote, of that moment: "As I jogged away alone into the Tennessee night I didn't feel joy. I felt empty and without purpose." Steene had won, and yet there was no sense of accomplishment, purpose, or positive emotion. What do you make of that? The hole where something should be but nothing is?

For a long time, I thought I ran, and competed in sport, as a way to use the metaphor of sport to understand life. Life is a marathon, I was often told. I remember watching and re-watching *Chariots of Fire*, particularly that moment in the rain when Eric Liddell, just minutes after winning a race, states: "I want to compare faith to running in a race. It's hard. It requires energy of will." I loved that moment as a child, especially as someone who had, at one point, a deep amount of faith. But I always paused the clip before he stated what later became to me more obvious: "So who am I to say believe, have faith, in the face of life's realities…I have no formula for winning a race. Everyone runs in their own way." It's true, that everyone runs in their own way, which is a fact I've come to appreciate as I've grown older. Patience, both with my own peculiar movements through life and with those of others, is a skill I actively try to cultivate and maintain. And yet, even Liddell's quote has to do with winning. And that—the idea of winning, or finishing, or accomplishing—has become its own universal signifier. It's not about what you do. It's about what you have done.

For the past three years, my college running friends and I have, despite whatever physical distance separates us, met up each February at a farm in Brooklet, Georgia to run a 24-hour ultramarathon. Known as Farmdaze, the race is a small, weekend-long festival of lots of things, running being only one of them. Other things include, but are not limited to: pig roasts, folk music, beer, beer miles, campfires, hot dogs, friends, occasional nakedness, cute puppies, scary roosters, goats, family-friendliness, non-family-friendliness, karaoke, ecstatic experiences, tears, blood, trippy lights in the middle of the woods, emotional connection, the phrase "what the fuck," and a lack of sleep.

Each year, Victor and Andrew, the two founders of this "thing," sneak off in the middle of the night to hang neon lights in the forest and set up speakers that play beautiful, discordant, wonky music. There's one hill on the course. It's called Space Mountain. It's five feet tall.

The race begins at 9 AM on Saturday and ends at 9 AM on Sunday. Serious is not the best word to describe it, but people are serious about having fun, about testing limits, about being "out there," wherever there is. Past winners have logged upward of 110 miles over the course of a single day. The race follows one lap that is repeated again and again. The lap is approximately two miles. The lap takes you along cow paths and through wooded trails and on plowed fields stretching long and wide beneath the sky. The lap takes you back to where you began, and then you begin again. Not everyone runs for the whole 24 hours. Some people do the six-hour race. Some do the 12. Some are there mostly to have fun, see friends, commune with one another around a fire. Some are there to find their limit. Some are there to run the coveted distance that defines an ultramarathon: 100 miles.

My friends and I go there for almost all of those reasons. Last year, I ran 100 miles for the first time in my life at Farmdaze. I finished it in 19 hours, had a shot of whiskey given to me by Victor and Andrew, and waited for my friend Nick to finish not far behind me. At some point, Nick had run a lap naked. At some point, I had cried a waterfall of tears while listening to the entire discography of The National and stumble-walk-running through the night. We tried to drink beer and sit in the glow of our achievement, but we wound up asleep under the same blanket and awoke bleary-eyed and sore a few hours later, drunk from dehydration and exhaustion. I loved every second of that. I loved what it meant to share in that with somebody. To be joined in my present moment by someone else in theirs, and to not have to question what joined us, or why, or what we owed one another. To do it a little bit on my own, and a lotta bit with the help of my friends.

This year, though, my friends and I had no plan, which is a kind of lie. We had the energy that comes with being unsure of what we were capable of. We weren't sure about completing the full 100 miles, or just enjoying each other's company. One of the many knowable things about an ultramarathon is how so much of it feels unknowable, even when you are in it. The early hours of a 24-hour race are like the early hours of any morning: a little achy, a little stretchy, a little chompy-at-the-bit. You want the hours to giddy themselves up into a faster pace so you can find out, more honestly, just how much you hurt, and just how much you are potentially capable of. It's an impatient dance with patience. You want to get to the part where the dwelling happens. That place where you live, for an extended present, in the narrowed focus of exhaustion, where each small thing grows luminous with pain and light. My friends and I spent the first few hours loping around the farm, telling stories, catching up, playing music on a portable speaker we passed to one another.

This year, we orchestrated our own rendition of Jeff Buckley's "Hallelujah" around 30 miles into the race. It made me fucking weepy. This year was the year my friends realized I had never seen *Shrek*, and it was the year Nick spent an hour trying to explain it to me, and all I can remember was something about an onion. We did all of this while running, in the early stages of the day, but this essay isn't about running.

The day grew messy as the running went on. It had rained for days before, and most of the course was a slog: muddy, slippery, and cold. And, at about 12 hours in, every one of my friends, except for me, had stopped running, and I found myself where this essay begins: alone, in the dark, wrestling with meaning, unable to stop. I am scared of this impulse in myself. Once, during a high school cross country race, I fell and hit my head on a rock, suffering a minor concussion. I got up, and finished the race in what must have been last place. It was not brave, or courageous. It was dumb. But I did it, because I felt like I had to, because I was worried about what other people might think if I didn't. The truth is, those who loved me would have loved me regardless. How hard was that for me to understand? It's still hard. It's really fucking hard.

WHAT HAPPENS if what you once used to make sense of things no longer helps you make sense of things? What happens if the patterns and habits and metaphors we lean on do not serve us in the moments we need them? What happens if the stories we tell ourselves about our lives leave us lonely, wrestling with meaning? What then?

I grappled with these questions for hours on that farm in Georgia. Under the stars and all alone, I did not know what I was doing. Each lap, I shuffled past the bonfire, past my friends singing karaoke, past the laughter of strangers, and each lap I shuffled away from them, until they became the soft patchwork of voices traversing a distance, the kind of sound that hollows you to your core and fills you with a deep sense of missingness, a longing to be there and not wherever you are. At that point, the race had ceased to be a race for so many people, but it hadn't for me.

Two weeks after Farmdaze, I sat in my therapist's office wondering why I hadn't been able to stop when all my friends had. We talked about how I have a desire to tell a specific story: a story of perseverance, a story I have been telling myself for so long as a way to make sense of my own life, as a way to prove, to myself, that I could love myself, and deserve the love of others. For a long time I have believed that love and joy come after. They come after accomplishment. They come after pursuit. They don't live in the present. They have to be earned. But there is a kind of grace that comes at a place like Farmdaze, a place that calls itself a race but is really everything that a race isn't, an event that lets men give up if they want, that doesn't shame them for it, that lets them become present in the story that is, simply, all of us trying to love all of us, the story that Galway Kinnell calls, simply, "tenderness toward existence."

Each time I made it through another lap and then shuffled into the next one, the voices of my friends got a little quieter, until one lap, when I came around, they had gone to sleep. I felt suddenly selfish, and sad, that I had abandoned spending time with people I loved so that I could search for meaning by myself. One lap, I was alone under a field of stars, soaking wet, skin steaming. I tried to see the stars, to see all of them, but my headlamp's glare made it impossible. So I turned off my head lamp and offered myself to the dark. It was freezing, my lips trembled. What is the point of all of this, I asked myself, what is the fucking point.

I was thinking of my own story: the story I would tell after I had done the thing, a story of hardship, of relentless pursuit through struggle, of accomplishment. But while I was telling myself that story, I missed out on the story I was living in and choosing not to see: the story of my friend Nick belting what must have been a hits-of-the-80s-90s-and-today playlist next to a raging fire while my friends Andrew, Ben, and Matt all tried to sing along.

For so many hours, shuffling around that farm, I didn't want to be doing, I wanted to be done, so that when I was done, I could say I did a thing. This is the opposite of the spirit of ultramarathoning, of distance running in general, which is in many ways about being "Out There," caught up in a moment that divorces you from the world, from society, from anything other than self. Accomplishment happens in an instant. Accomplishment is awarded the moment the finishing is done. But being out there takes a long time, and if it is only done for the sake of accomplishment, then it feels like an even longer, more painful time. Our society offers up so much as reward, and yet rewards so little for the so-much of life.

IN ONE OF LISEL MUELLER'S POEMS, "There Are Mornings," she writes: "the plot / calls for me to live, / be ordinary." It's a moment of trascendental mundanity in a poem punctuated by a blazing sun, mirrors burning. So often, the plot of our lives seems like a clarion call for the extraordinary. It is, nearly always, how the world is marketed to us as consumers, and speaking specifically, how the world is marketed to me as a man. Think of how young you were when you first thought you had to be the hero of your own story. I must have been barely older than a baby. My father called me maverick. It made me feel like a rebel. I wanted to be a star. I had to win at all costs. And yet: when was the last time anyone ever told a man to be ordinary? Think of the difference that would make, to begin to dismantle our need to be heroes, to finish things, to consider ourselves defined by accomplishment, particularly in a world where women make less money on the dollar and yet are defined, in settings both casual or professional, by what they have done or failed to do. Living, as Mueller writes, is so often, and so deeply, an ordinary thing. And yet the extraordinary sits there like a burning sun on the horizon.

The thing about horizons is that, upon reaching one, you always encounter another. It's the in-between where life lives. In another poem, "On Duration," the poet Suzanne Buffam writes: "To cross an ocean / You must love the ocean / Before you love the far shore." This is a beautiful explanation of what it means, as so many endurance runners say, to be "out there." Out there is a place, but it is also a feeling. It is a series of moments stretched out across hours, or even days, that feel like one long moment. It is the act of building the bridge between two points and being the bridge at the same time. Out there is distance turned into feeling. It is metaphor actualized.

Our world does not like "out there." It likes here, or there, but not what is in between. Here is what you are before. There is what you are after. For a long time, as I mentioned, I have been self-obsessed with my body, and with my perceived fatness. I have hated how I do not look like a runner, but I have wanted to be respected as one. I have wanted to be done with enough things so that I would have an answer for anyone who doubted me. Oh you're a runner, I imagined someone saying, prove it, and I would hand them my medals, my countless marathons, my hundred miles and 24-hour races, and say see for yourself. The problem with that, however, is that such a conversation lives on two distinct poles: here and there, or before and after. I am not letting that person love the ocean with me. And I am not loving the ocean of myself. In that scenario, we are throwing ourselves across it together, trying to get from the here of doubt to the there of certainty without love, kindness, or compassion. We are being nasty, brutish, and judgmental, so much like men, so much like society.

How, then, can we learn to love the ocean that signifies duration, the ocean that takes time? How can we acknowledge the plot when it calls for us to be ordinary? It takes a certain kind of grace to give yourself permission to do this, a certain kind of grace to say to yourself I've done enough, and sit down for a second, a minute, a day, a long time. Love does not always have to come after. It can be right here.

THERE WAS A TIME IN MY LIFE when running served a clear and definable purpose. After my parents divorced, when I was not even a teenager, I ran a two-mile loop in my neighborhood as often as I could, endowed with reckless abandon, feeling like I was racing out of my own story, or racing into a story that I could control. When I became a competitive runner, I ran to make myself proud. Later, I ran to show my father how far I had come in loving him, recognizing how far he would go, the lengths he would travel, just to see me and my brother run. He never missed a race, even if it meant waking before dawn four hours away to see us race at dawn in another city, another state. Through all of that, I grew to love running, because it always meant something.

But I understand that no matter how much I love running, it still exists within a system that has said, essentially, if you want something better, here is what you have to accomplish. There is something about finishing that our culture is obsessed with. I even think of finishing school, that age-old culture-training course for women to enter into society. For them, finishing manifested itself as a right-to-enter. Which is the case so often, isn't it? The act of finishing allows someone in society to enter into another realm of society. Finish high school, college, graduate school. Finish a marathon to put that 26.2 bumper sticker on your car. Finish the race to get the beer at the end. Finish your meal to eat dessert. Finish what you are doing so that you might find joy. So you might cease to care. So you might find something new to finish before you finish your life. This kind of reduction—of linking personal growth to accomplishment—does not honor the inconsistencies of life, the in betweens, the moments when finishing something doesn't feel good enough, or when achieving something just makes you long for the next achievement. This is why tense matters. If we are defined by what we have done or what we will do, then we, each day, seem to forget the present tense: what we do. This tense is shifty. It elides. It loses itself in the past and drives off a cliff into the future. It is full of insecurity, of difference. But it is where we live.

When I think of a moment when the present was where I lived, I think of a Monday in Boston in 2015. It was raining, and the wind was in my face on a course that went in one direction. I was with my friend Matt, who was guiding me, gently setting the pace a little faster or slower when needed, sometimes touching my hip just to let me know he was there. We had settled into a pack with a bunch of strangers, and, when we passed a fan handing out water bottles, one fellow runner grabbed one, drank from it, and passed it to each of us, who took sips in turn. Soon, one of the elite women caught up with us, and the few of us around her took turns blocking the wind. We did this for miles, barely talking. It was the sound of muffled footsteps and rain dropping from the lids of hats and spectators thumping gloved hands together. At some point, nearing the finish, we separated. Matt took off, and I chased him. Others came with me and others fell behind. But because we shared something, because we were out there together, because, for a few hours, our stories were inexorably linked, I remember waiting at the finish, turning my head to see if these strangers would arrive at this one place where we all stopped and existed together again. And they did, and we recognized each other, and embraced.

In one of her seminal works, *The Years*, Annie Ernaux writes "The world is suffering from lack of faith in a transcendental truth." I think that transcendental truth is simple. I think that truth has to do with solidarity. I think it has to do with existing in service of others existing, and not in spite of, or despite them. With putting your own personal pursuit aside sometimes. With understanding, or attempting to understand, the various inconsistencies of others, the way we are made and unmade in a world that tells us, every day, a different way to be made and unmade. Sometimes the transcendental truth involves giving up the race and just sitting with your friends. It involves forgetting the phrase I just said: giving up, and other phrases, like quitting, or losing. It involves remembering that the word last doesn't just refer to last place, but also refers to lasting for a long time. Life gives me glimpses of those moments. I have run to find those moments. But I am also learning to live to find them. And learning to love to find them. And learning to miss them when they are gone.

I wish I had thought of those moments while I was in Georgia, but I was caught up in the idea of accomplishing. I was obsessed with having done something. I wish I had said: not finishing does not mean giving up. I wish I had said: it is alright to love your friends instead of trying so hard to love yourself. I wish loving myself did not always feel, each day, like an extraordinary task that took extraordinary lengths and impossible distances to achieve. I am still living in the consequence of a lifetime spent telling myself all the ways in which I did not have value, and all the ways I was supposed to. A lifetime spent telling myself I was not fast enough, fit enough, smart enough, driven enough, insert anything enough. Enough, enough, enough with that.

The truth is: when I finished whatever lap took me over 100 miles on that farm in Georgia, I don't know how I felt. Like Johan Steene, I felt partly empty, without purpose. It was 20-something hours into the race. An hour before that, I had seen dawn rise. It glistened all pink and hazy and melted the stars away and revealed a thin layer of frost atop the grass. I was, at that point, wearing two pairs of tights under a pair of pants. I hadn't really done anything resembling running for hours. Most everyone except for Victor and Andrew and the few others still running the race was asleep in their tents or RVs or cars. The truth is: I wanted to feel more. But I was mostly tired. I had a glass of champagne. I went to sleep. There was so much distance between what I felt and what I was supposed to feel. It made me sad. I was alone. Meaning unshared is barely meaning at all. My reasons for finishing, whatever finishing meant, were defined wholly extrinsically. I had believed in what society told me would happen: that I would push through a challenge and emerge, new and strong, on the other side, where love was. But I was left instead with the deep, profound emptiness that comes with knowing entirely for certain that what you were told by society was wrong.

When I woke up, I went looking for my friends. I slept so long that I missed the awards ceremony. But that wasn't the point. I saw them sitting by a pond. They had gotten my award for me, for third place: a silly hat with fire streaked across the brim. (Just kidding. It wasn't silly. It was fucking awesome. Am I wearing it now? Maybe.) But the award wasn't the point. I missed my friends. They had spent a morning walking along the farm, befriending horses. They showed me pictures, videos of what I missed the night before. I missed so much. They hugged me and said they were proud. And they were. But I know now that they would have been proud no matter what.

Today, I can still hear the echo of my friend Andrew singing Kenny Rogers from a mile away, somewhere on a farm in Georgia. You gotta know when to hold them, know when to fold them. How apt. I think you hold for as long as you can the moments that don't feel like you have to choose between holding and folding. I wish I had been there, right next to him, instead of where I was. But it's alright now. Because even though I'm no longer out there, in the middle of some unimaginable distance, I'm still here, which is a kind of out there, which is where all of you are. Each of you, in each of your out theres, trying to love the ocean you're in.

Devin Kelly is a high school teacher in New York City and the author of *In This Quiet Church of Night, I Say Amen (Civil Coping Mechanisms)*. A winner of a Best of the Net Prize, his work has appeared in Longreads, Lit Hub, *The Guardian*, and more.

Fifty Years After Its Unfathomable Loss, Marshall Spends Another Nov. 14 with Pain and Memories

CHUCK CULPEPPER

FROM *The Washington Post* • NOVEMBER 14, 2020

HUNTINGTON, W.Va.—Suddenly in the 7:30 a.m. of a cold, calm Saturday, the departed reappeared. They reappeared on banners, two to a lamppost, through a stirring turn of thinking and of art. They appeared as they have in recent months along these winding sidewalks and autumn trees of the Marshall campus, their 75 faces beaming out from high up, in black-and-white photos, some grainy.

In some curious way, they presided at the 50-year memorial service honoring the 75 victims of the worst plane crash in U.S. sports history, the Marshall team plane that struck a rainy hillside near landing after a game at East Carolina on Nov. 14, 1970. They helped hold vigil before the vigil while the sun tried to peek out through the fog. Adi Goldstein's slow-noted beauty, "Just A Little Hope," floated from the speakers over the chairs scattered during a pandemic, and two small children wore jackets reading "Coach Tolley," the Marshall head coach who died at 30 in the crash well, well before their births.

They reigned up there through the speeches and the placing of the flowers beside the memorial fountain a chaplain called "a

sacred site." They held sway while university president Jerome A.
Gilbert extolled the new banners and said, "I've had the privilege
to walk among the images of the 75 the past several months,"
saying he had made a point to visit each one. They were up there
during the quote, "Athletics serves as a laboratory for human
relations," which came in the speech of keynote speaker Lucianne
Kautz Call, who was 21 when her father, athletic director Charles
E. Kautz, died in the crash.

They hung through the words of Athletic Director Mike
Hamrick, that Marshall linebacker from 1976 to 1979, when he
got choked up briefly after saying: "It is the greatest comeback
story in the history of all sports. Our program came back from
ashes to glory." And the people they depicted might have felt
amazed to hear a veritable pup, student body vice president Kyle
Powers, say the fate of the 75 "still shapes the university and
impacts every one of us."

In some way, the banners ratified the unifying capacity of
sports, given who juxtaposes whom on the lampposts. There's the
local car dealer and fan Parker Ward in a tuxedo bow tie, adjacent
22-year-old center Rick Dardinger, who had made the trip despite
a leg injury. There's Helen Ralsten, the schoolteacher who died
with her husband, Murrill, next to Frank Abbott, the pilot who
had served in World War II and the Korean War. There's a Black
player from Dallas, all-everything standout Bobby Hill, next to
a White player from Columbus, defensive back Richard Lech.

They were all people—36 players, five coaches, five crew
members, eight athletic department staffers and 21 fans—and
so people called them nicknames such as "Shorty"; "Jemo";
"The Menace" (for a Dennis); "The Governor"; "Gator"; "Griff";
"Bobby Joe"; "Nutsy"; "Happy"; the quarterback, "Shoe"; the athletic director, "Charlie"; and the play-by-play man, "The Voice
of the Herd."

Four were 23 years old. Three were 22. Twelve were 21.
Thirteen were 20. Eight were 19. The oldest was 60. They hailed
from 13 states, with four Alabamian African Americans all

hailing from Tuscaloosa. Eight married couples were on board, leaving 27 children bereaved of both parents. A New Jerseyan identified on a banner with the honorary title "father," Arthur L. Harris, died in the crash at 53, as did his son, sophomore running back Arthur "Art" Harris, at 20.

At least seven of the passengers had served in World War II, including community member Rachel Arnold (as an Army nurse), Charles Kautz (also Korea), special teams coach Deke Brackett and the two guys who gladly gave their time to videotape games for the coaches, Donald Booth and Norman Weichmann.

It went—and goes—on and on and on, a continuing onslaught of grievous fate that leaves the bereaved fortified only by the art of remembering, and at that art, Marshall rivals England with Liverpool's 96 fans lost in a stadium tragedy in 1989. "I've learned the significance of celebrating someone's life," Hamrick said in his speech. "Yes, we grieve. Yes, we mourn. Yes, we're hurt. This [annual] event taught me to celebrate someone's life."

So they did, and before they did, four men with hair aged to white walked up the sidewalk beneath the banners, wearing purple rather than Marshall green. They were former East Carolina running back Rusty Scales, defensive tackle Richard Peeler, offensive tackle Grover Truslow and defensive tackle Chuck Zadnik, and they had driven eight hours from Greenville, N.C., to pay respects 50 years after a postgame in which they had hugged Marshall players and shaken their hands. "I remember having to chase that quarterback all over the field," Zadnik said of Ted Shoebridge, a crash victim. "It was a hard-fought game."

Then: "I remember when I first heard about it" as East Carolina celebrated its 17–14 win. "Somebody walked in and yelled, 'The Marshall plane crashed!'"

They began to hold memorials on their own campus—that night, that Sunday. Fifty years later, their chancellor, Ron Mitchelson, sent an email to Gilbert that concluded, "Today, we are all Marshall." The ex-players who represented Mitchelson's school milled about with Marshall fans, posed for photos, then made their way indoors.

"It's not our story," Zadnik said. "We're just a part of it."

Then, with a noon kickoff coming shortly and a scattered audience dispersing—with distancing instructions—a banner found some meaningful company. It showed the face of the late wide receiver who starred on the fields and courts and tracks of Bluefield, W.Va., Dennis "The Menace" Blevins. He shared the lamppost with Jeff Nathan, a student sportswriter who wrote a column for Marshall newspaper the *Parthenon*, regularly titled "Hoof Beats." Blevins was 22. Nathan was 20.

Seven of Blevins's family members had come as they do most years from Columbus, Ohio. The niece Blevins never got to meet, Stephanie Blevins, wore a shirt full of photos of her uncle. Blevins's sister, Sharon Anthony, wore a Dennis Blevins mask and his jersey numeral 80 on her necklace as she said, "That trip was my brother's first plane ride." She said her "tall, gentle giant" of a sibling had called before departure from Huntington at the outset and said, "This is my first time getting on the bird!"

They were a Black family from Bluefield, seven children, with Dennis the fifth and Sharon the seventh. "We were children of a coal miner," she said. "My father worked on a coal mine. My mother was a cook [at a restaurant]. Dennis was the first one in the family to attend college. He had a full ride here." She was 17 when the news came across the black-and-white TV that evening, and she said, "A couple of players rode back in an equipment van, and we didn't know if he was in the equipment van, and we just had to wait...."

"And then, all of a sudden, the phone started ringing, and people started coming [to the house], and the cars." A friend went to pick up their mother from working at a restaurant in nearby Princeton. "And then cars. We lived on the hill. And the cars started lining up."

Then she did recollect a detail often lost. Several Black students at Marshall, including Lawson Brooks, Jane English,

Macy Lugo and Dawn Evans, helped the Rev. Charles Smith of Huntington organize a bus. They traveled to Bluefield and to Tuscaloosa and to elsewhere, attending the funerals of all the Black players, hoping to make their families feel less alone. "They left Dennis's funeral, and they went to the next one and the next one," she said.

"So emotional," Marshall Coach Doc Holliday said five hours later. "So emotional, walking out on that field." His team, ranked 16th, had bunched in the end zone during pregame amid the playing of a video honoring the 75. It had walked dramatically and slowly, almost in lockstep, up the field to the 40-yard line before dispersing to the sideline. Then it had reached 7–0 by managing the moment for a 42–14 win over Middle Tennessee. "There were a lot of emotions to say the least," quarterback Grant Wells said, "especially coming out like we did."

Neither they nor some of their parents were born Nov. 14, 1970, yet they seem to uphold a quote their coach gave on video during the ceremony. "Everything we do is for the 75 who were lost 50 years ago today," Holliday said. "Everything—I mean, everything—is for them." That's because it turns out humans can excel at remembering—and remembering more and remembering still more—until in some very real way the departed never die.

A chronic wanderer, **Chuck Culpepper** of *The Washington Post* has written about sports for the late *Los Angeles Herald Examiner*, the late *National Sports Daily*, and seven entities still breathing: the *Lexington Herald-Leader*, the *Oregonian*, *Newsday*, the *Los Angeles Times* (based in London), *The National* of the United Arab Emirates (based in Abu Dhabi and Dubai), Sports On Earth/ *USA Today* (based without any residence), and *The Washington Post* since 2014 (based in New York and Miami). He began writing sports at age 14 for the *Suffolk* (Virginia) *Sun* supplement of the *Virginian-Pilot*, writing summaries of local Little League action while also playing Little League and omitting his occasional RBI singles from any mention. He began his career by driving across the country and reaching Los Angeles after having car trouble in Kansas City, figuring he might just go ahead and live there, then carrying on after learning he'd simply misapplied the oil filter.

Their Son's Heart Saved His Life. So He Rode 1,426 Miles to Meet Them

A.C. SHILTON

FROM *Bicycling* • JANUARY 24, 2020

I.

It took several drafts to get the letters right. To capture her boy who, just a few short months before, had been so full of life, energy, and love. To distill him into the two dimensionality of words on paper.

Three weeks earlier, the thread that held Christine Cheers's world together had been ripped clean away, sending her whole life spinning like an off-balance top. On Wednesday, February 21, 2018, someone on the other end of the phone had said the words that bring any parent to their knees: "There's been an accident."

Her son, 32-year-old Navy flight surgeon James Mazzuchelli had been injured in a helicopter training mission at Camp Pendleton. If she wanted to see him while he was still alive, she needed to get on the next flight from Jacksonville, Florida, to San Diego—and she needed to pray.

James was still breathing when Christine and her husband, David, arrived at Scripps Memorial Hospital in La Jolla, California, the next morning. But it soon became clear that his condition would not improve. Machines were keeping him alive, and the doctors told Christine that what she was seeing was likely his future—that her scuba-diving, world-traveling, over-achiever of a son was never going to wake up.

There in the sterile hospital room, Christine flashed back to James as a teenager, coming home from school and making a proclamation that surprised her. As he and his friends worked toward their learner's permits, they'd sat through a presentation on organ donation. James walked in the door and told his mother frankly that he wished to be an organ donor. "It was kind of unusual for a kid that age," she remembers.

Under the fluorescent lights, with the rhythmic beeping of life-sustaining machines punctuating the silence, it was time for Christine to finish what James had started on that day 17 years before. It was time to honor the spirit of a man who had switched his major from commerce engineering to pre-med because he wanted to help people. It was time to make her very worst day some stranger's best one.

Christine instructed the hospital to begin the organ donation process. She knew those few words, as hard as they were to say, were the right ones. What she did not yet know was the way those heavy words would ripple outward like a stone dropping into a still pond: allowing a man to return to work, a veteran to get his health back, and an ailing cyclist to get back on his bike. And how those little waves would slowly smooth out the edges of her own grief.

II.

Mike Cohen was in trouble. It was day one of his 1,426-mile ride across the United States, and his heart was not cooperating. They'd gotten a late start out of San Diego. Perhaps he had not eaten enough or hydrated properly, or maybe it was a lack of rest—the past few days had been packed with trip preparations. Whatever the cause, it didn't really matter. What mattered was that he had to keep his heart rate under 150 beats per minute, and the steep Cuyamaca Mountains east of San Diego were sending it sky high. The sun was setting, and he would soon be pedaling in the dark. But he had to take it easier: doctor's orders.

His friend Seton Edgerton rode alongside him. They had rigged up Mike's heart rate monitor so Edgerton could see it on his computer, and he watched the screen, helpless, as his friend's heart refused to cooperate.

Mike had done a cross-county bike ride once before, back in 2012. This time was different. He was different. His body had been through so much since then. Both men were thinking to themselves: This is just day one. Should we even be attempting this? Neither dared to ask the question out loud.

Eighteen months earlier, on February 24, 2018, Mike Cohen was in the Sulpizio Cardiovascular Center at UC San Diego Health waiting for a new heart. Heart transplant priority lists are tricky. You have to be sick enough to truly need the new organ, but not so sick you can't withstand the 12-hour surgery, says Anuj Shah, MD, an interventional cardiologist based in New Jersey. Mike fit those parameters. With an active clot and a left ventricular assistance device (or LVAD) literally pumping blood that his heart was too weak to move, he'd been at the top of the list for a month.

He'd turned 33 three days before, and as he blew out the candles, he wished for a new heart. Today, blood work showed the clot had dissolved enough that he could safely go home, but he probably wasn't going to get a new heart any time soon. Another tricky thing about the transplant list—you get a month at the top. Tomorrow he'd be kicked to the bottom.

Mike was just 18 when he'd been diagnosed with an aggressive form of leukemia in 2004. Doctors warned him that the treatment protocol could cause lasting damage to his heart. At the time, surviving cancer seemed like the more pressing concern. He took his treatment seriously, doing the radiation and chemo, and even moving from New York to San Diego for his last year of chemo because his oncologist felt mild weather would be easier on his body. The risk had paid off—two years after his diagnosis, he was cancer-free. And the move had been a good fit too. As soon as he was healthy enough to get outside, he was hiking in the nearby hills or riding his bike. A casual cyclist as a kid, Mike became bike-obsessed as a young adult, upgrading from a hybrid to a road bike, then adding a mountain bike to his collection.

To celebrate his sixth year without cancer, Mike decided to ride his bike from the hospital in San Diego where physicians had pronounced him cancer-free, to the hospital in Long Island, New York, where doctors had delivered his diagnosis. Like most grand adventures, the cross-country ride plan was hatched after a few drinks at his local bar. And like many alcohol-inspired adventures, it was kind of a disaster. Every day was a grind. Somewhere in eastern Arizona, Mike was so over it he nearly threw his bike into oncoming traffic. And between Kansas and the Eastern seaboard, his relationship with the friend accompanying him soured.

What Mike didn't know during that ride was that his heart was beginning to fail; and in the years that followed, his health continued to deteriorate. Even on days he didn't ride his bike, he always felt tired and could not make it through the day without a nap. One evening in 2017, he started having chest pains. "At first I thought it was indigestion," he says. (He'd just eaten a steak.) Then he felt a pain in his jaw and a shooting pain in his left arm. "I took an inventory in my head and I was like, I don't recognize these feelings." He texted his brother: Get here now. I think I have to go to the hospital. He didn't dare put in the message that he thought he was having a heart attack. "Who texts that?" he says.

At the hospital, tests confirmed that a golf-ball-sized clot had lodged in his left ventricle. They tried blood thinners, but the clot wouldn't budge. Soon hospital staff was preparing him for open-heart surgery to install the LVAD, which would do the pumping that his heart—now blocked by a clot—couldn't accomplish. The doctors told him the device could work for eight months or eight years. Six months later, though, he was back in the hospital with another clot. His heart was failing.

Mike's old life—where he rode his bike across the country and hiked and biked all over San Diego—seemed like a thousand lifetimes ago. His implanted LVAD required constant access to an electrical outlet, which meant Mike was literally tethered to the indoors by a cord that ran out of his abdomen. Even with an emergency backup battery pack, "You couldn't go out in public because you couldn't trust that someone wouldn't knock into the cord," he says. "I couldn't even shower." He sold his bikes, including the nearly new Trek Stache 9.6 he'd ridden precisely five times before his heart attack. It hurt to send them to a new home, but it hurt more to be reminded that he might never ride again.

In the cardiac unit on February 24, 2018, as Mike waited for his discharge papers, he walked a lap around the hospital floor, then packed his bag to go home. A nurse walked in. "I have good news, and I have bad news," she said. Mike asked for the bad news first.

The nurse announced that he wouldn't be going home that day after all. The good news? They'd found him a heart.

Mike knew better than to get his hopes up. Twice before, hospital staff thought they had a heart for him. But then the size wasn't quite right, or the organ wasn't healthy enough. Day stretched into evening. The signs started to look promising— no one had come to tell him it wasn't going to happen. Nurses double-checked his height and weight and got his vitals one more time.

A little before midnight, hospital staff wheeled Mike to an elevator. It was happening. He was more excited than nervous, ready to move on from the chapter of his life where he lived in a hospital full time. There was a chance that he'd never wake up, he knew that. But the chance of waking up with a healthy heart far outweighed it. "There's a photo of me hugging my girlfriend and crying in her arms. It was like, we're finally there. Maybe this is the end. Maybe it's the beginning," he says.

III.

Christine Cheers wasn't going home until every last one of James's organs left the building.

She and David watched hospital employees carry coolers from the operating room: his left kidney and pancreas en route to a man in San Diego; his right kidney to a veteran at Walter Reed Medical Center. Next James's liver headed to the Bay Area. His corneas went to the San Diego eye bank. Tissue and bone also went to nearby tissue and bone banks. All that was left was his heart.

"That was the one I cared about most," Christine says. James was more than just her beloved boy; as a soldier and physician, he embodied the ideals of bravery and altruism. "James had such an amazing heart," she says.

With organ donor surgeries, time is critical; organs must be harvested and transported within hours to stay viable, and transplant surgeons move efficiently. Interactions with the donor family can complicate things, and the person charged with transporting James's heart had only a few hours to get the precious cargo to its new home. He picked up his cooler and headed toward a rear exit so he wouldn't pass the family.

When a hospital representative delivered the news that James's heart had already gone, David Cheers felt a flash of anger. This was the one thing his bereft wife had asked for; the one thing. He ran into the hallway. He could see the image of someone holding a cooler reflected in a curved safety mirror. The person transporting James's heart had gotten turned around in the maze of hospital corridors and couldn't find his way out. Now he was backtracking. David yelled for Christine. The pair watched through the mirror as James's heart left the building.

IV.

Mike Cohen woke up in a hospital bed with a breathing tube in his mouth and James Mazzuchelli's heart beating in his chest.

A heart transplant is a major surgery, and Mike was prepared for an arduous recovery. He'd been sick for so long. First with cancer, then with a faulty heart. He'd spent nearly his entire young adulthood focusing on his health.

This time, his energy seemed to improve immediately: He took his first steps around his hospital room just five days later and was walking the hallways shortly after. "The old heart was like a two. With the LVAD my energy went to like four to five," he says. "This heart is a 10."

After a little more than two weeks, he was sent home with instructions to report to cardiac rehab, where, for the first few days, he was limited to slow walking on a treadmill. Across the room from the treadmill, he spied a stationary bike. He knew he wasn't ready yet, but it became a beacon. And two weeks later, with his doctor's okay, he finally threw a leg over and soft-pedaled.

From there, it wasn't long before he started thinking bigger. He itched to get back on a bike outside. The new heart felt so dramatically different that he even dared to imagine whether another cross-country ride might be possible.

V.

In the weeks after James's death, Christine Cheers descended into a grief so deep that climbing out seemed impossible. She found herself needing to know that James's organs had helped people. That the recipients were doing alright.

The one part of the letter that Christine wanted to get right was the part about what organ donation had meant to her son. How glad he would be that his heart and kidneys and tissue were helping someone else. She didn't want the recipients to feel guilty about the heft and gravitas of the gift they'd gotten.

Every day in America, 20 people die while waiting for healthy organs. James's decision to be an organ donor was unusual not just because he had been so young, but because just 58 percent of Americans follow through and tick that box at the DMV. "I didn't get involved with organ donation until graduate school," says Tobias Reynolds-Tylus, PhD, a researcher who studies organ donation at James Madison University in Virginia. When he filled out the DMV form as a teen, he saw the spot where you could opt to donate your eyes. "I felt so uncomfortable thinking about my eyes not being in my body, I just didn't sign up."

Discomfort is just one of several barriers Dr. Reynolds-Tylus has identified in his research. Another is medical mistrust. "This idea of, 'I can't trust doctors, they're going to steal my organs,'" he says. Of course, that's a fallacy. Even if your driver's license says you're an organ donor, there's a national registry that administrators must consult before your status can be confirmed. Doctors do not have access to that registry.

It's also not uncommon for donors to hesitate because of the notion that the body should stay intact after death. And sometimes people just forget to sign up—leaving the box unchecked while they think about what to do, and then they don't follow through.

Follow-through was not something James lacked. After switching to pre-med, he'd taught himself all the requirements to pass the MCAT (Medical College Admission Test). He became a Naval flight surgeon, but did additional air crew training so he could assist his team in the plane if needed. Of course he had checked the box to make sure he was an organ donor.

On March 19, Christine put the final copies of her letters in the mail.

VI.

Mike was trying to achieve some semblance of a normal life. It was early May, a little more than two months since the surgery, and he was finally back to living in a normal apartment, not a hospital room. Just as Christine had been told not to expect a response, Mike had been told he might never hear from his donor's family. Some are simply too tightly wrapped in grief to reach out. But one morning, Mike got a call from the organization that had coordinated the transplant. They had a letter for him.

He unfolded the typewritten pages and took a breath.

Christine described her son's love for serving his country, and the fact that he considered everyone a friend and never judged a soul. He was selfless, she wrote, had a quirky sense of humor, and was a brilliant and gifted doctor. She described his love for adventure, that he used his time off during a deployment in Japan to earn his scuba diving certification but also loved snowboarding and riding motorcycles. He was a frequent user of the phrase: "Go big or go home."

As Mike read Christine Cheers's letter, he began to understand just how special his new heart was. The average cardiac transplant recipient gets about eight years from their donated heart, says Dr. Shah. Reading the letter, Mike became determined to keep this heart as long as possible. "As cliché as it sounds, I wanted them to know that James's heart was in a safe place," he says. "That I was going to do everything I could to protect it."

Since his surgery, Mike had spent a lot of time wondering about the man who granted him life every day. But until he read Christine's letter, Mike had known nothing about the heart he got except that the person it had come from must have been exceptionally healthy. He describes his health upgrade as going from a Huffy to a full-carbon road bike—and strangely he found himself craving pizza, something he never had much of a taste for previously.

A curious thing that sometimes happens after a heart transplant is that recipients seem to take on one or two of their donor's traits. Food cravings are particularly common. Dr. Shah says there's no science to back this up, and never will be—you can't make transplant recipients do a double-blind, placebo-controlled study on whether food preference transfers. But he estimates that between 20 to 30 percent of his patients report unexplained changes after the surgery. And he doesn't dismiss it.

Regardless of the reason, for Mike, the change was marked and it was one tiny nugget he could grasp onto about this stranger whose life was now permanently plaited into his.

VII.

What Mike didn't mention in the letter he eventually sent to Christine was that the plan he'd hatched in cardiac rehab was beginning to solidify. As soon as he was really and truly healthy, as soon as his doctor gave him the okay, he was going to ride across the country again.

Eager to know more about James, Mike typed his name into the Google search bar and learned that James had been buried in Jacksonville, Florida. The end point of his cross-country ride came into focus. Mike wanted to pay his respects in person. It seemed fitting to make the journey by bike—to show just how transformative the heart was. Go big or go home.

The trip would be slow. Not because Mike wouldn't be fit, but because he had to be careful not to stress out his heart and immune system. Instead of 100-mile days like the last time, he began plotting a trip that would focus on fun: four hours of riding a day max, with his heart under 150 bpm, even if that meant crawling up hills. With a few days off in Tucson, El Paso, Austin, and Baton Rouge, he thought he could ride from the cardiac ward at UCSD to James's grave in Jacksonville in just under two months.

Transplant patients take immunosuppressants for life, which prevent their bodies from rejecting the foreign organ. It's well-documented that intense physical exercise can further weaken the immune system, making a person especially vulnerable to colds—which, in a transplant recipient, quickly can become very serious. So Mike recruited his brother, Dan (who had become certified as a medical assistant so he could care for Mike after his first open heart surgery), to tag along in an RV as support. Then Mike asked his friend Seton Edgerton to ride with him. This time, he wanted companions he could count on.

VIII.

There is no manual for navigating a relationship with the man who has your son's heart. No guidebook to figuring out exactly how you're related to the family that literally kept you from dying.

Christine Cheers sent a total of four letters, one to each of the individuals who had received her son's organs. She got a response from two. The first was from the man who got James's kidney and pancreas. He thanked her, saying how the organs had changed his life—that he could go back to work and provide for his family. But his letter had subtly hinted that the thank-you note was all the contact he wished to have.

It took Mike a week to process Christine's letter and another week or so to write back. He wanted to get the tone of his letter just right, to accurately express how grateful he was, how much this heart had changed his life, and how he was determined to keep it beating for years to come. He needed to communicate his desire to stay in touch with James's family, if that's what they wanted.

For Christine, Mike's letter was a balm for a wound that had begun to feel like it would never heal. And so began the emails, the texts, the mutual Instagram stalking. The two were so similar, with their love of San Diego and adventure. And, yes, James had loved pizza as much as Mike now did. What were the chances they'd be so much alike? Christine didn't know, but it was somehow comforting. Sometimes, she even read the captions Mike wrote on Instagram in James's voice. "Knowing he was doing well really helped," she says.

Even physicians who are schooled in science and facts and logic sometimes find themselves believing just a tiny bit in magic. Dr. Shah explains that when it comes to heart transplants, so much has to perfectly align. And in this case, it did. On the eve of Mike's rotation to the bottom of the transplant list, suddenly there was James's heart, in perfect health and an improbable 100 percent size and blood type match. The hospital where James had been taken after his accident was minutes from the facility where Mike was waiting. And James's accident happened on Mike's birthday—the day he blew out the candles and wished for a new heart. For Mike and Christine, the serendipity was profound.

By September, Mike was back to riding and building up his mileage. He hired Randall Fransen, a Portland-based coach, to build him a training plan. His physicians were impressed by his progress and his cautious approach—and ultimately gave their blessing for the cross-country ride.

Mike announced on social media that he was riding to his donor's gravesite. The Cheers family decided they would meet him there.

IX.

Across Arizona, then on to Texas, Mike and Seton roll in matching blue jerseys, the struggles of that first arduous day behind them—at least Mike's heart rate has settled down. Somewhere in the desert, they take a wrong turn and end up sloshing through deep sand. Somewhere in the middle of the country, Seton pins an American flag to his jersey. Somewhere in Texas Hill Country they get barbeque they still talk about three days later. In the first 1,000 miles, they get a combined 24 flat tires. Every time they fix one, another thorn or shard of glass seems to find its way into their lives. They try not to think about how many hours they lose to fixing flats.

From Florida, Christine and David follow along on social media, worrying about traffic and dogs and all the things that can befall a rider in the middle of nowhere. A few times, when Mike and Seton can't find roads suitable for riding (or even just a direct-ish route), they detour onto the interstate.

"That's illegal," David, a former police officer, says to Christine when he sees Mike's post about it. "You should tell them they can't do that in Florida."

Christine winces at the thought of semis whizzing by those boys, that heart. If it had been her son, she might call him and dress him down for riding on the freeway. But Mike isn't her son; he is a stranger with her son's heart.

On November 20, 2019, Mike and Seton leave the Flamingo RV Park in Jacksonville and pedal the last dozen miles of their trip. It doesn't feel at all like the final day of his previous cross-country ride. "Last time, I was limping toward the finish," he says while slathering thick white sunscreen onto his freckled skin. He warms up slowly on the road and thinks about what a gift it is to be healthy. How he doubted his body for so long, but how now he finally feels like there's a normal life ahead of him. He ignores the niggling pain in his knee, and the fact he has the beginnings of a cold, and instead focuses on how well his body has handled this challenge over the past two months.

Mike's nerves kick in as he gets closer to the cemetery. He's not so much worried about whether the Cheers family will like him or not, but about what kind of emotion may be attached to meeting strangers who have already come to mean so much to him. "It's just such an intense moment to share with someone I've never met," he says.

Christine and David Cheers get to the gravesite early. They want some time alone with their son before Mike arrives. It's a perfect Florida winter day: sunny with a high of 72 and just a few passing clouds. They hear the whir of hubs as Mike and Seton coast into the cemetery.

Mike unclips from his pedals, hands his bike to Seton, and walks straight to Christine. At a loss for words, he manages a quiet "Hi."

In that moment, Christine feels a deep sense of calm, as if she's known Mike her entire life.

They fold into a deep hug. Then the tears start, silent and punctuated by a few sniffles. These are not the deep weeping tears of grief. They are tears of relief—from knowing that you've done right by someone you love, and from knowing that you've been accepted, or at least forgiven, by the family whose worst day was your best one.

The two release, and together they walk to James's headstone. Mike squats down, balancing on the balls of his feet, and takes a deep breath, feeling the strong pulse of James's heart in his chest. Silently, he tells James how thankful he is for his sacrifice, and how sorry he is they'll never get to be friends. He promises to take care of his heart.

Someone runs back to the R.V. to grab the stethoscope from Dan Cohen's medical kit. Christine Cheers slides the cold metal head underneath Mike's blue jersey and listens. She shifts the instrument up, then down, and a little to the left.

Then there it is, loud and clear. The best part of her son still very much alive.

A.C. Shilton splits her time between freelance investigative work and feature writing. You can see her investigative work in the Netflix docuseries *The Innocent Man*. She resides in Tennessee on her 45-acre farm.

Advisory Board

The Year's Best Sports Writing 2021

Ben Baby is a reporter for ESPN's NFL Nation. Previously, he worked for the *Denton Record-Chronicle*, the *San Antonio Express-News*, and the *Dallas Morning News*, where he covered Texas A&M football. Ben is a graduate of the University of North Texas and a member of the Asian American Sports Journalists Association. He and his wife, Heather, currently live in greater Cincinnati.

Alex Belth, the editor of Esquire Classic and The Stacks Reader, is one of our foremost magazine archivists, dedicated to preserving magazine culture from the pre-digital era. His work has appeared in *Sports Illustrated*, *Esquire*, The Daily Beast, Deadspin, and *The Best American Sports Writing*. He has edited literary anthologies *The Best Sports Writing of Pat Jordan*, *Lasting Yankee Stadium Memories*, and most recently a collection of the work of journalist Jon Bradshaw, *The Ocean Is Closed: Journalistic Adventures and Investigations*. He is also the author of *The Dudes Abide: The Coen Brothers and the Making of The Big Lebowski*.

Howard Bryant is the author of nine books: *Full Dissidence: Notes From an Uneven Playing Field*, *The Heritage: Black Athletes, A Divided America and the Politics of Patriotism*, *The Last Hero: A Life of Henry Aaron*, *Juicing the Game: Drugs, Power, and the Fight for the Soul of Major League Baseball*, *Shut Out: A Story of Race and Baseball in Boston*, the three-book Legends sports series for middle-grade readers, and *Sisters and Champions: The True Story of Venus and Serena Williams*, illustrated by Floyd Cooper, and contributed essays to 16 others.

He is a two-time Casey Award winner (*Shut Out*, 2003, *The Last Hero*, 2011) for best baseball book of the year, and a 2003 finalist for the Society for American Baseball Research Seymour Medal. *The Heritage* was the recipient of the 2019 Nonfiction Award from the American Library Association's Black

Caucus and the Harry Shaw and Katrina Hazard Donald Award for Outstanding Work in African American Studies awarded by the Popular Culture Association.

He joined Meadowlark Media in 2021 and has been a senior writer for ESPN since 2007. He has served as the sports correspondent for NPR's *Weekend Edition Saturday* since 2006. In 2017, he served as the guest editor for *The Best American Sports Writing* anthology.

Previously, Mr. Bryant worked at *The Washington Post*, the *Boston Herald*, *The* (Hackensack, N.J.) *Record, The* (San Jose, CA) *Mercury News*, and the *Oakland Tribune*.

He has won numerous awards, is a three-time finalist for the National Magazine Award (2016, 2018, 2021) for commentary, and earned the 2016 Salute to Excellence Award from the National Association of Black Journalists. In addition, Mr. Bryant has appeared in several documentaries, and served as a consultant for *Baseball: The Tenth Inning, Jackie Robinson, Hemingway*, and *Muhammad Ali*, all directed by Ken Burns, *Major League Legends: Hank Aaron*, produced by the Smithsonian and Major League Baseball, and *College Behind Bars*, directed by Lynn Novick.

Kim Cross is a *New York Times* bestselling author, journalist, and historian specializing in meticulously reported narrative nonfiction. Her stories have been recognized by *The New York Times*, the *Columbia Journalism Review*, Harvard University's *Nieman Storyboard, The Sunday Long Read, The Best American Sports Writing*, and the Society of American Travel Writers. Her first book, *What Stands in a Storm*, was named one of Amazon's Best Books of 2015, a Barnes & Noble "Discover" pick, and a finalist in the GoodReads Choice Awards. A graduate of the University of Alabama, before beginning a freelance career she worked at the *New Orleans Times-Picayune*, the *St. Petersburg Times*, and served as a senior editor with *Southern Living*. She was also a National Champion and Collegiate All-American in water skiing and is a certified mountain-bike skills instructor.

Roberto José Andrade Franco is from the El Paso–Juárez borderland. He's a writer-at large for *Texas Highways*. Among other places his work has also appeared in the *Los Angeles Times*, ESPN, the *Dallas Morning News*, Bleacher Report, *Texas Monthly*, and Deadspin, where his article, "As the Border Bled, Juárez Watched the Game it Waited Nine Years For," was nominated for the 2020 Dan Jenkins Medal for Best Sportswriting Award and anthologized in *The Best American Sports Writing 2020*.

Latria Graham is a journalist and fifth generation South Carolina farmer. Her work stands at the intersection of food, social justice, sports, and culture and she has written longform pieces about everything from NASCAR to chitlins. She is a three-time *Best American Sports Writing* notable selection for her stories on athletes in places of tension—primarily Standing Rock, North Dakota, and Flint, Michigan. She received a Bronze level CASE Award for her reporting on immigration policy that stemmed from 2017's Executive Order 13769, often referred to as the "travel ban." After years of traveling the country to cover systemic injustice in underrepresented communities, she recently decided to turn her focus to small towns in the American South at risk of disappearing due to gentrification and Southern expansion. In 2019 she was awarded the Great Smoky Mountain Association's Steve Kemp Writer-in-Residence position, and for two years she has been in and out of conservation spaces, intent on unearthing long forgotten Black history that she finds crucial to the narrative we tell about the American South. Her work in the region centers on the lives of the enslaved population that lived on the Tennessee side of what is now Great Smoky Mountains National Park. She holds contributing editor positions at *Garden & Gun* and *Outdoor Retailer*. Her work has been featured in *The Guardian*, *The New York Times*, the *Los Angeles Times*, espnW, *Southern Living*, *Bicycling*, and *Backpacker*. You can find more of her work at LatriaGraham.com.

Michael J. Mooney is a *New York Times* bestselling author. He writes for *The Atlantic*, *GQ*, *ESPN The Magazine*, *Outside*, *Texas Monthly*, and *Popular Mechanics*. Several of his stories have been optioned for television and film. His work has also appeared in multiple editions of *The Best American Sports Writing* and *The Best American Crime Reporting*. Since 2010, he's been on the advisory board of the annual Mayborn Literary Nonfiction Conference, and from 2015 to 2020, he was the conference director. He lives in Dallas with his wife, Tara.

Linda Robertson writes for the *Miami Herald*, where she's been a sports columnist and news reporter. She grew up in Miami, and is a Michigan native, University of North Carolina graduate, former Knight-Wallace Fellow at the University of Michigan, former president of the Association for Women in Sports Media, mother of three, and spouse of a journalist. Still running, much more slowly, she made the first of multiple appearances in *The Best American Sports Writing* in the inaugural edition with the story "Pride and Poison."

Glenn Stout is editor of *The Year's Best Sports Writing 2021* and served as series editor for *The Best American Sports Writing* for its entire 30-year run. He is the editor, author, or ghostwriter of 100 book titles, among them *Red Sox Century*, *Fenway 1912*, *Nine Months at Ground Zero*, and, most recently, *Tiger Girl and the Candy Kid: America's Original Gangster Couple*. His biography of Trudy Ederle, *Young Woman and the Sea*, is in development as a major motion picture for Disney+. He also works as an editorial consultant on book manuscripts, long features, and book proposals. A graduate of Bard College, before becoming a full-time freelance writer in 1993 he worked construction, sold minor league baseball tickets, was a security guard, and a librarian. He lives in Vermont and is a citizen of the United States and Canada.

Notable Sports Writing of 2020

Selected by the Editor and Advisory Board of The Year's Best Sports Writing 2021

Henry Abbott
Exceptional, Ruthless. Truehoop.com, January 2, 2020

Andrea Adelson
"We're Truly Blood Brothers": Stanford Coach David Shaw and His Recent Fight to Save His Brother. ESPN, November 4, 2020

Dotun Akintoye
Inside Russell Wilson's Seahawks, Where Positivity and Corniness Reign. ESPN, January 2020

Akim Aliu
Hockey Is Not for Everyone. The Players' Tribune, May 19, 2020

Joel Anderson
Michael Jordan Is Exactly Who I Thought He Was. Slate, May 17, 2020

Malika Andrews
Jimmy Butler and the Miami Heat Are in a Barista Battle on Jimmy Butler's Coffee. ESPN, September 27, 2020

Harvey Araton
A Year When Even Sports Wasn't an Escape. The New York Times, December 16, 2020

Gustavo Arellano

Kobe Bryant Had a Special Kinship with Latino Fans and Culture. Los Angeles Times, January 27, 2020

Kevin Armstrong

"The Pain Never Leaves": The Promise and Tragedy of Aamir Griffin. Sports Illustrated, December 20, 2020

Katie Baker

Mark Cuban Once Crashed the NBA's Party. Now He Hosts It. The Ringer, January 22, 2020

Chris Ballard

Love and Lhotse. Sports Illustrated, February 6, 2020

Katie Barnes

Inside WNBA Legend Maya Moore's Extraordinary Quest for Justice. ESPN, June 18, 2020

David Barron

Taekwondo Aftermath: Two Friends, One Survivor. Houston Chronicle, May 16, 2020

Leo Baudhin

It's Hard to Write about Sports Right Now. The Victory Press, September 16, 2020

Kevin Baxter

As Big Leagues Prepare to Return Amid Pandemic, Memories of When Barrio Baseball Ruled East L.A. Los Angeles Times, July 23, 2020

She's One Girl with Family in Two Places. Los Angeles Times, June 30, 2020

Greg Bishop

An Ocean Separated Them. A Surfboard Connected Them. Sports Illustrated, October 22, 2020

David Bixenspan

Owen Hart's Widow Isn't Done Fighting the WWE over His Tragic Death. The Daily Beast, May 19, 2020

Nicole Blades
Alysia Montaño Is the Hero of This Story. Runner's World, August 26, 2020

John Branch
Adam Ondra's Race to the Top. The New York Times, March 6, 2020
The Summer without Rodeos. The New York Times, June 19, 2020

Blair Braverman
Everything on Naked and Afraid Is Real. Outside, March 17, 2020

Howard Bryant
MLB Can Add Negro Leagues to Official Records but Can Never Change What It Did to Black Players. ESPN, December 18, 2020

Candace Buckner
How Politics Transformed Kelly Loeffler from Hoops Junkie into WNBA Villain. The Washington Post, August 29, 2020

Tamika Butler
I Love to Ride My Bike. But I Won't Call Myself a "Cyclist." Bicycling, November 13, 2020

Collin Cable
How Luka Doncic Saved My Life. FanSided, September 25, 2020

Scott Cacciola
Running Past an Olympic Dream. The New York Times, July 10, 2020

John Canzano
Amid Crisis, Pac-12 Signed Agreement to Fund News Coverage from the Los Angeles Times. The Oregonian, July 31, 2020

Cat Cardenas
The Lion Tamer. Texas Monthly, April 2020

David Courtney
A Four-Day, 65-Mile Walk along the Texas Coast. Texas Monthly, August 2020

Chuck Culpepper
There Was Big Ten Football in Wisconsin But the Streets Weren't Jumping as Usual. The Washington Post, October 24, 2020

Bradford William Davis
Baseball Let Unity Stand in the Way of Protest. *New York Daily News*, July 28, 2020

Britni de la Cretaz
Maya Moore, W.N.B.A. Star, Marries Man She Helped Free From Prison. Refinery 29, September 17, 2020

Ross Dellenger
The Search for Normalcy in a Football Town Left in a Hurricane's Devastating Wake. Sports Illustrated, September 25, 2020

David Dennis Jr.
Drew Brees Doesn't Care About Black People. NewsOne, June 3, 2020

Daniel Duane
What's Wrong with Jeb's Brain? Outside, November 18, 2020

Michael-Shawn Dugar
Brandon Browner: From the "Legion of Boom" to Inmate No. BL7078. The Athletic, May 14, 2020

Jori Epstein and Daniel Libit
Texas Tech Women's Basketball Players Describe Toxic Culture: "Fear, Anxiety and Depression." USA Today, August 5, 2020

Jack Evans
Who's Killing Horses in Central Florida? Tampa Bay Times, February 4, 2020

Mirin Fader
> *The Legacy of Mambacita.* Bleacher Report, March 9, 2020
>
> *What Tyler Skaggs Left Behind.* Bleacher Report, September 1, 2020

Steve Fainaru and Mark Fainaru-Wada
> *ESPN Investigation Finds Coaches at NBA China Academies Complained of Player Abuse, Lack of Schooling.* ESPN, July 29, 2020

Wes Ferguson
> *The Great Texas Fishing Safari.* Texas Monthly, May 2020

Mike Finger
> *Pandemic Hasn't Dimmed Friday Night Lights.* San Antonio Express-News, September 5, 2020

Peter Flax
> *He Lost His Leg, Then Rediscovered the Bicycle. Now He's Unstoppable.* Bicycling, May 27, 2020

Juan Forero
> *How Do You Play Soccer in a Pandemic?* Wall Street Journal, August 24, 2020

Scott Fowler
> *83-Year-Old Charlotte Man Shot a 69 over 18 holes. Has He Figured Out Golf's Secrets?* Charlotte Observer, November 27, 2020

Roberto José Andrade Franco
> *SMU Football Picked a Horrible Year to Be Relevant Again.* D Magazine, November 2020

Matthew Futterman
> *Sledhead: Sledding Athletes Are Taking Their Lives.* The New York Times, July 26, 2020

David Gardner
> *"He Just Got Left Behind."* Bleacher Report, January 23, 2020

Jason Gay
"I Don't Want to Be an Oracle." Wall Street Journal, September 17, 2020

Ross Gay
Have I Ever Told You about the Courts I've Loved? Lit Hub, September 15, 2020

Roxane Gay
Reckoning with Kobe Bryant's Complicated Past. ESPN: The Undefeated, February 13, 2020

Brittany Ghiroli and Jeff Zrebiec
#MoStrong: The Boy Who Inspired Athletes and Rallied a City. The Athletic, August 12, 2020

Hannah Giorgis
When Your Hometown Gets a New Identity. The Atlantic, November 26, 2020

John Gonzalez
Where Does Allen Iverson Fit In? The Ringer, March 11, 2020

Jeff Goodman
Wichita State's Gregg Marshall Punched Player, Choked Assistant. WatchStadium.com, October 9, 2020

Devin Gordon
The Incredible and (Mostly) True Story of Bruce and Michael Buffer. ESPN, April 13, 2020

Latria Graham
Out There Nobody Can Hear You Scream. Outside, September 21, 2020

Sean Gregory
LeBron James, TIME Athlete of the Year. Time, December 10, 2020

Emma Healey
The Game Inside the Game. Hazlitt, February 27, 2020

Justin Heckert
Citizen Pain. The Ringer, October 21, 2020

David Hill
The Casino That Time Forgot. The Ringer, June 29, 2020

Will Hobson and Liz Clarke
From Dream Job to Nightmare. The Washington Post, July 16, 2020

Patrick Hruby
Volleyball Star Hayley Hodson Had it All, Until Blows to Her Head Changed Everything. Los Angeles Times, December 8, 2020

Jazmine Hughes
Learning to Swim Taught Me More than I Bargained For. The New York Times, March 23, 2020

Alex Hutchinson
How the Menstrual Cycle Affects Athletic Performance. Outside, February 8, 2020

Dave Hyde
We'll Never See the Likes of Don Shula Again. South Florida Sun-Sentinel, May 4, 2020

Marisa Ingemi
A First for Sarah Fuller, but That Wasn't the Last of It. The New York Times, December 17, 2020

Mitchell S. Jackson
The Sports Hero Was Redefined on May 25, 2020. Esquire, September 3, 2020

Kenny Jacoby, Nancy Armour, and Jessica Luther
Sexual Misconduct at LSU. USA Today, August 19, November 16, November 17, December 15, December 17, 2020

Sally Jenkins

The Thoughtless Husks Who Plunged This NFL Season into Chaos Deserve a Public Shaming. The Washington Post, December 2, 2020

Bomani Jones

College Football Players Are Unpaid Stars on the Field—and Have No Power off It. Vanity Fair, August 2020

Tom Junod

The Hero of Goodall Park. ESPN, July 7, 2020

Kalyn Kahler

Pray for Kabeer. Sports Illustrated, July 14, 2020

Jovan Buha Kawhi

Chemistry and a Failed Clippers Title Run. The Athletic, December 2, 2020

Tim Keown

A Week in Manila with Manny Pacquiao. ESPN, February 26, 2020

Sam Khan and Dave Wilson

"I Don't Wish Either of Them Well": The Demise of the Southwest Conference, 25 Years Later. ESPN, December 2, 2020

Brendan I. Koerner

The Cheating Scandal that Ripped the Poker World Apart. WIRED, September 21, 2020

Maria Konnikova

How I Became a Poker Champion in One Year. The Atlantic, June 23, 2020

Mark Kriegel

Séances, Tattoos and the Unbreakable Bond between Mikaela Mayer and Al Mitchell. ESPN, October 30, 2020

Paula Lavigne and Elizabeth Merrill
Death at The U: Who Killed Bryan Pata? ESPN, November 6, 2020

Tim Layden
Deep Water. NBC Sports, January 8, 2020

Andrew Lewis
A Death at Sea on the "Row of Life." Outside, October 22, 2020

Daniel Libit
Spartan Accommodations. Sportico, December 30, 2020

Gloria Liu
Paul Basagoitia Said He'd Rather Be Dead Than Paralyzed. Bicycling, July 5, 2020

Tim MacMahon
Inside James Harden and the Houston Rockets' Breaking Point. ESPN, December 16, 2020

D'Arcy Maine
Naomi Osaka Cements Her Status as Leader on and off the Court with 2020 US Open Run. ESPN, September 13, 2020

Chris Mannix
The Tyson Fury Redemption. Sports Illustrated, February 23, 2020

Jack McCallum
The Big O: The NBA's Forgotten Trailblazer. Sports Illustrated, December 22, 2020

Gordy Megroz
Going the Distance (and Beyond) to Catch Marathon Cheaters. WIRED, February 14, 2020

Louis Menand
How Baseball Players Became Celebrities. The New Yorker, May 25, 2020

James Edward Mills
  These People of Color Transformed U.S. National Parks.
  National Geographic, August 5, 2020

Ben Montgomery
  Everybody Has a Tom Pritchard Story. Bicycling, October 2020

Michael J. Mooney
  *Inside the Summer Camp Where Jocko Willink Teaches Men
  to Fight. Men's Health*, March 15, 2020

C. Brandon Ogbunu
  *Can Artificial Intelligence Help Us Understand Racial Bias in
  Sports?* ESPN: The Undefeated, January 8, 2020

Ryan O'Hanlon
  Diego Maradona Was a Deeply Human Superstar. GQ,
  December 2020

Nick Paumgarten
  Survivor's Guilt in the Mountains. The New Yorker, February
  24, 2020

Michael Pina
  *What it's Like to Hang with Giannis Antetokounmpo in Greece.
  Vogue*, December 14, 2020

Craig Pittman
  *Hunting Pythons with the Ladies of the Glades. Flamingo
  Magazine*, July 1, 2020

Nora Princiotti
  Pity the Poor Punter During the NFL's Offensive Boom. The
  Ringer, November 11, 2020

Ray Ratto
  Billy Beane Finally Gets What He Wanted: Out Of Baseball.
  The Defector, October 13, 2020

Bridget Read
  The Eco-Yogi Slumlords of Brooklyn. The Cut, August 2020

Jason Reid
How Deshaun Watson Is Finding Inspiration Amid Chaotic Season. ESPN: The Undefeated, December 4, 2020

Dan Riley
Brooks Koepka, the World's Best Golfer, Has Some Issues with Golf. GQ, February 2020

Kevin Robertson
Living the Dream. Sports Afield, Winter 2020

Michael Rosenberg
In 1989, USC Had a Depth Chart of a Dozen Linebackers. Five Have Died, Each Before Age 50. Sports Illustrated, October 7, 2020

Tracy Ross
The Terrifying Whitewater Trip That Turned Into a Dream. Outside, November 2, 2020

When This Runner Faced Unspeakable Tragedy, Faith Kept Her Going. Runner's World, August 3, 2020

Ben Rothenberg
Olya's Story. Racquet, November 2020

Juan Manuel Rótulo
Diego Maradona, Argentina's Hero, and Mine. The New York Times, December 2, 2020

Leander Schaerlaeckens
Was Donald Trump Good at Baseball? Slate, May 5, 2020

Bruce Schoenfeld
LA Clippers Owner Steve Ballmer Wants to Save Sports by Reinventing the Way We Watch Them. Fast Company, May 4, 2020

Clay Skipper
How Patrick Mahomes Became the Superstar the NFL Needs Right Now. GQ, July 14, 2020

Bennett Slavsky

Why People Return to the Sports That Nearly Killed Them.
Outside, April 19, 2020

Doug Smith

*The Pascal Siakam Story a Great One at So Many Different
Levels. Toronto Star,* January 24, 2020

Rory Smith and Tariq Lanja

The Erasure of Mesut Özil. The New York Times, October 27,
2020

Emily Sohn

Meet the Woman Teaching the Psychology of Survival. Outside,
November 9, 2020

Luna Soley

My Priceless Summer on a Maine Lobster Boat. Outside,
November 11, 2020

Marc J. Spears

*From Russell to KG to Today's Celtics: Being a Black Player in
Boston.* ESPN: The Undefeated, February 29, 2020

Ben Strauss and Kim Bellware

*For Women in Sports Media, Dealing with Toxic Masculinity
Is Far from New. The Washington Post,* July 19, 2020

Barry Svrgula

*The Black Baseball Prospect, the Police Shooting and the Club
He Never Wanted to Join. The Washington Post,* December
31, 2020

Maxwell Tani

The Civil War Tearing Sports Illustrated Apart. The Daily
Beast, August 10, 2020

Shakeia Taylor

From Ghetto to Glory. Baseball Prospectus, October 16, 2020

Louisa Thomas
Nneka Ogwumike and the W.N.B.A.'s Big, Complicated Moment. The New Yorker, August 3, 2020

Alison Van Houten
This Adaptive Skier Wants Outdoor Sports to Be for All. Outside, April 24, 2020

Tom Verducci
In Cincinnati, It's Just Thursday. Sports Illustrated, March 26, 2020

Rhiannon Walker
"I Want to Move Forward from This." The Athletic, July 17, 2020

David Wharton
At Age 60 and Paralyzed, She Tried to Row Across the Pacific. Los Angeles Times, July 16, 2020

Seth Wickersham
The Story Behind the Split of Tom Brady, Bill Belichick and the Patriots. ESPN, March 2020

Jack Williams
Lockdown Kept Lonely Fans at Home. So Their Teams Went to Them. The New York Times, December 22, 2020